...ner

A Beginner's Guide

"Interesting, thoughtful, and well written. The book covers an admirably wide range of issues with clarity and assurance."

Barbara Graziosi, Professor of Classics,
Durham University, UK

"Barker and Christensen have written the best introduction I know to the Homeric poems. They explain the main themes, scenes, and characters in clear, jargon-free language that is a pleasure to read, whether for those new to Homer or advanced students."

Pura Nieto, Senior Lecturer in Classics,
Brown University, USA

ONEWORLD BEGINNER'S GUIDES combine an original, inventive, and engaging approach with expert analysis on subjects ranging from art and history to religion and politics, and everything in between. Innovative and affordable, books in the series are perfect for anyone curious about the way the world works and the big ideas of our time.

aesthetics	dewey	marx
africa	dyslexia	medieval philosophy
american politics	energy	middle east
anarchism	the enlightenment	modern slavery
animal behaviour	engineering	NATO
anthropology	epistemology	nietzsche
anti-capitalism	european union	the northern ireland conflict
aquinas	evolution	nutrition
art	evolutionary psychology	oil
artificial intelligence	existentialism	opera
the bahai faith	fair trade	the palestine–israeli conflict
the beat generation	feminism	particle physics
the bible	forensic science	paul
biodiversity	french literature	philosophy
bioterror & biowarfare	french revolution	philosophy of mind
the brain	genetics	philosophy of religion
british politics	global terrorism	philosophy of science
the Buddha	hinduism	planet earth
cancer	history of science	postmodernism
censorship	homer	psychology
christianity	humanism	quantum physics
civil liberties	huxley	the qur'an
classical music	iran	racism
climate change	islamic philosophy	reductionism
cloning	islamic veil	religion
cold war	journalism	renaissance art
conservation	judaism	shakespeare
crimes against humanity	lacan	the small arms trade
criminal psychology	life in the universe	sufism
critical thinking	literary theory	the torah
daoism	machiavelli	united nations
democracy	mafia & organized crime	volcanoes
descartes	magic	

Homer
A Beginner's Guide

Elton Barker and Joel Christensen

ONEWORLD

A Oneworld Book

Published by Oneworld Publications 2013

Copyright © Barker and Christensen 2013

The moral right of Barker and Christensen to be identified as the Authors
of this work has been asserted by them in accordance with
the Copyright, Designs and Patents Act 1988

ISBN 978-1-78074-229-8
ISBN (ebook) 978-1-78074-238-0

Typeset by Cenveo, India
Printed and bound in Great Britain by
TJ International Ltd, Cornwall

Oneworld Publications
10 Bloomsbury Street
London WC1B 3SR
UK

Stay up to date with the latest books,
special offers, and exclusive content from
Oneworld with our monthly newsletter

Sign up on our website
www.oneworld-publications.com

Contents

List of illustrations

Acknowledgements

There is no greater privilege for us than the chance to write a Beginner's Guide on Homer for a general audience. We would like to thank all the team at Oneworld Publications for giving us the opportunity, Mike Harpley, our series editor, who guided us through the edit of this little book on big issues, and Barbara Graziosi, from whose Homeric wisdom and skill we have learned much. Many other scholars have informed our understanding of Homer and his poems. We have tried to give some indication of our formative influences in 'Further Reading' at the end of the book. But for the record we would like to acknowledge Erwin Cook, Simon Goldhill, Bruce Heiden, and Lenny Muellner, whose lectures brought Homer alive for us and whose ideas may be found throughout this book. We thank too our students, both past and present, whose undiminished curiosity has kept Homer vibrant year after year. We are also indebted to the friends and colleagues who read through earlier drafts of the manuscript and spared us many blushes: Timothy Gerolami, Kristina Meinking, Alex Purves, and Sophie Raudnitz. Any nodding is ours.

Finally, we would like to thank our partners Kyriaki and Shanaaz for putting up with our affair, the late nights home from the office, the surreptitious checking of email at all hours, and the obsessive recounting of memories (those borrowed as well as our own). This book is dedicated to them, to our families, and to Homer's people everywhere suffering many pains because of the incompetency and greed of their leaders and the capriciousness of the 'gods' who rule our world.

Elton Barker
Reader in Classical Studies at The Open University and Research Fellow of the Alexander von Humboldt Foundation

Joel Christensen
Assistant Professor of Classics, University of Texas at San Antonio

A note on the text

We have translated Homer's words ourselves in order to help emphasise certain themes and ideas. But always near to hand are Richmond Lattimore's translations of the *Iliad* and the *Odyssey* (the former reissued in 2011 with an introduction by Richard Martin). While there are many fine and more up-to-date editions of both epics, Lattimore's translations match up with Homer's poems line-by-line and preserve the repetitions and special diction that are both characteristic of them and essential to their interpretation. It is important also to note that the names in Homer's epics have undergone many transformations from one language to another. In general, we have kept the more popular romanised and anglicised versions: hence Achilles for Akhilleus, Achaeans for Akhaians, Hecuba for Hekabe, etc. From time to time, a particular concept (highlighted in bold) has needed further elucidation: for this, we have used text boxes in order not to interrupt the flow of our story.

Introduction
O Homer, where art thou?

Beginning with Homer

The classical world begins with Homer. The ancient Greeks famously didn't have a sacred text like the Bible or the Qur'an. But they did have Homer. Homer, by some accounts, provided the origins of not only their literature, but also their religious, cultural, and political lives. Poets and scientists from the islands and mainland; Athenian tragedians, comic playwrights, and vase painters; Sicilian rhetoricians and temple-builders; politicians of all stripes and philosophers from every school – all these vastly different groups demonstrate intimate familiarity with Homer. Indeed, for disparate communities spread out across the Mediterranean from Massalia (Marseilles) in the west to Cyrene on the North African coast and the Black Sea in the east, Homer provided the glue for what we now call ancient Greek civilisation. The first-century AD Roman historian of rhetoric, Quintilian, likens Homer to the river Oceanus that the ancients thought encircled the world. Everything flows from Homer and back into him.

Even nowadays we find Homer everywhere. From the eponymous anti-heroic husband of the long-suffering Marge to the language used in everyday conversation, Homer lives on in the here and now. That use of the word 'heroic', for example, or 'epic', or 'Achilles heel', 'the Sirens' song', 'Trojan horse', an 'odyssey', etc. Or in the branding of everyday products, such as *Ajax*, the mighty household detergent, or *Trojan*, the make of condoms (naming a prophylactic after a city whose walls were breached is perhaps *not* the image the manufacturers were intending). More precisely, the two poems from which Homer's fame derives, the *Iliad* and *Odyssey*, continue to thrive in the popular imagination. Modern literary giants such as James Joyce and Derek Walcott parade their debt to Homer in the titles of their works, *Ulysses* (the Latin form of Odysseus) and *Omeros*, respectively. But the influence is no less marked elsewhere. Acclaimed sci-fi author Dan Simmons recreates the events of the *Iliad* on an alternate Earth and Mars in his 2003 novel *Ilium*, while Daniel Wallace's *Big Fish* (1998) adapts the *Odyssey* to the American South. Relatively 'straight' film adaptations include the Italian 'spaghetti epics' of the sixties and Hollywood's more recent *Troy*, starring Brad Pitt as Achilles. More 'inspired by' are the Coen brothers' *O Brother, Where Art Thou?*, featuring gorgeous George Clooney playing Ulysses Everett McGill complete with hair-grooming products and a song for every occasion, and Jean-Luc Godard's 1963 *Le Mépris*, in which the famous German director Fritz Lang plays himself struggling to direct a film adaptation of the *Odyssey*.

Indeed, ever since the *Iliad* and *Odyssey* were committed to writing, imitating Homer has represented something of the ultimate examination of an author's literary credentials or even of the cultural clout of their society, as epitomised by the 'national' epics of Virgil (the *Aeneid*), Dante (*Inferno*), and Milton (*Paradise Lost*). These examples alone demonstrate just how far Homer's stories have travelled through space and time, though epic has not been the only medium of transport: the Franco-Japanese cartoon *Ulysses 31* features a space-age Ulysses (Odysseus) travelling through the galaxy to the beat of eighties pop. Homer bequeaths far more to posterity than simply the raw materials of two epics. Homer gives us the art of storytelling.

The two poems with which Homer's name has been associ-
ated ever since antiquity, the *Iliad* and the *Odyssey*, tell the story
of two great cataclysmic events set in Bronze-Age Greece
(c. twelfth century BC). The *Iliad* describes the war at Troy, when
Greeks (or **Achaeans** in Homer's language) clashed with Trojans
over Helen, the most beautiful woman on Earth, and heroes like
Achilles and Hector won immortal fame (*kleos*). The *Odyssey* is
about the return home (*nostos*) of the Trojan War veteran
Odysseus, his adventures with fantastical creatures on the way, the
battle to reclaim his household, and his eventual reunion with his
faithful wife Penelope.

HOMER'S ACHAEANS

Homer has several names which he uses to refer to the heroic-age
Greeks. The most popular is Achaeans, which we use throughout
this book. Others Include Danaans and Argives. In the historical
period, Greeks referred to themselves by city of origin and, as a
group, Hellenes. Ancient Achaea was located in the north-west
portion of the Peloponnese In central Greece. Lattimore spells
Achaeans as Akhaians.

It is easy to feel overwhelmed by the size of these poems. The
Iliad runs to over fifteen thousand lines of verse, the *Odyssey* over
twelve thousand. It is also easy to feel lost in their alien world.
The total cast list runs to several thousands. The heroes who
bestride these verses can throw boulders it would take two men
of today to lift. All-too-human gods continually intervene in the
affairs of man as they squabble among themselves. But Homer's
epics are powerful, gripping, and exciting tales about the big
themes of human existence. They tell of the life and death struggle of battle; the love for a wife or husband, parent, sibling, or
friend; the desire for honour and glory set against care for one's

city, family, or comrades; respect for the gods and pity for the weak. They are also about the (re)discovery of identity, the longing for adventure, and the pleasure of storytelling. Above all, the poems invite us to contemplate suffering loss, enduring pain, and the basic human instinct for survival. Among our tasks in this Beginner's Guide is to help translate what made Homer's poems stand out some two and a half millennia ago, and explain why we should still listen to them now.

This means beginning with Homer himself. Should we conceive of Homer as an individual genius out of whose head these epic poems sprang fully formed? Or is it better to think of Homer as representing a tradition of storytelling that stretches back centuries over the eastern Mediterranean and beyond, of which the *Iliad* and *Odyssey* are a small part? Besides, where or how is the balance to be struck between the individual and his art, between originality and tradition? For the story of Homer – who he is, where he was from, whether he even existed – is also a story about epic poetry. How we answer these questions will make a difference to how we listen to his poems.

But that is not all. For Homer's story is also a story about us. It is about where we think poetic beauty and sublime meaning come from, about how we think about two poems that both belong to their own time and speak across the generations, about our basic assumptions concerning the nature of literature. In short, it is about why stories matter and the impact that they have on the world around them. This introductory chapter lays the essential groundwork for approaching just some of the complex cultural contexts through which we can learn to listen to Homer's songs.

Homer, singer of tales

Contrary to modern (and many ancient) assumptions, Homer is not the beginning of the classical world. The Homeric poems actually stand at the *end* of an epic tradition stretching back over many centuries and winding through the entire Mediterranean area, intersecting in various ways with other storytelling traditions such as the Babylonian *Gilgamesh* epic or the Hebrew Bible.

Signs of this larger world crop up over the course of both epics. First, unlike storytellers today, Homer rarely introduces a character and, even then, introductions convey only essential information, such as that Chryses is a priest of Apollo or that Nausicaa is the maiden daughter of the king of the Phaeacians. That Homer does not introduce at all featured characters like Agamemnon, Achilles, Odysseus (among others), or any of the gods suggests that his cast list was well known to the audience. Indeed, the Homeric epics assume that the audience not only know the major characters but are even familiar with the events themselves. At the beginning of the *Iliad*, for instance, we are not told why the heroes are before Troy, where Troy is, or who the Trojans are. We (should) already know that Helen, the wife of Menelaus, had run off with Paris, son of the Trojan king Priam. The *Odyssey* does not even bother to name its protagonist (it refers to Odysseus simply as 'the man of many turns'), what he was doing in Troy, or where his home is.

Numerous other sources allow us a peek under the curtain that has fallen on epic's grand stage. Fifth-century BC poets like Bacchylides and Pindar crown the victory of athletes at games around mainland Greece (including the ancient Olympic Games) by linking their protagonists' labours to the martial feats of bygone heroes. The content for nearly every plot of Athenian tragedy derives from the heroic 'other' worlds of Thebes or Troy. Visual culture especially adds significantly to our knowledge of Homer's mythical backdrop. Temple friezes all around the Greek world depict scenes from mythology, showing gods and sometimes heroes waging war on forces of disorder. The Parthenon, for example, has no fewer than three cosmic battles raging about its columns – the Centauromachy (the battle between Centaurs and Lapiths), the Amazonomachy (the battle between Greeks and Amazons), and the Gigantomachy (the battle between the Olympian gods and the Giants) – to accompany its depiction of the Trojan War.

Above all, vases of different kinds, the popular merchandise of the day, reveal knowledge of a truly rich and lively mythical landscape, in which heroes accomplished tasks that in one way or another helped clean up society. Featured are heroes such as Heracles (Latin: Hercules), whose twelve labours show him ridding the world of various monsters, and Theseus, whose own tasks (e.g. killing the Minotaur) led to him being celebrated as the founding hero of Athens. Or again there's Jason (of the Argonauts fame) in search of the Golden Fleece, Oedipus answering the Sphinx's riddle, or Perseus killing the gorgon Medusa. Some common depictions seem to correspond to passages from our *Iliad* and *Odyssey*, two of the most common being Achilles ransoming Hector and Odysseus blinding the Cyclops Polyphemus. But most, surprisingly, appear either to represent those episodes differently or to depict entirely different accounts from those captured in Homer. This is an important point: the pictures on pots (as elsewhere) are emphatically *not* 'illustrations' of scenes from the *Iliad* and/or *Odyssey*. But they do help to illustrate for us the breadth and popularity of stories from myth and the wide variety of Trojan War narratives available outside the Homeric epics.

So, Homer is emphatically *not* the creator of the Trojan War saga. Indeed, his epics in all likelihood represent the culmination of a tradition of storytelling that stretches back hundreds of years and reaches far and wide across the ancient world (into the ancient Near East, for example). Exactly why no other ancient Greek epic poems about these heroic myths, apart from the *Iliad* and *Odyssey*, survive is impossible to say. But certain features of Homer's epics hint at why *they* were recorded and preserved for posterity. As any good comedian knows about that other inherently traditional kind of speech, the joke, it's the way you tell it that counts. And Homer knows how to tell a good story.

First, plot. The Homeric epics stand apart from the myths of the Trojan War and set the standard for subsequent narrative traditions largely through *what they leave out*. According to the fourth-century BC philosopher and natural scientist, Aristotle, Homer excelled all other ancient Greek poets of the so-called '**Epic Cycle**' – a collection of epic poems that comes down to us in fragments and in the form of a late 'summary' – because he didn't try to tell the whole Troy story. (Makers of the Hollywood *Troy*, take note!) That is to say, the stories told in the Homeric epics are pointedly not narratives of the Trojan War; rather, they are tales set *in* the Trojan War. So, the *Iliad* concentrates on a handful of days during the ten-year war, homing in on a narrow strip of land between the Achaean ships and Troy, unified under the theme of Achilles' wrath. Even the *Odyssey*, whose range extends over both the known and unknown world and spans some twenty-odd years, is tightly woven around the final point of Odysseus's journey back to Ithaca and what happens when he arrives there: the hero's 'post-*Iliad*' adventures are mostly told in flashback by Odysseus himself. The compressed plots of the *Iliad* and the *Odyssey* imply that the epics were made for audiences who were entirely familiar with the general background of the Trojan War. The intricacy with which they engage with these traditions without repeating each other, moreover, indicates a sustained and dynamic rivalry with that mythic tradition.

THE 'EPIC CYCLE'

The 'Epic Cycle' refers to a group of epic poems that document the heroic age. They are first mentioned as a group by Aristotle, who compares them unfavourably to the Homeric poems (*Poetics*

1459a19–b18). We know them only as fragments preserved in other authors and in the form of a second-century AD prose synopsis, Proclus's *Chrestomathy*. As a collection, they provide the necessary background for a reader to understand the *Iliad* and *Odyssey*. For example, Proclus's summary tailors the beginning and end of each tale to provide one continuous narrative encircling the Homeric poems, without thought of appropriately dramatic beginnings or endings. The 'Epic Cycle' as we know it is made up of the following poems. The *Cypria* provides the origins of the Trojan War, including Helen's birth, the judgement of Paris, and their elopement to Troy. The *Aethiopis* gives the events of the war directly after the *Iliad* (including the deaths of Memnon, the Amazon Penthesilea, and Achilles). The *Little Iliad* details the war's final stages from the struggle over Achilles' arms to the wooden horse. The *Sack of Ilion* documents the fall of Troy and its destruction. The *Telegony* sketches out the events after the end of the *Odyssey* (specifically Telegonus's search for his father Odysseus).

Next, character. Aristotle also notes that Homer immediately 'brings on stage' his characters and creates a great deal of the drama and tension through what they say. The *Iliad*, for example, is over forty percent direct speech. Allowing others to speak has the effect of opening up the tale to different perspectives, which in turn encourages empathy with the characters. Memorably, we feel the intense pain of Andromache, as she laments over her husband's body. We learn what Hector, the city's protector, meant to her. We get a sense of her devastating loss, the loss of a last whispered word with him in the bed they shared (*Iliad* 24). We must confront our own contradictory and shifting opinions, as Achilles goes from a man protecting his people to one who damns them to hell, and from a man who abuses the corpse of his enemy to one who weeps with that man's father. The *Odyssey* puts the audience to the test in different ways. By having Odysseus tell his own story of his journey from Troy for three whole books of the epic (*Odyssey* 9–12), Homer makes the audience distinguish truth from lies for themselves, as the spinner of tales explains just how he lost all of his men. While these poems are entertaining, they also demand emotional intelligence on the part of, and critical reflection from, their audiences. The Homeric epics rarely present simplistic ideas or outcomes, rendering it difficult or problematic to take sides (say, against the Trojans or the suitors) or maintain unflinching, unproblematic support (with, say, Achilles or Odysseus).

Third, theme. We have already mentioned that Homer refrains from telling the whole story. Rather, he stitches his narrative together around one central theme. In the *Iliad*, that is Achilles' *rage*, the poem's first word. Achilles rages against Agamemnon, whose kingly prerogative runs roughshod over collective opinion. But Achilles also rages against all the Achaeans for – as he interprets their silence – consenting. He rages too against Hector and the Trojans, for the death of his friend Patroclus. One could say that he rages even against human (and divine) codes of behaviour, as he tries to deny burial to his fallen enemy. Through this theme, the *Iliad* relentlessly questions what the Trojan War is really about: why *are* the Achaeans fighting on the plain before Troy (or Ilion, Homer's other name for Troy)? And it represents conflict in such unflinching detail that limbs are severed, organs skewered, eyeballs roll in the dust, and the souls of heroes scurry off to a gloomy afterlife.

The *Odyssey* has a somewhat different focus. Its first word is *man* (*andra*). This is *the* man, Odysseus, the hero of this epic. *Andra* also means husband, and Odysseus's role as Penelope's returning *husband* spells doom for the suitors. But *andra* also denotes *a* man; that is, man in general. And Odysseus's role as representative somehow of the mortal condition comes under intense scrutiny. His ability to say one thing while keeping another in his heart led to his being adopted as a model for stoic philosophers, with their special dedication to putting up with the hardships of life.

But, less favourably, Odysseus was also the go-to figure for Greek and Latin literary representations of politicians or special advisers, in whose words one can place no trust.

Fourth, spectacle. Both Homeric epics powerfully exploit the potential of the imagination to conceive of whole worlds. Whether it is the ability to range over massed ranks on the battle-field, or the capacity to penetrate the innermost workings of a character's mind, Homer's skill is to reconstruct the world's epic scope from the perspective of the gods. His vision of the Trojan War comes from the Muses, whom he addresses in his proems (the introductions to his epics). This poetic licence enables him in particular to enter two worlds strictly off limits to ordinary mortals. In *Odyssey* 11, for example, we accompany Odysseus as he somehow enters Hades (the ancient Greek underworld, meaning literally 'the unseen place'), where he interviews famous figures from the Trojan War and receives a prophecy of his own fate. More frequently, Homer takes us to the heights of Olympus to witness the grand politicking of Zeus, Poseidon, and the other gods (*Iliad* 1, 4, 8, 14, 15, 20, 24; *Odyssey* 1, 5, 24). Yet Homer's privileged access to the divine adds depth to human suffering. In *Iliad* 3, Aphrodite invites the audience into Paris and Helen's per-fumed bedroom, which both jars with the scenes of battle raging around Troy's walls and re-enacts the cause of the war (the cou-ple's elopement). In *Iliad* 24, Hermes leads us into Achilles' tent, where Priam will debase himself by kissing the hands of Hector's killer in an effort to secure his son's burial. In *Odyssey* 19, Athena stages a conversation around the hearth between Penelope, des-perate to hear some word of her husband, and Odysseus himself, in disguise as a beggar. The gods are everywhere in the Homeric epics – in the flight of an arrow, in the decision not to unsheathe one's sword, in the manic laughter that echoes through Odysseus's halls and condemns the haughty suitors to death. Through the gods, paradoxically, much of the poems' humanity – their pathos, humour, and tragedy – is derived.

Fifth, tone. Homer reaches the sublime heights of Olympus. But, even with the gods, he's not averse to bringing us crashing down to Earth, as he does with the foul-mouthed 'lesser Ajax', who ends up with a mouthful of dung for failing to pray to Athena before a foot race. Homer translates epic into a more memorable register by drawing on scenes from nature, using a figure of speech known as simile (comparing one thing to another). Menelaus is compared to a mountain lion keeping dogs at bay as he defends the body of the fallen Patroclus. In the eyes of Priam, Achilles appears like the Dog Star, shining bright and banefully, bringing destruction to Troy as he prowls the battle-field in pursuit of Hector. Homer uses similes to support themes and to advance the plot subtly. In *Iliad* 2, the near-mutinous Achaeans are compared to waves sent spraying in contrary directions, only to be brought together as one wave slamming against a single cliff once the threat to army unity has been faced down. The simile also offers rare occasions for Homer to moralise. In *Iliad* 16, the onslaught of war is compared to a flood sent by Zeus to punish men for their wickedness, in perhaps what is a distant echo of Near-Eastern or biblical tales of divine wrath. Similes in the mouths of men help to unveil their character and some universal traits of humanity. Achilles compares Patroclus – weeping at the fate of their Achaean comrades – to a young girl running after her mother, while he compares himself to a mother bird bringing food to its young. But the similes also may make the ravages of war both more common and precious. Agamemnon cries like a woman in childbirth after he is wounded. The two sides coming together in battle are compared first to two men arguing over field boundaries and then to wool being weighed out by a woman who must provide for her children. Finally, the similes themselves can approach the sublime. Odysseus, washed up naked on the Phaeacian shoreline of Scheria and near dead, is compared to a glowing coal wrapped for a future fire, as he covers himself in leaves during the dead of night.

By means of these five elements (among others), Homer communicates the continuing resonance of this lost heroic age for our present circumstances. His epics sing about the brutality of war, the value of friendship, the importance of the community's survival, the omnipresence of the gods, the troubled humanity of heroic actions, the loss of a loved one, and even the dangerous seductiveness of the story itself. But, before we can embark on epic's much-resounding sea (to borrow a line from Homer), we first need to learn to listen to this kind of poetry. Words, phrases (such as 'much-resounding sea'), and even whole scenes in Homer are frequently repeated, transposed to other contexts, and echo throughout the whole body of epic, beyond even Homer. For, unlike poetry as we know it, whose form, content, and very composition derives from the mind of an individual, ancient Greek epic is not the invention of one man but the product of centuries of innovation and evolution in far-flung storytelling traditions. But, if one person didn't invent the story of the Trojan War and the returns home, then who is Homer?

In search of Homer

There is no simple or easy answer to *the* Homeric question. Homer appears as someone or even something different depending on who is asking the question. For the Romans, Homer was the inventor of epic, an inspiration to Ennius, Lucretius, and Virgil. For the Italian humanist Giambattista Vico or eighteenth-century German classicist F.A. Wolf, Homer was a nationalist idea containing the spirit and communicating the essential nature of a Greek people. Even the Greeks of the classical period disagreed about where Homer came from, which epics he composed, and when he lived.

The problem derives from the fact that the *Iliad* and *Odyssey* belong to a culture that was predominantly *oral*. The Homeric poems were not originally disseminated as books with the author's name clearly printed on the spine. Like other poems of the same form – that is to say, **archaic Greek hexameter poetry** – they would have been performed at public events or festivals, where the author or, better, *poet* (from the Greek *poetēs*, meaning 'maker') would have been obvious. A good example of a likely scenario occurs in Homer's epic rival Hesiod. In his *Works and Days*, Hesiod describes performing in a poetic competition and winning first prize for an earlier work (perhaps his *Theogony*). Apart from this reference, however, there is only one other archaic Greek hexameter poem that has an 'autograph' of sorts. This is the *Hymn to Apollo*, which refers to its author as 'the blind poet from Chios'. Nowhere in the whole of either the *Iliad* or *Odyssey* is an author named. Rather, both works are imagined as emanating from the Muses, goddesses who, as Hesiod relates in his *Theogony*, oversee poetic memory. The epic poet appeals to the Muses for the authority to sing about the past and about events that involve the gods.

ARCHAIC GREEK HEXAMETER POETRY

Archaic Greek hexameter poetry refers to those oral poems composed in the same dactylic hexameter metre as Homer's *Iliad* and *Odyssey*, using the same artificial language, and even deploying many of the same formulae. The only other two epic poems to have survived in full are Hesiod's *Theogony* and *Works and Days*, though the few fragments of poems that have been assigned to an 'Epic Cycle' also appear in hexameter. The *Theogony* gives an account of the creation of the cosmos down to Zeus establishing his reign (the Greek gods are conceived as part of the world, not prior to it). The *Works and Days*, which sets out man's place within the world, is perhaps best known for its two mythological examples that explain the toil and pain that define the human condition: the story of

Prometheus and Pandora, and the myth of the Five Ages of Man. Also ascribed to Hesiod are the fragmentary *Catalogue of Women*, which explores the age of heroes (thereby offering a transition between the divine sphere of the *Theogony* and the human focus of the *Works and Days*), and the *Shield of Heracles*, which narrates one of the adventures of the great hero Heracles (Latin: Hercules). Also belonging to this category of poetry are the *Homeric Hymns*, a collection of thirty-three anonymous ancient Greek hymns celebrating individual gods.

A further problem lies in the fact that Homer's poems operate on a scale far removed from any other text of the period that comes down to us. For example, both the *Hymn to Apollo* (546 lines) and Hesiod's *Works and Days* (somewhat over one thousand lines) could have been performed easily in one evening. In contrast, the performances of the *Iliad* and *Odyssey* would have been a massive undertaking for a single individual: it is thought that each epic would require at least *three entire days* to stage. No performance context recorded fits the bill, although in fifth-century Athens tragic performances also spanned three days, with one playwright putting on his quota of plays (three tragedies and a satyr play) each day. Significantly, the one reference that we do have to the Homeric poems being performed is at the Great Panatheneia, a four-yearly Athenian festival established in honour of Athena by a family called the Peisistratids. As part of their strategy to curry popular support (for political office), they were apparently responsible for instituting performances of the *Iliad* and *Odyssey* as part of the festival programme. Indeed, such is their alleged influence that many scholars think that this is when the Homeric poems were written down and fixed in form (the so-called 'Peisistratid recension'). It should be noted, however, that there is no evidence that the *whole* of the *Iliad* and *Odyssey* were performed. For most Greeks of the archaic period, experience of epic poems would have been episodic. Professional singers called rhapsodes (they who 'stitch verses together') would typically perform the best bits of epic. We see just such scenarios (albeit on a smaller scale) in the *Odyssey*, when the Ithacan bard Phemius entertains the suitors with songs about the 'returns' of the Trojan War veterans, or when the Phaeacian bard Demodocus provides hospitality for Odysseus by singing about the conflict between Achilles and Odysseus, the adultery of Ares and Aphrodite, and the fall of Troy. Epic poems (in part as well as in whole) were both composed for performance and recomposed in reperformances, meaning that audiences would not only know the tales (and their manner of telling) but also learn to be sensitive to variations in theme, content, and focus.

It is in this context of rhapsodic performance that the name Homer first emerges. When the poems' performances (by rhapsodes) became detached from their composition (by poets), the name of an author (in this case, 'Homer') was attached to the circulating poems (or sections of poems) as a marker of authority. In turn, the performance tradition also began to generate details of the life and origins of that authority. None of these 'biographies' of Homer is worth much as evidence of an actual living, breathing Homer. But they do give an impression of how his poetry was received in antiquity. The fact, for example, that none of the biographies can agree on a place of origin mimics the wide dissemination of Homer's poetry throughout the Greek world and his pan-Hellenic ('all-Greek') appeal. An anonymous fourth-century BC text reconstructs a contest between the two giants of epic poetry, Homer and Hesiod. The work, called simply the *Certamen* ('Contest'), dramatises the critical importance of competition for literary productions of this kind. The second-century AD philosopher-cum-satirist Lucian directly poses the 'who is Homer?' question and indulges the scholar's fantasy of travelling all the way to Hades to interview Homer to find out (in his '*True*' *Story*). Lucian lists the places that claim Homer as their own – the eastern Aegean islands of Chios and Samos, or the coastal town of Smyrna (modern-day Izmir). Wrong, says this 'Homer'. The answer's *Babylon*! While the former listing points to the 'Ionic' origins of epic dialect, it is more arguable whether the answer of Babylon suggests an awareness of epic's Near-Eastern connections. But giving Homer a foreign birthplace certainly fits Lucian's predilection for controversy.

Questions about Homer tend to lead back to poems themselves. So, what do we know about the *writing down* of the *Iliad* and *Odyssey*? Some scholars suppose that the Homeric poems were fixed when writing was reintroduced to the Greek world sometime in the eighth century BC, while others see their written transmission as a process that lasted centuries (seventh to fifth centuries BC). However, we lack any hard evidence for the original recording of the epics. Did an oral poet learn to write down his poems? Did he or a group of poets dictate to a scribe? Did oral performers have 'scripts'? Nor do we know the motivation for that fundamental shift in medium: *why* write down an oral poem? It is also misleading to insist that once the epics were written down they were fixed once and for all, or to suppose that the epic tradition stopped evolving once the new technology of writing had been widely adopted. Be that as it may, by the fifth century BC, authors such as the historian Herodotus are openly referring to Homer's version of the events at Troy and differentiating it from others, while a generation or two later Aristotle uses Homer's *Iliad* and *Odyssey* as model narratives which he can use to come up with a rudimentary literary theory.

In the wake of Alexander the Great's conquests in the fourth century BC and the Hellenisation of the Mediterranean, examples of Greek literature were gathered, recorded, and stored as part of an advertising campaign by ruling elites of their cultural heritage and political legitimacy. As a result, this age witnessed the flourishing not only of museums (from the Greek *Musaion*, literally 'a temple to the Muses') but also of libraries, while new occupations grew up around the collection and authentication of works of literature. Activity centred on Homer, demonstrating the cultural capital his poems provided for the Greeks, in much the same way as Shakespeare's works have been essential for the construction of an English literary tradition. It wasn't enough now to listen to Homer: given the prestige involved, it became imperative to get the *right* texts of the *Iliad* and *Odyssey*. The vigorous editing of the Homeric poems in fact gave rise to the discipline of scholarship. Scholars such as Aristarchus, Zenodotus, and Aristophanes of Byzantium (modern-day Istanbul) became the gatekeepers of culture, policing 'authentic' texts of Homer and cracking down on alternative versions. While their activity may have distorted our subsequent conception of a fixed text of Homer, at the same time it is likely that without their activity we may not even have had the chance to enjoy Homer at all.

By this period, because of his two epic poems, Homer was considered the font of everything. In a marble relief by Archelaus of Priene (probably second century BC), Homer – flanked by his literary progeny, the *Iliad* and *Odyssey*, and proclaimed by all manner of personifications ('Myth', 'History', 'Poetry', 'Tragedy', 'Comedy', 'Nature', 'Excellence', 'Mindfulness', 'Trustworthiness', and 'Wisdom') – is depicted being crowned by 'Time' and the 'Inhabited World'. Homer's poetry is everywhere and for all of time. With the rise of Rome, Homer's star remained undiminished, serving as the model for its great epic, Virgil's *Aeneid*, as well as providing the examples on which rhetoricians or scholars based their observations about literature, in works such as *On the Sublime*.

Once Rome falls, it becomes more difficult to trace the history of Homer's poems. It is clear they must have remained highly valued, if not widely disseminated, by the fact that they are preserved in mediaeval manuscripts. It is to the monastic industry of manuscript production, which saw texts painstakingly copied by hand over the centuries, that we owe our knowledge of nearly all ancient Greek and Roman literature, Homer chief among them. One of the earliest and finest examples is the tenth-century AD Venetus A (so called because it resides in the Biblioteca

Marciana in Venice) manuscript of the *Iliad*. The twelfth-century Archbishop of Thessaloniki, Eustathius, compiled an epic commentary on Homer. But it is the movement known as the Renaissance (fourteenth to seventeenth centuries) that reaffirms Homer's cultural capital. Dante (c. 1265–1321) refers to Homer as *Omero poeta sovrano* ('Homer the sovereign poet'), though most readers now experienced Homer second-hand through translations, a trend that has continued to this day.

The so-called 'Apotheosis of Homer', Archelaus of Priene, probably second century BC, British Museum

In this marble relief, Homer is represented as being flanked by his literary progeny, a kneeling *Iliad* and *Odyssey*, while being heralded by all manner of personifications: 'Myth', 'History', 'Poetry', 'Tragedy', 'Comedy', 'Nature', 'Excellence', 'Mindfulness', 'Trustworthiness', and 'Wisdom'. Behind him, and crowning him, stand 'Time' and the 'Inhabited World'.

Mount Parnassus, Raphael, 1511, Vatican Museum, Vatican City

The fresco shows Mount Parnassus, the residence of Apollo, god of poetry, who is surrounded by the nine Muses, nine poets from antiquity, and nine contemporary poets. Homer forms a group with Virgil and Dante, representing the world's best epic poets.

The picture of Homer as the Muse-inspired blind bard favoured by Renaissance artists, as in Raphael's famous *Mount Parnassus* fresco in the Vatican, proved to be highly influential. It served as the basis and inspiration for the Romantic poets and painters, who emphasised Homer's genius, originality, and the **sublime** – a concept that could be traced back to Homer through the treatise *On the Sublime*. Artistic responses to Homer during this period (eighteenth and nineteenth centuries) impacted heavily on scholarship, to the extent that appreciation of the poet's originality prompted a renewed search for the poems' sources. So-called 'Analyst' critics broke the Homeric epics down into their constituent parts – episode archetypes or core 'lays' – in an effort to get back to an 'original' 'Iliadic' or 'Odyssean' kernel, such as Achilles' anger with Agamemnon, or Odysseus's return to his wife. Even their opponents, the 'Unitarians', who argued for the artistic unity of these poems, nevertheless based their arguments on the same premise of Homer's priority. Instead of trying to strip away the elements that had accreted to the poems, these scholars simply argued that all these elements could be traced back to an individual genius, known as Homer. Here we are back with the Alexandrian idea of Homer as the font for all subsequent classical literature.

THE SUBLIME

In ancient literary theory, the sublime was a desirable and exceptional quality sought out in great literature. It is intimately bound up with Homeric epic, since size matters: *hypsos*, 'sublimity', can also be translated as 'height' or 'loftiness' (*On the Sublime* 9.4–15). Such a quality in a work of art was often thought to correspond with genius and to be able to produce enjoyment, wonder, inspiration, and transformation in the reader/viewer. The classic work *On the Sublime* is dated to around the first century AD, and attributed (probably incorrectly) to Longinus. Whoever the author, *On the Sublime* has been highly influential. It was revived as a category of literary criticism and philosophy during the Enlightenment. By virtue of its wide dissemination in the nineteenth century in the wake of the Romantic movement, the sublime even became a central subject of debate for aesthetic value and, in wider parlance, a description of general and unqualified positive worth.

The growing literary culture of the twentieth century presented a bleak outlook for Homer. The tangled textual transmission of the epics, alleged errors, and inconsistencies within them, and the repetition of epithets, phrases, and even whole scenes (sometimes verbatim) throughout them, left critics either searching for the original stories that had been artlessly combined or else explaining away the author's style as naive and primitive. Between the two World Wars, however, advances in linguistics and a revolution in academic fieldwork were about to take Homeric scholarship beyond the hyper-literary Analyst/Unitarian divide into the world of oral poetics.

Learning to listen to Homer

In the 1930s, two young American scholars, Milman Parry and Albert Lord, made a trip that would revolutionise Homeric studies. Parry had previously studied with the famous French linguist Antoine Meillet, who conceived of Homeric epic as being entirely made up of formulae handed down from poet to poet. Meillet not only introduced Parry to Slavic scholars (such as Matija Murko) working on their own heroic epic traditions, but also encouraged him to test the idea of the formulaic composition of Homeric epic 'in the wild' by conducting field research on oral traditions in Yugoslavia. What he and Lord found was a living, breathing poetry, where bards were hired to perform a combination of history, myth, or folktale at public gatherings. What is more, these singers weren't memorising their performances but composing them on the spot, drawing on a store of traditional stories and story patterns. Thus, a whole new field of enquiry was born – oral-formulaic theory.

Oral-formulaic theory explains repetition as the heartbeat of Homer's kind of poetry. Individual components – whether they are conceived of as words (epithets such as 'rosy-fingered' Dawn, the 'wine dark' sea, 'ox-eyed' Hera), phrases (e.g. 'once they had put away their desire for food and drink'), type-scenes (e.g. arming, giving or receiving hospitality), or even whole story patterns (the sack, the return) – were not only repeatable but also encouraged highly versatile verse making. The poet could vary the type-scene or story pattern, depending on what effect he wanted to achieve. So, for example, Homer highlights the glitzy show of Paris's armour to indicate his singular lack of martial prowess, while Achilles' own armour is made to order from Hephaestus, the smithy god, in order to underline this hero's godlike stature.

Fundamentally, this versatility derives from two specific details about Homeric poetry. First, this poetry is metrical. Each line is made up of six units, each unit consisting of one long syllable followed by another long syllable or two short ones. This 'line in six units' gives the name to Homer's kind of poetry, '**dactylic hexameter**'. In addition, each individual word has its own metrical value, meaning that the singer has to choose carefully which words to use in combination in order to slot them into the line without coming up short of or spilling over the verse end. The sheer variation of epithets used to describe a particular hero demonstrates well the different metrical values of set phrases or 'formula'. So Achilles is not only 'swift-footed' but also, depending on line position, 'swift of foot' or alternatively 'godlike', 'lion-hearted', or 'son of Peleus', while Odysseus is 'much turning', 'much enduring', 'wise', 'sacker of cities', 'son of Laertes', etc.

THE DACTYLIC HEXAMETER

The hexameter line is made up of six units, or feet. Each foot comprises either of two long syllables (a 'spondee') or one long syllable followed by two short ones (a 'dactyl'). This is why Homer's poetry is often referred to as 'dactylic hexameter' verse. To see what this looks like, and how this determines the composition of a hexameter line, we provide an example relating to Hector as the subject of the sentence:

Héktôr / Priamí/dês - /- ∪∪ / - ∪∪ / - -
Héktôr / Priamí/dês broto/loigôi/ ísos Arêi
Héktôr / Pria/moio pá/is phlogí / eíkelos / alkên
- Hék/tôr méga/thumos ∪ / - ∪∪ / - ∪∪ / - -
- - / - Priá/moio pá/is koru/thaíolos / Héktôr
- ∪∪ / - ∪∪ / - ∪mé/gas koru/thaíolos / Héktôr
- ∪∪ / - ∪∪ / - ∪∪ / - koru/thaíolos / Héktôr
- ∪∪ / - ∪∪ / - ∪∪ / - ∪∪ / phaídimos / Héktôr
- ∪∪ / - ∪∪ / - ∪∪ / - ∪∪ / óbrimos / Héktôr

But there is more to the effect of oral poetry than mechanics of metre. Recognising the fundamental rhythmical basis for each line, comprised of a treasure-trove of reusable units that function as the building blocks of each line, allows us to understand why the Homeric epics read so differently from modern writing. And yet the functional nature of repeated lines and scenes does not undermine the importance of each particular appearance of a phrase or scene. Even our everyday language relies upon widely accepted assumptions about the meaning of certain phrases, which can be exploited by practised speakers for particular effect. (Think, for example, of JFK's 'ask not what your country can do for you, ask what you can do for your country', or Tony Blair's 'tough on crime, tough on the causes of crime'.) The effect is heightened in the case of archaic Greek epic with its special artificial language. (Ancient Greeks didn't go around speaking like Homer.) This means that an audience would be highly attuned to the moments when Homer's epics exhibit a similar tension between inherited usage and the current application. In each individual oral performance of epic, words, phrases, type-scenes, and even story patterns are drawn from prior performances, thereby creating a rich web of associations on which each audience member can hang their interpretation of, and appreciation for, the current poem-in-composition. What is more, the more experience of oral performance that a member of the audience gains, the richer that web of associations becomes for them. Even as this traditional language resonates within contexts of significance beyond any specific example, the wider tradition can be heard through each individual case. Fundamentally, oral poems are not constrained by the conventional story. Rather, part of their force and meaning derives precisely from how they position themselves in and against other versions.

Arguably, the nearest modern equivalent of such poetry is rap, which not only possesses a similar set of stock scenarios, images, and language, and has a strong metrical basis (which must aid memory and recall for poet and audience alike), but also is composed in performance before a discerning audience. Such a scenario is reimagined by Eminem in the film *8 Mile*, in which we see the 'poet' draw upon a store of common phrases and traditional motifs as he composes on the spot (albeit based on a 'script') in competition with his rivals before an audience of judges. This image might not get us any nearer to a real-life 'Homer' – the sheer scale of the *Iliad* and *Odyssey* far exceeds any comparable context, ancient or modern. However, it does at least allow us to imagine how an individual poet – let's call him Homer – might operate in and against the epic cosmos he inherits.

The first instance in the *Iliad* of the phrase 'swift-footed' Achilles is a good example of how Homer's echoic language can work. Achilles has just called the Achaeans to assembly. 'When they were gathered together,' Homer relates, 'swift-footed Achilles stood up and addressed them' (*Iliad* 1.57–8). Logically, this line begs the question: why should Achilles be described as 'swift-footed' when he *stands* to speak? Oral-formulaic theory helps us part of the way – namely, that the use of the epithet 'swift-footed' is determined by metrical need. In other words, Homer, who has several other epithets for Achilles such as 'godlike' or 'son of Peleus', uses 'swift-footed' here because that phrase fits the demands of the current hexameter line. While this explanation satisfies the logical reason for its occurrence, however, it hardly does justice to Homer's skill. It demands that we accept the scenario in which, as Homer composes 'in performance', he runs out of space at the end of the line and, in need of an epithet to describe Achilles, comes up with 'swift-footed' off the top of his head even though it hardly suits the context.

But there is an alternative interpretation that takes into account both the mechanics of oral verse *and* its effect, which allows added meaning to be ascribed to the event being narrated. This is possible if, instead of trying to explain the phrase from the poet's perspective, we think rather about how this phrase is *heard* by the audience. Epithets point to something essential about each character's identity – his or her epic DNA as it were. Just as Odysseus is the man of 'many turns', or Hector is 'horse taming', Achilles *is* 'swift-footed', as well as 'godlike' and 'son of Peleus'. That is to say, Achilles is recognised as being 'swift of foot' based on the audience's familiarity with this character in epic poetry. Indeed, a fragment of that tradition (assigned to the *Cypria*) tells the story of Achilles hunting down and killing Priam's youngest son, Troilus, by virtue of his speed of foot. The *Iliad* preserves a memory of this knowledge when, as the epic draws near to its climax about the story of his wrath, Achilles chases Hector around the walls of Troy (*Iliad* 22). In this replaying of a traditional scene, however, Homer provides a twist since Achilles is *not* quick enough to catch Hector. Rather, it takes the intervention of a god (Athena, disguised as Hector's brother Deiphobus) to bring the two into fateful confrontation. Thus, when Homer sings of Achilles 'swift of foot' standing up to speak, the phrase points to his previous career, (re-)establishes economically and effectively his traditional identity, and resonates with examples from the tradition of when he truly was swift-footed.

That is not all: for it also points to what is unique about *this* particular retelling. The fact that we will later see Achilles *failing* to catch Hector already may suggest to us that Homer has an unusual take on Achilles' swiftness. It may also prompt us to look for another reason why Homer uses the phrase when Achilles rises to speak in the assembly. The context is precisely at odds with what Achilles is famed for – namely, being swift of foot on the battlefield. Heard in these terms, the expression draws our attention to a disjunction between what is expected of Achilles in traditional storytelling and the crisis about to be described. In the *Iliad*, Achilles' swiftness will be in speech, the challenge he will pose in words to his comrades in the assembly, as much as flight of foot on the battlefield and the physical threat he poses against the Trojans. Furthermore, this take on the story relates to his 'swift-fatedness' (1.417) and represents his role as a paradigm for mortals. In this way, the phrase 'swift-footed Achilles', while being entirely traditional and a product of the oral tradition, also gestures towards the *Iliad*'s uniqueness.

Homer and history

The subject of Homer's innovation within a tradition of storytelling brings us on to the question of the poems' historicity – that is, their relation to real-life events and their function within society. For us, this story begins in 1871, when a German entrepreneur by the name of Heinrich Schliemann started excavating the site at Hissarlik, on the Ionian coast of Turkey just to the south of the Gallipoli peninsula. He was there in search of Troy. After being raised on a diet of the *Iliad* and *Odyssey* from an early age, Schliemann had become obsessed with recovering that lost world and finding evidence that the grand events they told of really happened. In semi-retirement, he devoted his life and fortune to digging up Troy and the palaces of those great Achaean heroes who had gone to fight there, legendary men like Agamemnon and Nestor. And find palaces of enormous size he did, at Mycenae and Pylos, respectively, and treasure too, not least of all – according to Schliemann – Agamemnon's golden mask and the jewels of Helen. Through this process, the reception of Homer helped to give birth to another discipline – archaeology.

Schliemann's accomplishment is noteworthy now because, before his excavations, few scholars would have taken seriously the question of whether the Trojan War really happened. During the nineteenth century, critics believed that the Trojan War belonged wholly to the province of myth. When he ignored academic consensus and excavated in the Peloponnese and Asia Minor, Schliemann not only proved scholars wrong but also illustrated the folly of denying any truth to myth. Myth, as the ancient Greeks knew very well, is concerned with neither truth nor fiction. It is about storytelling, of making the past speak to present concerns. From our own perspective one hundred years on, it is clear that Schliemann overstated the case. The so-called death mask of Agamemnon, for example, pre-dates Agamemnon's supposed career by some several centuries, while further excavations at Troy have revealed a number of cities, none of which clearly fits the scenario of a devastating sack c. 1350 BC (the traditional date of the Trojan War). Even so, this amateur archaeologist revealed that many cultural features were shared between the region of Troy and mainland Greece, that the famous cities of the Homeric poems did exist and with similar traits to those in the epics, and that the myths of the Trojan War probably indicate cultural memories of sea-faring conflicts among the Mycenaean people. Subsequent generations of scholars have undermined many of Schliemann's claims. But his discoveries made it possible to talk about Homer and history again.

The idea that Homer's epics were historical would not have struck an ancient Greek as strange. For the ancient Greeks, Homer *was* history. Herodotus, the inventor of the genre of history, looks back to Homer as the precedent for the great clash of civilisations that his own generation experienced when the Persians sought to bring Greek territories to heel. Even Herodotus's sceptical successor, the Athenian Thucydides, draws heavily on Homer's account of the Trojan War in sketching out history from earliest times to the present day. While it was always possible to quibble with details in Homer (the poet Pindar famously claims that Homer lies about Odysseus to present him in a better light), there was very little debate about the essential facts of the Homeric world. For Greeks in the classical age, Homer's epics were stories from a war that really occurred, from a moment in the past that joined the genealogy of the gods to the race of men. Well after the archaic age (c. 800–480 BC), some Greeks still looked to Homer to adjudicate geographical boundaries (the Athenians were suspected of manipulating the text of the *Iliad* in order to lay claim to the island of Salamis) and negotiate political, ethnic, and cultural identities.

There are several challenges to understanding the dynamic relationship between Homer's poems and what we call history. First, one must distinguish between various layers of 'historicity' with respect to the poems, such as between the historical period of their performance (discussed earlier) and the historical character of the world they depict. The society that they represent is another thorny issue. The epics depict objects datable to diverse historical periods and describe a society with aspects from many different eras or that are entirely made up. Even more problematic is the chaotic picture of warfare that Homer paints, with bronze and *not* iron, the real-world choice of weapon, chariots used only to transport heroes around the battlefield (one of the more laugh-out-loud moments of *Troy*, the movie), and individual duels instead of scenes of massed ranked fighting.

Political and social arrangements are similarly unclear. Take the *Iliad*, where the political picture of the Achaeans seems to have no historical precedent. Agamemnon is in charge overall, as the brother of the wounded party, Menelaus. But he does not (and cannot, it seems) enjoy unquestioned authority over other leading figures, such as Odysseus, Nestor, Diomedes, and, of course, Achilles. Instead, Achaean society appears to operate on a 'first among equals' principle, whereby the leaders of the many contingents of the coalition vie for honour and glory from their peers in a more or less chaotic free-for-all in battle or in assembly. Indeed, it is only in the institutions of the public assembly and the council of elders that the *Iliad* appears to echo the political entities of historical Greek city states (*poleis*; singular, *polis*, from where we get the word politics). Even then the echo is distant. Neither institution functions in quite the same ways as their real-life historical equivalents would have. Nevertheless – and this is important – they would have been recognisable to the people, say, of both Corinth (where power lay in the hands of the few, as an 'oligarchy') and Athens (where the general mass of citizens – the *demos* – ruled as a 'democracy'), allowing any group to have some stake in what was being described. The political situation back on Ithaca (in the *Odyssey*) is similarly unclear, because its institutions have fallen into disuse during Odysseus's long absence. What the precise social status is of a Homeric 'king' or 'lord' like Odysseus and Agamemnon and how their power functions in relation to the community at large are questions posed, not answered, by the Homeric poems. In their representations of heroic society, neither poem aims to provide a realistic snapshot of a political order at a particular period.

This same engagement with, and departure from, the real-world experiences of the audience can be seen in the *Odyssey*'s adventurous geographical scope. By having Odysseus chart out the known places of the real world, as the hero returns home to Ithaca from Troy gathering stories from places like Crete, Egypt, and Sidon, the *Odyssey* belongs to a series of stories (including the labours of Heracles and the voyage of Jason and the Argonauts) that reflect an expanding Greek awareness from the eight century BC onwards of geography, place, and civilisation. For this was an age of discovery, as Greeks took to the sea to settle in far-off places or to trade wares much like Odysseus trades stories, rendering the Mediterranean Sea the ancient equivalent of the world wide web. And, in his own account of his adventures, we can see Odysseus giving voice to these pioneering concerns, when he reflects upon the favourable harbour and uncultivated land of the Cyclopes' island (*Odyssey* 9.132–9). Here Odysseus comes across with the same kind of inquisitive spirit that took Greeks through the Mediterranean and beyond, with an eye always on the possibilities of settlement, cultivation, and profit. Paradoxically, however, Odysseus's description acts as a prelude to a series of adventures (in *Odyssey* 9–12) that become ever more fantastical (starring one-eyed monsters, a witch who turns men into pigs, ghosts of heroes past, etc.). So, the *Odyssey* hardly aims at a realistic depiction of voyaging. But, by portraying a world beyond what was known and recognisable, Odysseus can act as a model for all adventurers. Even as the map of the Greek world gets ever larger and ever more detailed, the ambiguous locations of Odysseus's wanderings allow them to continue to speak to those charting new ground or waters. The *Odyssey* reaches parts other tales cannot reach.

Problems with the lack of realism exhibited by Homeric poems can be partly explained by poetic concerns. First, the oral tradition of epic developed over countless generations, during contrasting and distinct historical periods. In all probability, as a result, Homer's epics inherited many conventions and elements that were functionally obsolete for their audiences but were still part of the poetic repertoire. Just as scientists have shown that DNA contains a historical record of our earlier development, including forgotten fragments and no-longer-understood structures, so too the Homeric epics could not abandon the imprint of previous generations. In addition to this, audience expectations were different. Homer's audience would not know what the Mycenaean period was like or which tools and weapons belonged to which eras. All that really mattered was that the poems present a believable past. Narrative rather than historical consistency reigns supreme in epic storytelling. So, it is not surprising to find recent archaeological research showing that, while the Homeric epics generally refer to the people and palaces of late Bronze-Age Greece, they contain references to materials spanning a thousand years. Meanwhile, Homeric geographic knowledge fits roughly into the world of the eighth century BC. Such a range, depth, and assortment of inconsistencies has led historians to characterise the world within the epic poems as a realm of fantasy with just enough tethers to 'reality' to render it understandable for poet and audience alike.

Above all, the poet had to weave tales that were convincing, meaningful and entertaining. These factors explain the presentation of warfare especially. For example, Homer's interest in depicting individuals fighting each other probably derives from the dramatic impact of such encounters rather than an interest in representing a specific era or method of ancient warfare. Here one might think analogously of recent efforts in our world of cinema to represent large-scale battles. Particularly successful in conveying the sheer magnitude, and terror, of massed armies fighting each other is Peter Jackson's *Lord of the Rings* trilogy, which not only highlighted individual endeavour in battle (such as that of the dwarf Gimli or the elf Legolas) and even attributed distinct character traits to certain Orcs, but also showed the potentially horrendous consequences of a siege by taking us inside 'Helm's Deep' to see the terrified women and children – as, indeed, Homer does in *Iliad* 6. All of these strategies are aimed at making the chaos of war not only more comprehensible but also more affecting. We *care* what happens to the people involved. Contrast this to the rebooted *Star Wars* franchise (episodes 1–3), with its massed ranks of anonymous armies of drones fighting each other, or Michael Bay's *Transformers* trilogy, with a similar penchant for machines hitting each other very loudly and very frequently: both of these examples demonstrate the *failure* of dramatic impact and emotional involvement in spite (or because?) of advances in 'special effects' technology. Homer's use of ahistorical – and, at times, unbelievable – depictions of encounters in war evokes the character and effect of violence on the participants of the narrative in a way that is sensitive to, and has the most impact on, the audience.

But there is another reason for the poems' presumed historical inconsistencies, and this has to do with how each poem presents itself within the inherited oral tradition. We noted above how the *Odyssey* positions itself as a model for the pioneering spirit characterising the Greek world of Homer's day. In fact, both Homeric poems use the past to speak to the present. They are narratives that set out to explain where we come from, as we shall see in the next chapter.

1
Homer's epic cosmos: a world full of gods, heroes, and men

Epic is a world full of gods and heroes. Near-Eastern epic has Gilgamesh, two-thirds god and one-third man. The Bible stars God himself and introduces his son, part god and – crucially – part man. Norse sagas contain a dizzying array of gods and magical creatures. Central to all is the question of where we – humans – come from and how we (should) live. The same is true of Homer. His poems belong to an epic cosmos largely lost to generations of readers by virtue of having been composed and performed orally. But two other archaic Greek hexameter poems also survived the precarious transition to writing, and they help us make sense of Homer's world.

These two poems are Hesiod's *Theogony* and the *Works and Days*. They present a picture of the cosmos from opposite ends of the spectrum, so to speak, from the birth of the gods (*Theogony*) to the everyday lives of the archaic audience (*Works and Days*). Significantly, Homer's poems can be read as part of this picture. The *Iliad* takes up the story of the world from where the *Theogony* leaves off, as men born from gods ('demigods' or heroes) begin populating the Earth and making it human. The *Odyssey* depicts a stage further on in evolution, as gods appear largely absent and men must face up to taking responsibility themselves – which is the explicit and insistent demand of the *Works and Days*. In fact, by being seen in relation to Hesiod's poems, some of the oddities in Homer can be better appreciated. Why, for example, the gods appear frivolous, why heroes die, or why Odysseus is the only man left standing at the end – these questions are less intractable for someone who knows the poems of Hesiod. It can also help to explain that confused portrait of society that we have just observed. For Homer's poems do not present a historical reality: they represent *foundational* narratives. They help us explain and understand where we come from.

The age of heroes

At the beginning of *Iliad* 12, more or less at the exact centre of the epic, Homer places his version of the battle for Troy against a cosmic backdrop. Using a technique that in modern film we recognise as panning out, Homer starts with the picture of fighting on the Trojan plain that he has been describing up until this point; then, as he slowly draws back the lens, he puts that scene into a mythical framework. First, he details the mass slaughter of those who fought at Troy. Then he mentions the fall of the city itself. Finally, he explains why it is that the Trojan War has been lost from view, before, that is, his (re)telling of the story: all evidence of the event has been washed away by the gods, in a great deluge to rank alongside the biblical Noah's flood. And so it came to pass that the 'race of demigods' was dust.

Homer's label of 'demigods' occurs only once elsewhere in the literature surviving from the ancient world, and that is in Hesiod's *Works and Days*. Like Homer, Hesiod has been recognised as composing (at least) two epic narratives, composed in the same hexameter verse as Homer and sharing many linguistic features. These are: the *Theogony*, which tells of the birth of the cosmos up to the point when Zeus assumes control, and the *Works and Days*, which represents a plea for justice and an exhortation to work in contrast to the moral bankruptcy and laziness of the narrator's brother, Perses. To prove his point, in this latter poem Hesiod presents a myth of decline, akin to the Garden of Eden in Genesis, whereby each successive race of man, being ever more degenerate and immoral, finds life harder as the gods withdraw their favour. Once upon a time there was a golden age of men, who lived harmoniously with each other and Earth offered up her fruits easily and freely. But, as these men began to get ever more greedy and jealous, so they became corrupted into silver, and their lives became much harsher. In turn, this silver race gave way to a bronze age, famous for its dreadful wars. Nowadays, we – the hapless audience of this poem – have the misfortune to live in the iron age, where men routinely cheat each other and work is unending.

But there is a break in the chain of this obvious serial decline. Hesiod also relates that there was a generation before our own, a race of 'demigods', an age 'of heroic men'. Of particular interest here is Hesiod's association of two 'events' to epitomise this heroic age of men. There was a war at Thebes over the 'flocks of Oedipus' and a war at Troy over Helen. The former seems to refer to the stories surrounding the siege of Thebes, a lost epic tradition, attested in fragments, art, and other literary forms such as Greek tragedy (notably the Theban plays by Sophocles). The latter war appears straightforwardly to refer to the Troy story tradition, as exemplified by our *Iliad* and *Odyssey*. In other words, this race of 'demigods' or heroes refers exclusively to the mythical stories of epic, whether represented by oral poems such as Homer's or in visual culture.

Seen from this cosmic perspective, the *Iliad* and *Odyssey* can be regarded as 'history' in the sense that they depict the world *before* ours came into being. This interpretative framework can help make sense of a simple, but frequently overlooked, feature of the *Iliad* and *Odyssey*. Homer's heroes aren't a clearly defined group of star performers, as one might suppose given our vernacular usage of 'hero' to denote someone who does something outstanding. Nor is there any direct statement about what being a 'hero' entails, or indeed of any 'heroic code' of behaviour. Rather, Homer emphasises the distinction between his characters *and people nowadays*, as when Hector is said to lift a boulder that 'two men now' could not lift. In fact, the term 'heroes' describes the group of warriors who are fighting at Troy en masse, indiscriminately, in a way that links Homer's heroes to the race that Hesiod describes. It is just such a usage that occurs in the proem to the *Iliad*, where Homer describes how Achilles' wrath led to the souls of *heroes* being sent to Hades (1.3–4). The mention of heroes right at the beginning of the poem acts as a kind of generic label of heroic epic poetry, signalling to the audience that the tale being spun before them will be about the early history of mankind.

But there is a further aspect to the idea that Homer's heroes represent a bygone age. In a very real sense, myth is a precursor to history. Myth (generally) and archaic Greek hexameter poetry (specifically) deal with and explore contemporary issues but in the framework of a distant past. They use the past to explain, make sense of, and, even, shape the present. Hesiod's two epic poems importantly map out a movement on a cosmic scale from the past to the present – from the very beginning of things (the *Theogony*) to our everyday, humdrum, and burdensome existence (the *Works and Days*). The *Theogony* is all about the 'birth of the gods'. It moves from the dawn of time with the ancient Greek equivalent of the big bang theory (chaos), through the various successions of male deities (first Ouranos, then Cronus), until we get to Zeus, who, by seeing off various challenges, makes sure that his reign will be forever more. One way in which he does this is implied by the *Theogony*'s rather confused ending, which sees Zeus beginning to populate Earth (Gaia) with heroes, which brings civilisation and order to the cosmos.

At the other extreme stands the *Works and Days*, which presents a contemporary perspective on hard work and respect for justice. Its focus is on human endeavour, a moral lesson for leaders to rule free from bribery, and an exhortation to his brother (the poem's direct addressee – and so, by implication, any of us) to work hard. The gods are absent, save the abstract figure of Justice and Zeus himself, who appears equally distant and impersonal, far removed from the affairs of man.

The key point for us to note, and the most relevant for our book, is that the Homeric poems fit into this pattern. They too chart a movement from a past in which gods walked among men to a present where the gods are absent (overtly at least). The *Iliad* begins in a world full of (interfering) gods, and gradually over the course of its narrative moves to a world of men. Crucially, it ends with a scene of humanity between two enemies with the gods notably absent from the scene (though not uninvolved in its staging). For its part, the *Odyssey* begins with a world in which the gods are already more detached, with a divine apparatus stripped down to its bare essentials, Zeus and Athena, who oversee the action. And that action sees Odysseus escaping the clutches of a goddess, and rebuffing the prospect of immortality, in order to make his way back home to the arms of his mortal wife.

The divine comedy?

Homer's gods do not fully represent the pantheon and ritual traditions celebrated throughout the Greek world. Two Olympian gods who enjoyed major festivals in ancient Greece, Dionysus and Demeter, as well as other divine powers who were important in daily life, such as Hecate (goddess of crossroads and entrances), the Furies (avenging spirits), or the Fates, barely get a mention. The Olympian gods who do appear are not named by their local epithets, even though in everyday life this is how they would have been invoked most frequently. In short, Homer's heroes do not seem to celebrate grand festivals or participate in many of the rituals that were a significant part of Greek cultural life. What we find instead is a very selective representation of the Greek religious activity, which conforms more to the grand cosmogony of Hesiod's *Theogony* than to real life.

The gods we do find can seem part of an elaborate Olympian soap opera. In the *Iliad*, Zeus, the father of gods and men, is constantly hassled by Hera, his henpecking wife (and sister), about his many love affairs. Poseidon plays the brother resentful of Zeus's supremacy. As for the children: Athena, who sprang fully formed – and armed – out of Zeus's head, acts the daddy's girl. Apollo is the favourite son; his twin sister Artemis the silent moody type prone to occasional bursts of anger (as in *Iliad* 21). Aphrodite is all grace, charm, and sex appeal. Hephaestus is devoted to his mother Hera (from whom he was born without Zeus's seed). Ares is the unruly teenager who creates havoc on the battlefield. Additional cast members include: Iris and Hermes, who act as messengers between the worlds of god and man. The river Scamander rises up to confront Achilles about choking his waters with dead bodies. Sleep has a short walk-on part as the one god who can pull the wool over Zeus's eyes. Above all, there's Thetis, Achilles' mother, who has something on (and, perhaps, something with) Zeus. The *Odyssey* features the pairing of Athena and Zeus stage-managing events, with some minor deities in supporting roles.

Read in this way, Homer's gods have always been something of an embarrassment to critics. The early Greek thinker Xenophanes (c. 570–475 BC) complains that 'Homer and Hesiod attributed everything to the gods that is reprehensible and shameful among men: stealing, committing adultery, and deceiving one another' (fragment 21). Plato's Socrates, who has issues with the ambiguity of Greek myths generally, disapproves of a number of details, such as when the Olympian gods laugh at the cripple

Hephaestus at the end of *Iliad* 1 (*Republic* book 2, 389a), or the fact that in *Iliad* 14 Zeus is so impatient to have Hera that they have sex in the open (*Republic* book 3, 390c). He similarly objects to the story in *Odyssey* 8, which depicts Aphrodite committing adultery with Ares (*Republic* book 2, 390c–d). According to Socrates, if Homer's epics were really educative – as the historian Herodotus believed – then no one would have let him wander around singing songs. They would have installed him as a teacher or a ruler instead (*Republic* book 10, 599–600)!

Already a bone of contention in the ancient world, the problem of Homer's gods is compounded for readers coming to the topic from largely monotheistic cultures. In viewing Greek representations of the divine as bizarre and unlikely to have been taken seriously, some critics have even questioned whether the Greeks really believed in their gods. The ancient Greeks, however, were not, as Socrates fears, rabid literalists. Concepts such as literalism and fundamentalism are largely characteristics of modern religious movements, which confuse polytheism with primitivism. But ancient Greek religion was not a dogmatic centralised hierarchy that propagated official doctrine. Rather, it was a loose de-centralised association of rituals, stories, and beliefs that permeated and dominated everyday life through the power of tradition and cult. Religious rituals and beliefs developed in something of an ungoverned market, whereby practices would gain a foothold and become an essential part of local traditions. Whether or not an individual Greek from, say, Syracuse or Samos would have believed the story of Cronus eating his children as being *true* is impossible to answer and beside the point.

The gods were a permanent and indelible feature of Greek culture in much the same way that we may think of banks. That is, mysterious and capricious but absolutely essential to the functioning of everyday society (try to imagine a world without a banking system), complete with a basic daily transactional relationship between the ordinary consumer and the 'high priests'.

Despite gradations in belief, the Greeks' relationship with their religious traditions was complex and nuanced enough that Homer could depict the gods as players in a bizarre sitcom in order to develop a meaningful contrast to the high risks of human conflicts. Greeks were free to revise their view of the gods, but only to a point. Intellectuals like Xenophanes and Socrates could criticise their contemporaries' religious attitudes and traditions but not without risk. We shouldn't forget that one of charges for which the Athenians condemned Socrates to death was that he didn't believe in the city's traditional gods and taught others the same.

Our real difficulty is appreciating the extent to which the gods are present in Homer's poems. At one level, their presence is clear. In the first book of the *Iliad* alone: Apollo sends a plague on the Achaean troops, after Agamemnon insults his priest; Hera puts the idea into Achilles' head to call the Achaeans to assembly; Hera sends Athena to stop Achilles from killing Agamemnon; Apollo is given sacrifices to make up for his priest's humiliation; Thetis, Achilles' divine mother, intervenes on her son's behalf to make sure he will be given due honour; finally, Zeus nods in promise to Thetis, which shakes Olympus such is its profundity. Even the question that helps to begin the epic – 'which one of the gods set Achilles and Agamemnon at odds with each other?', 1.8–9 – immediately presumes divine involvement and depends on the poet's privileged access to affairs on Olympus through the authority of the Muse ('sing goddess', 1.1). At every turn, the gods are involved, even if (as we can see) humans are still responsible for their actions.

But it is more complicated than that. We know from other sources (such as the *Cypria*) that the ultimate cause of the Trojan War goes back to the marriage of Peleus and Thetis, the parents of Achilles. It was the *Paris Match* magazine wedding of the age. Thetis was not only an immortal sea nymph, but also highly desirable, while Peleus was a mighty fine hero: strapping, handsome, and ambitious. It was the wedding to which everyone wanted to go and to which all the great and the good had invitations. Bar one figure – not surprisingly, the goddess 'Strife' was left off the guest list. Nevertheless, she went and, doing what she did best, sowed strife by rolling through the assembled dignitaries an apple engraved with the legend 'to the fairest'. The resulting chaos pitched Zeus's consort Hera against Athena and Aphrodite in a dogfight for possession of the apple and the title of 'the fairest of them all'. Called in to offer judgement, Paris, the son of the Trojan king Priam, chose Aphrodite. (While Hera had offered Paris power of dominion, and Athena wisdom and military skill, Aphrodite had promised him the most beautiful woman in the world: Helen.) Winning also the undying enmity of the slighted Hera and Athena, Paris's choice precipitates the Trojan War.

Homer knows this background but doesn't feature it. In fact, we only hear passing mention of it when, at the beginning of the last book of the *Iliad*, Hera accuses Apollo of forgetting that Achilles is divinely born, even though he attended (and entertained at) Peleus's wedding (24.59–63). Yet the antagonism of Hera and Athena towards the Trojans – which would otherwise seem senseless and unmotivated – is apparent throughout. By not using the myth explicitly, Homer offers a different take on strife, as we shall see in the next chapter. But it is important for us to know a little more about this immortal sea nymph Thetis, which casts her marriage to Peleus in a rather different, and more sombre, light. According to the fifth-century BC poet Pindar, Thetis was so desirable that both 'Zeus and glorious Poseidon strove to marry [her]; each wanted her as his lovely bride'. So, Thetis *could have* been Zeus's wife. But there was a problem: there was a prophecy. The goddess Themis ('Custom', 'Right') revealed to the gods that 'it was fated for the sea-goddess to bear for a son a lord mightier than his father' (*Isthmian* 8.26–48).

Jupiter and Thetis, Ingres, 1811, Musée Granet in Aix-en-Provence

In this painting, Ingres captures the moment when Thetis appeals to Zeus ('Jupiter' in Latin) to honour her son. The ritual act of supplication is captured by Thetis's position of subordination, kneeling down in front of Zeus and holding Zeus's chin. The striking pose that Zeus adopts resembles closely Ingres' 1806 portrait *Napoleon I on his Imperial Throne*.

Two important consequences follow for our understanding of the *Iliad*. First, had Thetis married Zeus, she would have born to him a son greater in might, as she did for Peleus – indeed, Achilles proved to be far mightier than this father. And had Thetis given Zeus a son greater than him, this would have ushered in another chapter in the kind of succession myth narrated by Hesiod in his *Theogony*, with this other Achilles challenging and usurping Zeus for the throne of Olympus. This 'history' between Thetis and Zeus informs the events on Olympus at the end of the *Iliad* 1. When Hera notices that Zeus and Thetis have been taking counsel with each other, she threatens to bring the strife that we have just witnessed in the Achaean camp (between Achilles and Agamemnon) to Olympus. The *Iliad* here almost *does* break out into a full-scale battle among the gods. It almost becomes another *Theogony*. The implicit threat of divine queen and king arguing over their heir is picked up by Hephaestus's immediate reaction. He recalls a time when he took Hera's side against Zeus and was subsequently thrown out of Olympus by Zeus (1.590–4). Hephaestus bears the living proof of Zeus's power on his crippled body. Zeus cannot be challenged, since, as Hephaestus puts it, 'he is far *mightier*' (1.581). Thetis's son is *not* his after all.

But strength is not everything. Zeus rules supreme because he harnesses the power of the Olympians as a group. The corpus of poems known as the *Homeric Hymns* (most dated roughly to just after the Homeric poems) describes Zeus's distribution of honours among the Olympian gods. Each granting of honour that Zeus makes secures his status as the Supreme Being. Homer makes passing reference to that kind of divine political settlement here. The end of *Iliad* 1 describes the gods settling back to enjoy their feast, laughing unashamedly while the crippled Hephaestus bustles among them serving them drinks – and 'none of them lacked their rightful share' (1.602). This picture of the gods frivolous and partying is the image that strikes many modern readers as grotesque, especially given the scene of human strife that we have just witnessed. But it is *good* that it is so, since the alternative – a Theogonic battle between the gods on a cosmic scale – is too awful to contemplate. For it would mean the destruction of everything we hold dear and the end of the world as we know it. As it is, Zeus is the power and glory forever and ever. Amen to that.

But this is only the case because Thetis was married to a mortal. Behind that glossy image of the happy couple we presented, we should bear in mind the humiliation that Thetis suffers in being forced to marry a mortal. Nor should we overlook the mother's pain that this union will cause her, not least of all because her son, Achilles, will die.

Achilles and the plan of Zeus

In its very first line the *Iliad* names Achilles as the 'son of Peleus' and, at the end of the proem, in line 6, 'godlike'. The tension between these twin aspects of Achilles' nature is a central dynamic of the poem. In *Iliad* 1, Achilles appears indeed to be godlike. It is Achilles to whom Hera turns when she looks to initiate a response to Apollo's devastating plague that rampages through the Achaean camp – and he calls an assembly. In the subsequent debate, Achilles is the one figure to stand up to the leader of the expedition, Agamemnon, when the latter demands a replacement prize for giving up his own to pacify Apollo's anger. When Agamemnon threatens to take Achilles' prize, Athena intervenes to stop Achilles drawing his sword. Her singular, and strikingly physical, epiphany, when 'no one else saw her' (1.198) pulling Achilles back by the hair, underlines his special connection to the gods, particularly when it is she who immediately agrees that Agamemnon has done him a grave insult. Nowhere is this direct line to divinity clearer than when he goes

to his mother, Thetis, to take his demand for reparation to
Zeus himself. Achilles has the ear of the gods. Yet, as his mother
is only too acutely aware, Achilles is doomed to live a short
life – her 'swift-footed' son is, in Thetis's words, 'swift-fated'
(1.417). Whether Thetis means by this expression a general
reflection on the short lives of mankind is difficult to say
initially. But it is certainly the case that the gods are conscious of
the brevity of human life. Later, Apollo characterises men as
'wretched creatures who like leaves on a tree / flame to life at
one moment, eating the fruit of the fields, / and then wither and
die at another' (21.464–6).

It soon becomes clear that the brevity of Achilles' life in particular is a central theme in the poem. When the Achaeans finally
offer reparation to him in *Iliad* 9, Achilles rebuts their proposals.
It is evident that, during his absence from battle, he has had time
to reflect on his situation at Troy, and what particularly preoccupies him now is the memory of his mother's warning (9.410–6).
According to her, he has a stark choice: either he gives up on the
war and returns home to live a long, but unspectacular, life; or
else he dies in a blaze of glory at Troy and receives immortal *fame*
(*kleos*). The two choices would appear to be imbalanced. Even an
exceptionally long life at home pales in comparison to everlasting glory. At this point, however, Achilles remains unmoved by
the possible attraction of immortality. Instead, and this is the
important point to note here, Achilles *knows* that if he stays at
Troy he *will* die. Unlike all the other heroes, who put their lives
on the line, his death is not only a possibility; it is inevitable. This
is the extent of his divinity now – the sure knowledge of his
impending death.

In fact, arguably the most important theme of the *Iliad* is
Achilles' growing recognition of his mortality. He begins the
epic rubbing shoulders with the gods. As the last movement
begins, he becomes a force of death, meting out slaughter indiscriminately, because he was unable to prevent his best friend

from dying. By its end, he shares grief with the king of Troy in, incidentally, one of the most memorable scenes in the whole of ancient Greek literature. By then, he truly has become the 'son of Peleus': a hero conscious of his own mortality, a warrior willing to show humanity to an enemy, a son his father would be proud of. But it is not just Achilles learning about death and humanity. We too learn what it is to be human, for it is embedded within the fabric of epic poetry and the very structure of the *Iliad* itself.

Hesiod's *Works and Days* briefly refers to two wars that brought the age of heroes, the superhuman race before our own, to an end: the war for the flocks of Oedipus (the Theban tradition) and the war for Helen (the Trojan War tradition, represented by Homer's poems). The *Iliad* alludes to the annihilation in its proem when it reveals that the souls of heroes were sent into Hades (1.3–4). But a supposedly rival poem, the *Cypria*, which comes down to us only in fragments and a (much) later summary, makes the connection explicit. In what appears to be its proem (fragment 1), the *Cypria* explains that Zeus, 'taking pity' on Earth – for 'she was burdened by the sheer weight of man's numbers' – resolved to 'stir up the strife of the Trojan War' and kill off the race of heroes. Such holocaust narratives are a feature of Near-Eastern epics. Think, for example, of the biblical Noah's flood, which too has connections to similar floods in the Babylonian *Gilgamesh* and Sumerian *Atrahasis* poems. It is significant that in Greek epic, however, the top god uses war as his chosen weapon of mass destruction, for this allows more space to examine human motivation and responsibility.

Moreover, the *Iliad* and *Cypria* proems are connected by a line that appears in them both – 'and the will (or plan: *boulē*) of Zeus was being accomplished' (1.5) – which places emphasis on Zeus's *intellect* not his might. (As Hesiod's *Theogony* showed, Zeus is beyond challenge in either.) Thus, Homer immediately locates his epic world in the space between the souls of heroes being sent to Hades and the will of Zeus being accomplished such as that described by the *Cypria*. But he does so in a way that puts less emphasis on the aim of diminishing mankind's numbers (as apparently the *Cypria* did) and more on the aftershocks. That is, Homer focuses on the ways in which the heroes, like Achilles, learn to face their mortality, and the situation left behind for the present generation of mankind (us), now deprived of superheroes or direct communion with the divine.

Moreover, Zeus's will is not accomplished in a straightforward way. On first impressions, it seems self-evident that Achilles initiates Zeus's involvement in his quarrel with Agamemnon. Not content with assurances from Athena that he will be compensated three times over for Agamemnon dishonouring him, Achilles persuades his mother to supplicate Zeus on his behalf to make the Achaeans collectively pay for their leader's insulting behaviour. At the beginning of the very next book (*Iliad* 2), we witness Zeus pondering how best to put a plan (*boulē*) into action that will satisfy Achilles' demand. He settles on sending a lying dream to Agamemnon that convinces the king that Troy would fall that very day were he to launch a full assault against the Trojans. He does so, and the results are catastrophic: without Achilles, the Achaeans no longer hold the whip hand and are beaten back behind hastily constructed walls.

By *Iliad* 8, the Achaeans are faring so badly that Hera and Athena, their trusted divine allies, have to resort to direct intervention on the battlefield. In response Zeus articulates for the first time what he has in mind (8.470–7) and outlines the events of the next eight books or so. It is worth reiterating that, while it may seem curious to us, whose artistic creations lend so much emphasis to originality and surprise, that Homer anticipates much of what is to happen, for an audience raised on oral poetry there weren't the same expectations of surprise and innovation in subject matter. Achilles always dies at Troy; Troy always falls; Aeneas always lives to fight another day; Odysseus always makes it home. Instead, the surprise comes in how the poet handles his material. Nothing that Zeus says here would have been considered a plot spoiler. In fact, such a strategy helps the audience discover a deeper significance to events and gain a perspective certainly not available to the characters involved in them.

Nevertheless, there is still anticipation and the unexpected in the *Iliad*. The tension resides in the balance between this narrative and the fixed demands of the tradition. In this sense, Zeus's plan is less transparent if we consider what it *leaves out*. The episode immediately succeeding this event describes the Achaeans' petition to Achilles to return to battle, the critical 'embassy scene' of *Iliad* 9, which leads to Achilles making a decision – not to fight – that lies outside Zeus's basic outline. Also left to surprise the audience are: the night raids in *Iliad* 10, in which the Achaeans win a small success and relieve their general suffering. Zeus's speech does not anticipate the subsequent intensity of the battles from books 11–15, as a result of which all of the major Achaean heroes become wounded. It also reserves the surprise irony of the battle being waged over the *Achaean* fortifications rather than over Troy, as the besiegers become the besieged. Last but not least, Zeus fails to foresee his own deception by Hera in *Iliad* 14, as her lovemaking with Zeus allows Poseidon a free hand to support the Achaeans in the battle. Two points stand out from this list. First, while Zeus sets a broad outline for the plot, the events always seem on the verge of veering past these boundaries. Second, while the audience knows what the plot of the epic is, its players *do not*. As the struggle for life and limb continues on the plain before Troy, the heroes make decisions and live on (painfully) ignorant that the plot – if not the story – of their lives has already been composed.

This tension between divine plan and human decision – one that recalls the *Iliad*'s opening division between immortality and mortality – is encapsulated by the relationship between Zeus and Achilles. In the embassy scene of *Iliad* 9, Achilles asserts that he will leave Troy in the morning, finds himself besieged by protestations from a dearest colleague, and finally has to come to some kind of compromise. During this process of give-and-take, it is all too easy to forget that Zeus has *already* ordained that Achilles will eventually return to battle, when he articulates his plan in *Iliad* 8. Despite this preordination, Homer presents Achilles in the process of making a critical life-and-death decision, which has devastating consequences for both him and his comrades-at-arms – that is, whether he should stay (and fight) or go (home), and ultimately doing neither. As Zeus anticipates, Achilles won't return at this point. However, the fact that his decision has been pre-empted and undercut by Zeus's plan does not lessen the effect of the scene or the heart-wrenching crisis that Achilles goes through. Instead, it shows the dual determination, by which we see god and man in a dance around fate.

In the aftermath of Achilles' decision to remain at Troy (but out of the fighting), events go more or less as planned until Hera seduces Zeus, which allows Poseidon to recover some of the losses that the Achaeans had suffered. But it is only a temporary reverse. When, at the beginning of *Iliad* 15, Zeus awakens from his post-coital slumber and becomes aware that his narrative has gone off the rails, he puts Hera in her place and the poem back on track with the fullest and most explicit articulation of his thinking (15.49–77). This new and improved plan is not only about making the Achaeans suffer (as Achilles had requested), but also about those elements absolutely fundamental to the traditional account of the Trojan War: Hector's death (narrated by the *Iliad*) and the fall of Troy itself (which isn't). This plan of Zeus clearly resonates with an epic world in which Zeus rids Earth of her burden. But it also provides more detail, notably that Patroclus will die after being sent into battle by Achilles. *Iliad* 16 then opens with Patroclus, who has witnessed at first hand the Achaean suffering, returning to Achilles in tears. In turn, Achilles reluctantly allows his best friend to take his armour and fight in his place. Once again, Zeus's articulation of his plan fatefully, and fatally, foreshadows a decision that Achilles is going to make, without in any way depriving the hero of responsibility for that decision. Achilles does not know that Zeus has outlined this plot; for him, the decision to send Patroclus in his place is emotionally difficult and a struggle which he concedes to his best friend. The audience, in turn, is given the choice of attributing the action to man, god, or even both.

Furthermore, if one contemplates the exact points at which Zeus articulates his plan and Achilles makes his critical decisions, an interesting and significant pattern emerges. Zeus maps out his plan for the first time at the end of *Iliad* 8; the very next book (9) is all about Achilles' deliberation whether to stay or go. Zeus asserts his plan for the second and final time in *Iliad* 15; in the very next book (16), Achilles makes the fatal choice to send his friend into battle. This summary draws attention to how Zeus's plan and Achilles' decision making structures the *Iliad* into three 'movements' – 1–8, 9–15, and 16–24. Each movement ends with Zeus setting out his plan; the next begins with Achilles' own decision. This dynamic between Zeus and Achilles not only provides coherence to the lengthy narrative, but also lends meaning to it. It shows how the human and divine worlds are closely synchronised with each other, but with the mortal Achilles making a decision after Zeus has always already laid down the boundaries to it.

This structure also forces a reconsideration of the events of the first book. On the face of it, Zeus comes up with his plan (*boulē*) *in response to* Achilles' demand for honour (as delivered by his mother, Thetis). But the proem's introduction and, in particular, the resonant hexameter phrase 'and the will (*boulē*) of Zeus was being accomplished' is significantly ambiguous. First, this phrase only loosely links back to Achilles' wrath, the topic of the first sentence, leaving the causal relationship unclear. Does Achilles' wrath lead to, or spring from, Zeus's plan? In short, what is cause and what is effect? Second, the tense of the verb in the phrase 'and Zeus's will was being accomplished' denotes a past action that is incomplete and continuous, indicating that Zeus's plan is in process, that it has already begun but is not yet done. In other words, the grammar of the proem leaves open the possibility that Achilles' wrath is not so much the cause of the *Iliad* as *part of* Zeus's plan (to rid the world of the race of heroes). Or perhaps one should say that it is *both* the cause *and* the effect of Zeus's plan(s). This explanation in turn casts in a new light Achilles' initial decision to seek Zeus's guarantee for honour. He is, in effect, signing the death warrant of his friend, Patroclus, and, consequently, his own. How far removed, it seems, are men from the gods in all aspects – life, knowledge, power – even, *or especially*, one so close to the gods, like Achilles. In spite of being set in the age of heroes, the *Iliad* is all about humanity. It is about the recognition and acceptance of mortality by the godlike Achilles and the death of the race of heroes.

Divine care

Even as the *Iliad* gradually enacts the separation of the worlds of men and gods, the gods are invested in the outcome of mortal events. And that happens even if they don't have ties to specific men and women. The divine comedy is only part of the picture: all is not frivolity and ease among the gods. The lives of humans affect them in many ways, so that they experience grief, disappointment, and even rage at the death of their favourites. Homer's gods *care*.

Why gods care for mortals is tied both to individual identity and their own stories. We have already mentioned Hera's care for the Achaeans in *Iliad* 1 (using the label 'Danaans', 56), when she first prompts Achilles to call an assembly. She is also responsible for sending Athena to stop Achilles from killing Agamemnon, again because she '*cares* for them both' (196). A good part of her motivation on both occasions, however, is her hatred of the Trojans for having been slighted by Paris in the beauty contest. Indeed, she reveals in *Iliad* 4 that this hatred trumps her love for the four most favoured cities in the Peloponnese, all of which she is willing to sacrifice just to see Troy fall. Similarly, Aphrodite's interest in protecting Paris – he voted her the fairest – means that she rescues him from being killed by Menelaus in a duel, leading to the death of countless heroes on both sides. She also rescues her son Aeneas, though in his case the other gods know that he is fated to preserve the Trojan race. Ares typically throws a tantrum when he discovers that his son, Ascalaphus, has been killed.

The gods who have genealogical connections to certain mortals cherish them all the more because of their frailty. The figure through whose eyes we see this concern most acutely is Thetis. Just as her son represents the paradigmatic hero who risks his life in war, so Thetis represents the paradigmatic mother who has to face his impending doom and mourns his loss of life – all the more severely because of her own immortality. Even as Achilles asks her to secure Zeus's support, she bewails her son's 'swift-fatedness' (1.417). More strikingly, when Achilles lies stretched out in the dust mourning the death of Patroclus, Thetis leaves the sea to hold his head in her hands (18.70–3), anticipating the ritual gesture of mourning that she herself will go through when her son dies (described in *Odyssey* 24.36–94). In fact, Achilles' very act of lamentation here seals his doom, for now he commits himself to re-entering the fray.

Even Zeus finds himself similarly affected when faced by the prospect of his son, Sarpedon, being killed by Patroclus. Sarpedon's epic career intersects with Achilles' in ways that continue the *Iliad*'s questioning of war and glory. At *Iliad* 12.310–28, Sarpedon reflects on the high status that he and his cousin Glaucus enjoy in society. Since they receive, literally, the best cut of meat at feasts, they have a duty to risk their lives and win renown, even if it would be safer not to fight. Like Achilles, as a son of a god, Sarpedon cuts a dashing figure, though his ruminations on the nature of nobility and heroism differ somewhat from Achilles' and show Homer's keen sense of diverse perspectives. Now, as Patroclus and Sarpedon come together in *Iliad* 16, the audience hold their breaths while Zeus deliberates. As the father of gods and men, Zeus *could* do something about his son's fate, were he so minded, and he actually contemplates intervening to rescue him. Hera immediately objects, but not because Sarpedon is not worthy of pity. Rather, she worries that Zeus would set a danger-ous precedent, since, as she puts it, *all* the gods would want to intervene to save their favourites, though as mortals they are doomed to die. Seen in this light, the gods actually care *too much*. Hera instead gives Zeus an alternative. She recommends that he protect what men can't control once they're dead – ensuring burial in his homeland so that his friends and family can mourn him (16.450–7). In this way, Homer creates a kind of founda-tional myth for society to bury its fallen warriors. Even the chil-dren of gods cannot escape death, but they may be honoured by virtue of the gods securing for them a proper burial and allowing the community to give them due rites. This, indeed, is the 'prize' that a hero might hope for now in this world.

Sarpedon's death triggers a series of deaths – first Patroclus, then Hector – which, ultimately, will lead to Achilles' own death outside the frame of the *Iliad*. But equally important is another chain of events triggered here: that is, the gods' intervention to secure the hero's body for burial. As Achilles chases Hector around Troy, the gods look on as if spectators at some competition, a scene that is usually taken to show the gods' detachment from the suffering of men. But Zeus raises the same question he asked before: should he intervene to save the hero whose life is threat-ened? Unsurprisingly, it provokes the same indignant response from Hera, who again emphasises that it is fate that Hector should die here: Zeus *could* go against fate and save Hector, but the other gods wouldn't thank him for it. Yet there is an important distinction too. Earlier Zeus wanted to save Sarpedon, *his* son. Here, Zeus wants to save Hector, not because of some genealogical connection, but rather because Hector always made sacrifices to the gods: 'My heart mourns / Hector, who burned in my honour many thigh pieces of oxen / On the peaks of many-folded Ida, and at other times / On high in the city' (22.169–72).

This important shift in Zeus's stance towards humans signals the *Iliad* developing towards a world without heroes. Since he can boast Zeus as his father, Sarpedon is a classic case of a 'hero' who is literally 'godlike', 'divine-born', 'semi-divine'; Hector, strictly speaking, isn't. But that is why he is such an important character among the *Iliad*'s class of heroes. It is not his intrinsic nature that is being recognised here by Zeus, but the behaviour he has shown throughout his life. In particular, his piety is recognised as something important and valuable, worthy of the gods' attention and care. Since we too are not born from divine parents ourselves, we could never aspire to be a Sarpedon or an Achilles. But we *could* be like Hector.

The difference between the two heroes also points to an evolution that takes place over the course of the *Iliad*'s narrative. Even as the divine and mortal realms become ever more distinct, the gods themselves begin to recognise human mortality and its evolving value. The last book of the *Iliad* opens with the gods debating what to do with Hector's *body*. Burial is the one thing that we, as humans, have no control over. As the poem draws to a close, the *Iliad* depicts the gods as taking an interest in it above all other human concerns – honour and glory, fear and anger, etc. Times *have* changed. In *Iliad* 1, Apollo intervenes directly in human affairs because of an insult to his priest. Here, he takes his complaint to an assembly of gods, over which Zeus presides. Moreover, his complaint has to do with a general principle – the right to burial – not a personal affront that he has suffered. In addition, whereas before Achilles had persuaded his mother, Thetis, to exert influence over Zeus to grant him due honour, now we hear an echo of that communication in reverse – Zeus sends Thetis down to Achilles in order to ensure that he gives up Hector's body for burial. The gods, working now collectively under Zeus, show their care for a man who deserves the 'gift' of burial because of pious behaviour (he burned many sacrifices). And they show their care, not by intervening directly themselves, but by preparing a context in which Achilles and Priam, Hector's father, can come together and negotiate a settlement. The structural mirroring serves to emphasise this evolutionary change. It draws attention to the human response to conflict (Achilles' decision to hand back Hector's body), rather than the divine action that initiates it (Zeus's plan).

In the very end, the gods appear in the background, preparing the ground for great deeds of humanity to take place, all the while looking out for the man who shows piety towards them. The *Odyssey* takes this world as its starting point.

Heroes and immortality, men and women

We have seen how the *Iliad* begins in a world full of gods, and only gradually moves to a point where the gods, while still concerned about events on Earth, remain more in the background, stage-managing events (such as the meeting between Achilles and Priam). The *Odyssey* also makes the most of divine activity at its beginning. Zeus, no less, is the first speaker of the epic! But the tone of divine engagement with human life has shifted significantly. Thus, while the *Iliad*'s dissection of conflict begins with a direct question to identify the gods as its ultimate cause, their involvement – whether Apollo supporting his priest, or Hera caring for the Achaeans – takes place within the narrative of events. In contrast, the *Odyssey* begins with the gods already more detached, with Zeus presiding over an assembly in much the same way as he does at the end of the *Iliad*. In fact, the

Odyssey's Zeus may even have the end of the *Iliad* in mind when he complains: 'Oh for shame! How mortals always blame the gods! / They claim that ills come from us, while it is / because of their own recklessness that they have pains beyond what is fated' (1.32–4). In *Iliad* 24, Achilles complains that Zeus hands out ills mixed with blessings for some people, while the unlucky just get the bad stuff. Zeus's musings here in the *Odyssey* function as a gloss on that sentiment, which places responsibility for evils squarely back with men. How each man meets that fate and whether he makes it better or worse is up to him.

These comments echo throughout the *Odyssey* and frame the suffering of the people involved: of Odysseus and his family (Telemachus, Penelope, and Laertes), of Odysseus's companions, who don't make it home, and of the suitors, who are courting Odysseus's wife back on Ithaca. The suitors' suffering is the clearest case. They continually receive warnings that their behaviour flouts conventions, but heed none. As a result they meet a gruesome death 'because of their own recklessness'. Odysseus's companions, who accompany him on the way back from Troy, also die 'by their own recklessness', for making the poor choices that lead to their demise. Telemachus is a more difficult case, since his suffering – seeing the suitors eat him out of house and home – comes about because of his youth. He needs time to learn to assume his father's mantle. Nor is Odysseus immune from moral judgement. He suffers so long because – as we learn in flashback (in *Odyssey* 9–12) – Poseidon has been angry with him for blinding the god's son, the Cyclops Polyphemus, and then boasting about it. By the end of the epic, human suffering is motivated equally by human notions of retribution and justice. The gods preside, but from a distance. We are now in a world almost like Hesiod's *Works and Days*, where the poet invokes Zeus to ensure that just deeds are rewarded and the unjust punished.

We say *almost*. For, notwithstanding its more human focus, the *Odyssey* remains in the realm of heroic epic with connections to, as well as distance from, the world of the *Iliad*. The strongest of these links is Odysseus himself. It is not only the case that this hero is a survivor from Troy and the *Iliad*, but also the story of his fate directly looks back to one of the lessons of the *Iliad*. As we have just seen, Zeus cares about Hector and guarantees his proper burial because of that man's piety. Hector's lifelong dedication to divine rites sets him apart from a godlike hero like Achilles, who was deserving of attention because of his divine parentage. In the opening scene of the *Odyssey*, Athena objects to Odysseus's inclusion in Zeus's blanket indictment of mankind's irresponsible behaviour (1.45–62). In response, Zeus is minded to agree for the same reason as he favours Hector – Odysseus always showed piety towards the gods (1.65–7). As a result, three times in the epic, in *Odyssey* 1, 5, and 24, Zeus and Athena form a war cabinet to stage Odysseus's return home. In *Odyssey* 1, Zeus sends Athena (in disguise) to initiate Telemachus's search for news of his father. In *Odyssey* 5, he sends Hermes to initiate the final leg of Odysseus's return home. In *Odyssey* 24, the pair of them oversee Odysseus's victory over the suitors' families. Yet, the clearest example of their plot management comes from the fact that the *Odyssey* starts with Poseidon – the one god obstructing Odysseus's return – *absent*. This is the window of opportunity that Athena has been looking for and she is quick to take advantage in order to speed Odysseus on his way. Thus, even though Odysseus is closer to the world of men than, say, Achilles, he enjoys the support of the gods in a far more direct and explicit way than anything for which we could ever hope. Unlike Hesiod, Odysseus doesn't just express hope that Zeus punishes transgressors. He himself becomes Zeus's instrument to ensure divine will is done.

The developing withdrawal of Zeus and the absence of the other deities illustrate how the poem probes the widening of the gap between gods and men. The *Odyssey* explores the margins of the epic cosmos as Odysseus literally moves from the world of epic fantasy, gods, and monsters back to reality and human existence.

We first find Odysseus languishing on a desert island held captive as the lover of the goddess Calypso. We should expect offspring from the union of a god and her lover, as indeed we do with Peleus and Thetis, whose union acts as such an important genesis to the events of the *Iliad*. Yet, the *Odyssey* offers none, in spite of the fact that Odysseus has been having sex with Calypso for some seven years. Later, we learn that Odysseus also enjoyed a year of intercourse with the witch Circe. In one of the 'Epic Cycle' traditions that come down to us, Odysseus and Circe are said to have had a child (in the so-called *Telegony*). Not so in the *Odyssey*. The *Odyssey* admits a magical (and monstrous) world that was absent from the *Iliad* (if part of its backstory), only to deny its continued relevance. In spite of appearances, this is *not* a world in which gods and mortals couple to produce a race of semi-divine heroes. Instead, the *Odyssey* charts a route away from such a fantastical realm. The land of the Phaeacians is the last fantastical place Odysseus visits before Ithaca. Significantly, it is described as a 'golden age' land, where crops grow without effort and gods walk among men. The help that they give Odysseus actually draws a curtain over their existence, as Poseidon seals off their world forever. The *Odyssey*'s statement could not be clearer. The heroic age has passed. The world of men is forever separated from the world of gods.

In this growing chasm between gods and men, women find a place. In the *Iliad*'s poem of force, women are rarely heard. But their perspectives play a crucial role in giving the events added emotional charge, such as when Andromache or Hecuba express what Hector means to them, or, more remarkably, when the slave girl Briseis mourns the gentle Patroclus. In contrast, the *Odyssey* abounds with women – so much so that the Victorian critic Samuel Butler claimed that a woman must have authored it. Its cast list of women extends from gods and magical creatures (Athena, Calypso, the Sirens, Circe) to human, yet still significant, characters (Nausicaa, Arete, Helen, Anticleia, Eurycleia, Penelope).

These women all play a critical role in Odysseus's return home. But they are also important because of the kind of world the *Odyssey* presents. Women are the great survivors of epic. In this transition to the world of man, which the *Iliad* and *Odyssey* map out, the race of heroic *men* die, while women live on. They represent the future promise of immortality, now conceived not as everlasting life for the individual but as generational continuity. In fact, the only women to die in epic are the maidservants of Odysseus who have been sleeping with the suitors. By having them gruesomely executed, the *Odyssey* demonstrates its moral concern with legitimate progeny. More than anything, the poem is deeply concerned with Odysseus's legacy with the like-minded woman he left behind and the son who will take his place.

In actual fact, the poem's denial of a heroic cosmos extends to Odysseus's role in it. When Hermes arrives on Calypso's desert island to initiate Odysseus's departure, the nymph offers Odysseus immortality only for him to refuse. Every day, for seven years, Odysseus has risen from his lover's bed to sit by the shoreline and weep. For all this time, his sights have been fixed on getting home to Ithaca and returning to the arms of his wife, Penelope. Odysseus asserts the poem's *human* focus. But, in a paradoxical twist, Odysseus's refusal of immortality also represents the poem's *epic* focus. For, by refusing immortality in body, Odysseus ensures immortality of his *fame* (*kleos*).

In providing one of the last steps before cosmic history arrives at a place near us, the *Odyssey* depicts domestic life – slaves, family, hospitality, and leisure – in ways that the *Iliad* cannot. In part, this is a function of this poem's focus on a post-war society. But it is also part of the function of epic more generally. Since men cannot fraternise with the gods anymore, much less be (demi)gods, epic narrative needs to set out what men are now and how they define themselves. Of course, the gods remain important, but now the focus is on how men relate to them. Thus, the *Odyssey* depicts religious behaviour and observance from small sacrifices before meals to grand sacrifices to Poseidon. When Alcinous, the king of the Phaeacians, (finally) asks Odysseus to reveal his identity, he specifically asks him to talk 'about the people and well-populated cities, / those who are cruel, wild and unjust, / and those who respect strangers and have a mind that is god-fearing' (8.574–6). The introduction of right and wrong as a crucial aspect of fearing the gods indicates another way in which the *Odyssey* separates itself from the age of heroes and anticipates the life of its audiences. While the gods no longer intervene directly in human affairs, they still offer the promise of acting as guarantors of righteous behaviour. Judging it and this *man* (*andra*, 1.1) of many ways will be key.

The two Homeric epics each in turn give differing but complementary visions of the world of gods, the society of men, and the intercourse between the realms. Such perspectives reflect not only the narrative interests of each poem but also the general development of these themes in Greek myth. Homer's epics project upon a mythical past a world that is at once like ours enough to be familiar, but separate enough for gods and men to negotiate their relationships in anticipation of the world of the audience. They provide a foundational story for the nature of man and his responsibility to the gods. They also provide the basic framework for starting conversations on important issues like the value of a life, the meaning of violence, the proper behaviour of men, and, as we shall see next, the governance of cities.

2

The *Iliad*: the poem of politics

Homer's *Iliad* arguably stands as the first literary classic of the Western tradition. In it, Homer tackles some of humanity's big questions. What's it like to face death and how should you face up to it? What role do the gods play in human existence? How can you be adequately compensated for putting your life on the line? How can the competing demands of winning honour and protecting the community be balanced? What are the consequences of intense emotion and extreme violence? How should you treat the enemy or behave towards those less powerful? What is truly worth living, and dying, for? Homer explores these themes (and more) at the same time as having a keen sense of the minutiae of life – the close word of a husband to a wife, the silent loyalty of a friend, the toil of battle, the burning sense of injustice that is so difficult to put away. Part of what makes the *Iliad epic* has been precisely its ability to speak to successive generations, and to mean something different for different peoples at different times.

But the *Iliad*'s relationship to its own tradition is also exceptional. The *Iliad* is pointedly *not* the story *of* the Trojan War, but rather a story set *within* the Trojan War. Even so, it still manages to evoke the concerns of the entire conflict. In the catalogue at the end of *Iliad* 2, Homer provides a roll call 'of the thousand ships' launched to secure Helen's return and the mustering of the combined Trojan forces as the two sides prepare to face each other in battle for the first time in the epic – *as if it were* the first time in the war itself and not sometime in the tenth year of conflict.

In the very next book, he introduces the primary Achaean heroes to us through the eyes of Helen, as she answers Priam's questions about them from their vantage point on the city's walls (though logically he must have been sick of the sight of them by now). Soon after, Homer imagines the conflict played out as a long-awaited duel between Menelaus, rightful husband of Helen, and Paris, her Trojan lover, before re-enacting the lovers' original elopement by having Aphrodite spirit Paris from the battlefield to have sex with Helen in her perfumed chambers back in Troy. Homer also anticipates a 'future' beyond the poem. Achilles' doom is foreshadowed (and determined) by the deaths of Patroclus and Hector. Agamemnon's murder on arriving home at the hands of his wife, Clytemnestra, is hinted at by his slighting of her in favour of a slave girl (Chryseis), particularly since he will arrive home with another slave girl (Cassandra, daughter of Priam). Memorably, Homer describes the mourning of Hector as lamentation for the destruction of the city. The poem's capacity to stand for the whole tradition while telling just a part is, in fact, one aspect that Aristotle singles out to indicate its greatness (*Poetics* 1459a).

In many ways, the *Iliad* offers itself as the master narrative not just of the Trojan War but of all and any wars. It was this impulse that prompted in 1939, on the eve of another war to end all wars, Simone Weil's famous essay on *The* Iliad, *or The Poem of Force*, in which she reads the *Iliad* as a brutally honest interrogation of the realities of conflict. Weil's remarkable insight into the poem's exposure of the emotional and psychological trauma that violence inflicts on those who are both victims of it and aggressors in it still has resonance today: but it is not the complete picture. For, as part of its challenge to the Trojan War tradition, the *Iliad* subverts the famous statement by Carl von Clausewitz that 'War is the continuation of politics by other means', by using politics as a means to reframe, and reimagine, the war at Troy. By focusing on conflict within the Achaean camp, the *Iliad* highlights the importance of public speech, in particular of having a place where men can do battle with words. In fact, a critical feature of its foundational narrative is its exploration of the assembly as an institution in which people can challenge the king. Man is a political animal, contended Aristotle, because of his capacity to speak. But, unlike the gods who can live alone (as Aristotle suggests), men need *each other* for protection and sustenance. Homer, who uses the war at Troy as a prism through which to explore the complex personal and public relations among the warring heroes, might have agreed.

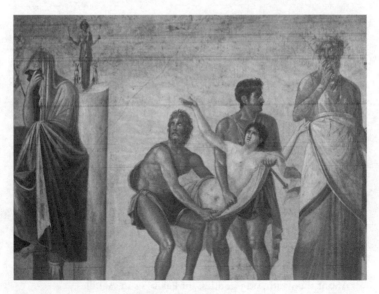

Sacrifice of Iphigenia, fresco from Pompeii, first century AD, National Museum of Naples

In addition to his returning home with a slave girl to enjoy in bed (Priam's daughter, Cassandra), Clytemnestra has other reasons to hate her husband, Agamemnon. As the Greek fleet gathered at Aulis (Euboea) to sail for Troy, the winds dropped and they couldn't set sail. (According to some accounts, this was because Agamemnon had killed a stag sacred to Artemis.) In order to gain a favourable wind, Agamemnon had to propitiate the gods. And, to do this, he sacrificed his daughter, Iphigenia. The story is memorably referred to in Aeschylus's tragedy *Agamemnon*, while Euripides stages it in his *Iphigenia at Aulis*. In this wall painting discovered at Pompeii, Agamemnon is presented as the figure on the left, covering his face, as his daughter is led away to sacrifice.

Anger and strife

With remarkable economy, the *Iliad*'s opening lines present its unique take on the Trojan War. In the tradition, the goddess Strife rolled an apple down the aisle at the wedding of Peleus and Thetis, resulting in three goddesses, Hera, Athena, and Aphrodite, battling it out to be recognised as the 'fairest of them all'. Paris judges Aphrodite the winner, and wins for himself Helen, the most beautiful woman in the world, and Menelaus's wife, as his bride. As a result, the Achaeans, under Agamemnon, Menelaus's brother, send an expedition to Troy to get Helen back, thereby bringing strife to the world of the heroes.

The *Iliad* begins in the tenth year of that war. It puts strife at the heart of its narrative, but in a way that radically departs from this story:

> About the wrath, sing goddess, of Peleus's son, Achilles,
> Destructive, which put pains thousand-fold upon the Achaeans,
> And sent many mighty souls to Hades
> Of heroes, and made them food for dogs

And birds of all kinds, and the will of Zeus was being
accomplished,
From that time when first the two of them stood apart in strife,
Atreus's son lord of men and godlike Achilles.

(*Iliad* 1.1–7)

The epic's first word is 'wrath', an almost godlike anger. It belongs
to Achilles, the Achaeans' champion. Its destructive impulse spells
doom for the heroes at Troy, all in the name of Zeus, whose plan
for the age of heroes is being accomplished. To this extent, the
Iliad clearly aligns itself with its epic inheritance.

But a closer examination reveals what is arguably a marked
departure from the Trojan War tradition. As a hero, we expect
Achilles to be wrathful and for his wrath to be destructive. But
the surprise is that the heroes who die are identified as *Achaeans*.
Achilles' wrath damns his *own* side. This point is worth stressing.
In the war between the Achaeans and Trojans for Helen, Achilles,
the greatest Achaean hero, is, according to the *Iliad*, responsible
for the deaths of his own people. The *Iliad*'s extraordinary take on
the fall of Troy immediately challenges audience expectations.
Rather than a tale of 'us' (Achaeans) versus 'them' (Trojans), the
main thrust of its narrative will be on *internal* conflict. This radical
shift in target complicates many of the themes central to the
Trojan War – themes such as honour, fame, shame, friendship, and,
above all, relations between individual and group. The traditional
story of strife speaks powerfully to a contemporary audience whose
own societies were undergoing revolutionary change.

The last line of the proem presents the central conflict as one
between Agamemnon and Achilles, between the 'lord of men'
and the 'godlike' hero. In the mythical tradition, heroes born of
gods, like Achilles, Heracles, Theseus, Jason, or Perseus, make the
world safe for mortal men by killing dangerous beasts (many-
headed Hydras, grotesque composite creatures, dragons, etc.) or
dangerous men (brigands, traitors, foreigners, etc.). The Athenian

hero Theseus was even said to create laws and encourage people to live together in larger communities instead of villages – which is why he could be considered the founding father of their democracy. On the other hand, the tradition also documents the dangers of such figures. Heracles goes mad and kills his first wife and children (his last wife also dies horribly). Theseus accidently brings about the death of his father. Jason's children with Medea are murdered. From the beginning of this epic, the audience are invited to question what kind of a hero this Achilles will be – whether the promise of benefaction will be worth the destruction. Furthermore, in spite of his semi-divine status, Achilles is not pre-eminent absolutely. Instead, he is paired with Agamemnon, addressed, according to his social status, as 'lord of men'. Elsewhere, Agamemnon is called 'shepherd of the people', a metaphor of some pedigree in the ancient world – Jesus, too, is a shepherd after all. Like Jesus, Agamemnon is responsible for his group's welfare and safety. The question is how these two figures, godlike Achilles and Agamemnon lord of men, fit in Zeus's plan and the story of this poem.

Homer strikes at the heart of the matter by immediately posing the question: 'which one of the gods set the two of them [Agamemnon and Achilles] fighting?' (8). An answer (of sorts) is immediately forthcoming: 'Zeus's son and Leto's, Apollo, who in anger at the king / sent foul pestilence among the army, and the people perished' (9–10). The poem's opening gambit reveals the hands of gods. Apollo is the ultimate cause of Achilles' anger; the Muses, the generator of this poem; Zeus, the author of the plan. But it also identifies human agency – the king, Agamemnon, insulting Apollo – and human suffering, as the people die from plague as a result of the king's (as yet unspecified) actions. While it takes barely two lines to deliver the divine perspective on events, it will take the rest of the poem to work through the consequences of Apollo's anger with the king. Translating a god's word into a human story is a messy, and complicated, business.

It involves the issue of man's *responsibility* for his actions, particularly when that man is a leader of men.

Though, for the most part, the *Iliad* does not represent the thoughts and feelings of the group at large, their wellbeing is a major concern of the narrative. From the beginning, Homer draws a direct connection between the warring strife of the two greatest Achaean heroes and the suffering of the people. His story questions the decisions and behaviour of the commander-in-chief. It investigates the role of the greatest warrior, allowing him full licence to vent his frustrations at heroic society and reflect on his place within it. Above all, it encourages the audience to think about the very survival of the people, both with and without heroes like Achilles. The *Iliad*, by subjecting the relationship between individuals and the group to such intense scrutiny, makes the story of Troy *political*.

Homer has identified the actions of the leader of men, Agamemnon, as causing Apollo's wrath. But just how did Agamemnon anger the god? Here Homer springs another surprise that directly reflects on internal strife in the Achaean camp. The first character on Homer's stage is neither Achilles, nor Agamemnon, nor in fact any of the Achaean heroes, an enemy warrior or a god. It is someone called Chryses (11), whose daughter Chryseis was taken when Achaeans sacked their town, Chryse. Chryses, Homer tells us, is a priest of Apollo, bearing the trappings of his office. Homer communicates this essential information in a rare introduction. Since we need to be told who Chryses is, in all probability he represents a minor character in the tradition, if not a complete innovation. Indeed, his name 'speaks'. Other, more familiar names mean something too. 'Hector' means 'protector', since he's Troy's bulwark. 'Achilles' derives from two nouns, *akhos* ('grief') and *laos* ('the people'), denoting the 'grief' that he brings to 'people' – an apt description. Chryses' name means 'the golden one', thereby underlining his affiliation with 'golden' Apollo (who, at some point, probably later, becomes associated with the sun; in Homer's world, Helios is the god who drives the sun in his divine chariot). The poem of force's first speaker is a minor character, from the opposing side, whose only significant attribute is his association with Apollo. Moreover, he comes to the Achaean camp to appeal for the return of his daughter. Contrary to expectations, the *Iliad* puts the *cost* of war at the heart of its narrative, not the glory that is said to come from it.

The challenge is about to become greater still. In offering a 'boundless ransom' (20) for his daughter's safe return, Chryses addresses his words to the Achaeans and the sons of Atreus, Agamemnon and Menelaus, 'the guardians of the people' (16). The views of the Achaean group are not articulated. But, importantly, we are told what they think: 'then all the rest of the Achaeans cried out in favour / that the priest be respected and the shining ransom be taken' (22–3). When this acclaim is ignored by Agamemnon, who sends Chryses away 'with a mighty command' (25), a dangerous political moment has been reached. The Achaeans and their leader should be in a symbiotic relationship. In the epic formulas, 'shepherd *of* the people', 'lord *of* men', the group are dependent on the individual, and he in turn is defined by them. Here, however, they are in conflict.

This king's speech is particularly shocking for several reasons. First, and most reprehensibly, Agamemnon disregards Chryses' status as Apollo's priest. The old man may *look* powerless (as his swift departure testifies), but he is still the god's servant, and bears that proof for all to see. The king, no matter how high and mighty, should respect that office. The clash between priest and king opens up a debate about the limits of human power. As if to emphasise the point, Agamemnon flaunts his power by threatening the priest with grievous bodily harm should he hang around, and by boasting how Chryses' daughter serves him in bed as well as in other duties (1.31). But almost as shocking is Agamemnon's assertion of his personal whim over the will of the community.

This first episode sets the overt expression of physical power against the marginal authority of the priest, and the desire of the king versus the will of his community. Both points act as a prelude to the catastrophic quarrel that follows.

Achilles calls an assembly

Once thrown out of the Achaean camp, Chryses retreats to the shoreline where he appeals to Apollo for revenge over the insult he has suffered. Apollo's vengeance is swift and deadly. With only the sound of arrows clanking in their quiver, Apollo descends from Olympus and rains a plague down on the Achaean host. And for nine days the people die because their king disrespected the priest. Then, on the tenth day, Hera puts it into Achilles' mind to call an assembly (54).

This event raises some important issues. A god's involvement marks the action out as significant. Hera intervenes because she 'cares about the Danaans [Achaeans]' (56). The assembly is set up under the supervision of a god for the benefit of the community. This will be important. But what of the instituting figure? At first sight, it may seem odd that it's not Agamemnon, since he's the leader of the expedition. But then he's the cause of the plague in the first place: so, perhaps he's either disinclined to address a situation he caused, or too blind to see the connection between his behaviour and their suffering. At the very least, we witness rather underwhelming leadership, since for nine days Agamemnon has stood by while his people suffered. When Hera turns to Achilles, perhaps because of his godlike quality or else because of his standing among his community, her act occurs in a political vacuum and will have fundamental political consequences.

Arguably the most important is Achilles' establishment of an assembly. At one level, the fact that calling an assembly is heralded as Achilles' first act in the epic points to the *Iliad*'s radical take on its tradition. Achilles, the hero of swiftness and fury, starts out *this* story by instituting a process of (peaceable) political redress to protect the people *we already know* he is bound to destroy. The extraordinary moment in Achilles' career is marked by the tension between his conventional character, the formulaic epithet 'swift-footed', with its battlefield associations, and the context in which it first applies – standing to speak in the assembly (58). But the act of calling an assembly itself may possess greater significance, if we reflect on the context. Prior to Hera's intervention, Homer makes no mention of the assembly (even though the Achaeans are gathered to hear Chryses' plea). This lack of detail may simply be a result of an economical and fast-paced narrative. But, because of what we have just said about Hera's role and Agamemnon's dereliction of duty, it is also an invitation to regard this event as something special, perhaps even new. Without question, assemblies must have played a role in epics prior to the *Iliad*. The elaborate formula for gathering an assembly, used when Agamemnon calls an assembly in *Iliad* 2, testifies to its presence in the tradition. But it remains true that when Achilles calls the assembly in *Iliad* 1 at this specific time for a specific reason – to address a threat to the people caused by their leader – he establishes a far more general principle for dealing with a crisis in the community.

The idea that we may be witnessing the tentative beginnings of a political settlement helps to explain some of its oddities. Achilles begins the debate (59) but, apart from citing Apollo as the plague's cause (Apollo is the god of health and sickness after all), he doesn't offer any solution himself. Instead, he calls upon 'some seer or bird interpreter' (again, note the connection to Apollo, the god of prophecy) to say what he knows. One such seer, Calchas, answers Achilles' invitation. But he refuses to say more unless and until Achilles can guarantee his safety, since (he fears) his revelation will anger a king (74–83). When Achilles offers this assurance, Calchas identifies Agamemnon as the cause, for having so brutally sent away Apollo's priest.

To us, these opening manoeuvres can seem strained, if not contrived. One might even suspect that Achilles and Calchas have staged the whole affair to undermine Agamemnon's authority. (Achilles glosses Calchas's vague worries by immediately pointing the finger at Agamemnon (91).) But, for an assembly that was established to address a specific topic, it is striking that it raises fundamental questions of *procedure* – who can speak, and how, and with what consequences. Achilles heralds the assembly as a space for *anyone* who can help the group to speak. (By the time of classical Athens in its fifth-century democratic heyday, these tentative first steps have become crystallised in the heraldic formula, 'Who wishes to speak?') Yet Calchas hesitates to speak for fear of upsetting the king. Such a fear would still be uppermost in the audience's mind, coming so soon after Agamemnon's violent dismissal of Chryses. But the risks are even greater in the case of Calchas, for suppression of his voice threatens to deprive the people of important knowledge. So, with another surprise turn, the champion of frank and open discussion turns out to be Achilles (at least initially). As much as paving the way to resolving the crisis within the Achaean camp, these opening manoeuvres in the assembly invite audiences to consider the interplay between personal desire and public need, free speech and the threat of violence, multiple viewpoints and a single authority.

Therefore, this first assembly functions in at least two ways. First, Homer expertly captures the cut-and-thrust of a real-life quarrel, involving a clash of egos between two powerful figures. Even as Agamemnon agrees to return Chryseis, he demands a prize (another woman) in return (118–20). When Achilles questions his right to do this, Agamemnon names and shames prominent leaders, including Achilles, whose own prize (the slave Briseis) Agamemnon could take, were he so minded (135–9). When Achilles threatens to leave, then and there, Agamemnon calls his bluff and sarcastically taunts him to 'go home then' (173). Events are spiralling out of control, as the speeches get angrier,

lengthier, and ever more personal. Homer also allows his protagonists' characters to come through. Agamemnon makes con-
cessions alongside new and surprising demands; Achilles seems
unnecessarily provocative. Thus, Achilles assures Calchas that he
will stand up to anybody, including he who '*claims* to be the best
of the Achaeans' (92) – an obvious dig at Agamemnon. Soon
after, he taunts Agamemnon by labelling him 'the greediest of
men for gain' (122).

But the assembly also functions in a more abstract sense as
well. The audience are invited to consider the political ramifica-
tions in the tensions between the selfish leader and the overzeal-
ous dissenter. The importance of this dissent, however, is elevated
by Hera's opening sponsorship; the subsequent moves may even
anticipate basic values of public assembly. Achilles makes the
ability to speak without fear of physical reprisal sacred with his
oath to Calchas. In addition, the fact that he can dissent from a
foolhardy authority, and that this protest results in a correction of
a mistake, emphasises the potential strength of the assembly (just
as the strife that issues from the personal argument indicates
potential weakness). By establishing the fundamental importance
of – but also difficult problems with – free speech in the assembly,
Homer primes his audience to look for the development of these
themes as the poem unfolds. The subsequent Achaean assemblies
of *Iliad* 2, 9, and 19 continue the investigation of this institution
as a way of facilitating both the participatory behaviour critical
for the salvation of the people and the success of the Achaean
coalition in the wake of the death of the age of heroes.

Achilles calls the assembly to find a solution to the community's crisis. He then promises the seer support so that the cause
of the crisis can be revealed. When Agamemnon first threatens to
take another prize (a woman), in compensation for having to
give up his own (Chryseis), Achilles defends the welfare of the
group. He speaks up on behalf of their interests and in support of
the principle of the public distribution of goods. 'We know of no

common store,' Achilles explains, adding: 'But what we took from
the cities by storm has been distributed; / it is unbecoming for
the people to call back things once given' (124–6). Yet, faced
by Agamemnon's intransigence and the silence of the crowd,
Achilles feels impelled to assert his own effort and poor returns.
Before too long, he is even swearing an oath not to fight again
until the *people* have suffered for their tacit support of Agamemnon.
For his part, Agamemnon does the right thing by promising to
return Chryseis to her father, but mismanages the situation by
making the argument personal. When he threatens to take Achilles'
prize, he makes his position dependent upon putting Achilles in
his place. At the heart of what began as a political crisis, Homer
exposes individual motivation and the role of the emotions.

One Achaean sees enough that he tries to intervene in the crisis.
Nestor, who has lived through two generations of men (so Homer
tells us at line 250) and advised mighty heroes like Perithous and
Theseus, asks everyone to listen to him again. Representing
something like the voice of tradition, Nestor tries to redirect the
heroes' anger against its proper target. As he puts it, the Trojans
must *love* seeing the Achaeans fight among themselves (255–7) – a
sentiment that also serves to remind *us* just how far the *Iliad* has
departed from the traditional story of the war at Troy. In a desperate
attempt to build bridges, he directs Achilles, though 'divine-
born', to give up his anger, since Agamemnon 'rules over most
men'; in turn, the king should relinquish his claim on Briseis.
Yet Nestor *fails* to persuade either man, which leaves us with
an uncomfortable question: just why should such a reasonable
compromise not succeed? One answer is that both men are too
stubborn and have invested too much to capitulate. Thus, while
Agamemnon pays lip service to Nestor's sound advice, he also
obsessively recounts Achilles' impudence (accusing him of wanting
to rule over them all himself (287–89)). When he derides Achilles'
status by labelling him a 'spearman', Achilles interrupts – a unique
event in epic verse – and tells Agamemnon where to go.

Another possibility is that Nestor intervenes *too late*. In fact, a god has already interceded, and changed the rules of the game. When earlier Agamemnon calls Achilles' bluff and taunts him, Achilles loses his temper and reaches for his sword (188–94) – at which point Athena suddenly appears. Appearing to him alone (underscoring Achilles' closeness to the gods), she pulls Achilles back by the hair to stop him from killing the king. As much as Achilles' defence of Calchas sanctions the right to speak without fear of violence, so now Athena's intervention ensures that dissent does not spill over into physical assault. By wholeheartedly supporting Achilles' conviction that Agamemnon has badly insulted him, she promises that he will receive material compensation from Agamemnon for this slight. (Not content with this promise, Achilles will go to his mother, Thetis, to enlist an assurance from Zeus himself.) Yet, crucially, Athena also invites Achilles to transform his rage into *words* instead of actions (210–11). It is because of Athena's intervention that Achilles feels free to launch into a vicious tirade against Agamemnon, in which he calls the king a 'wine sack with dog's eyes' and finishes by hurling down the sceptre (245). The sceptre symbolises the right to speak publicly on public concerns: by throwing it to the ground Achilles rejects all that it stands for. In turn, these insults he has just thrown (sanctioned by a god to do so) represent a departure from the kind of speech appropriate to the assembly.

Athena's intervention demonstrates that violence has no place in the assembly – for how could that help communities gain from open debate? Typically, however, divine intervention merely defers the crisis rather than resolve it. Athena, that aide of heroes from a bygone age, directs Achilles to use his words as weapons, the assembly as a battleground, and *public speech* for a private assault. Complementing this picture, Nestor's failed intervention shows that the personal interests of the combatants make them blind to the public good. Both mediations prompt the audience to think about the issues of this assembly and proper behaviour in its context. Dissent is necessary and useful; but it is not the same as abuse. Public speech should always be directed towards the public good, not individual profit.

Achilles acts as the catalyst for these issues to be aired and explored. Upon his entry into the epic, he is fundamental for sanctioning public debate by calling the assembly and sponsoring Calchas's speech. But, in his own use of speech, he is unnecessarily provocative, using his defence of Calchas to undercut Agamemnon's claim to be the best. After Athena's intervention he is all too quick to use angry words. By being 'godlike', Achilles enjoys an ambiguous status, which is both a blessing (his closeness to the gods brings him their aid) and a curse (inhuman action). Homer uses this duality to have Achilles both lay down the foundations to save the community (by establishing the assembly) and threaten its very existence (by withdrawing from it). In turn, Agamemnon is lord of men, shepherd of the people. He *ought* to have his people's best interests at heart, like the portrait of the good king at the beginning of Hesiod's *Theogony*. By showing Achilles' challenge to Agamemnon, the *Iliad* suggests that absolute power and authority in one man can threaten communities. In contrast, with the establishment of an assembly, the audience glimpses the possibility of a different world, one where political institutions exist to assist leaders and to ensure the cultivation of the public good. Furthermore, it is no accident that the assembly at the beginning of the *Iliad* might recall similar contexts in the world of Homer's audiences. As a foundational narrative that illustrates and explains the extinction of the race of heroes and the separation of the worlds of man and god, the *Iliad* offers a political drama that looks forward to the future present of its audience.

Still, these initial steps are only tentative and restricted at first to Achilles. Subsequent assemblies extend the *Iliad*'s investigation of politics by integrating other members of the Achaean host into the process of working through the political fallout from

Achilles' challenge. In *Iliad* 2 and 9, Agamemnon establishes assemblies in order to recommend swift flight – the first time as part of an elaborate trick, the second time in despair, but on both occasions with near-disastrous consequences. In the assembly of *Iliad* 2, Agamemnon's 'test' of his troops' resolve demands that each man must think whether it is still worth fighting at Troy – and to a man they rush to the ships. Then there would have been a 'homecoming beyond fate' (Homer again testing how far he can rework the tradition), had not Hera intervened and, with Athena's help, roused Odysseus to get the men back in line. Even then a crisis looms, as a perpetual dissenter by the name of Thersites takes up Achilles' mantle and roundly chastises Agamemnon. Odysseus beats him up for his pains (whether because Thersites is a commoner or because he doesn't take dissent seriously enough, we aren't told), but the effect is to unite the crowd in laughter. Speeches by Odysseus and Nestor then use the assembly to ensure that their fragile coalition doesn't fracture completely, by rallying the men behind Agamemnon, however disgruntled they might be.

When Agamemnon again recommends flight in the assembly of *Iliad* 9, this time in all seriousness, his speech again meets resistance, this time in the form of the youthful Diomedes. This hero, who has already proven himself in battle (in *Iliad* 5), appeals to the precedent that Achilles has laid down, describing how he will do battle in words with the king as 'is the custom' (9.33). By book nine, dissent is now being configured as something routine and *traditional*. Even so, Nestor intervenes, this time to move the discussion to the more intimate surroundings of the 'council', in which only the Achaean leaders could participate. He understands that standing up to Agamemnon still requires careful management.

These different responses to Achilles' challenge continue the exploration of assembly talk, of what kind of dissent is legitimate, and how far, as well as how best, debate should be managed. What isn't resolved, however, is what to do with Achilles.

The embassy to Achilles

For eight books, Homer removes from the scene the 'best of the Achaeans', whose wrath so violently begins the poem and disrupts the political status quo. At long last, we return to Achilles in *Iliad* 9. When the focus returns to him, however, once again it is not physical action that drives the day, but speech; not the war against the Trojans, but politics. While the assemblies of *Iliad* 1, 2, and 9 emphasise the development and importance of public debate, the embassy – involving three hand-picked Achaeans journeying to Achilles' tent to offer him recompense for Agamemnon's insult – turns attention back to social relationships and personal worth. Through the different responses elicited from Achilles during the negotiations, the embassy scene invites reflection not so much on what a hero is but what it means to be a man, what men hold dear, and how and why men should get along with each other. In turn, the embassy scene presents among the most powerful and majestic speeches of the whole epic, revealing the character, hopes, and fears of the people involved.

By the end of book eight, the Achaeans' predicament is perilous: the Trojans camp on the plain for the first time in the war and their fires surround the fearful Achaeans. After Agamemnon's near-disastrous recommendation of flight, which Diomedes successfully rebuts, Nestor immediately calls a council for the leaders to deliberate on what to do, since their position remains precarious. In this more private setting, Nestor speaks what until now would have been considered unthinkable: he advises Agamemnon to offer 'gifts and sweet words' to win over Achilles (111–13), advice to which the king readily assents. To attract Achilles back, Agamemnon offers a mightily impressive catalogue of stuff: seven tripods, twenty cauldrons, a dozen horses, seven women, the hand in marriage of one of his daughters, rule over seven cities in the Peloponnese (115–61). Yet, in spite of its size and quality, problems remain. For one thing, Agamemnon promises some gifts that will be Achilles' only once the Achaeans have sacked Troy and returned home safely – a point which, as we shall see, has particular meaning for Achilles. The number of the gifts also points to Agamemnon's power – he has them to bestow because of his superiority. Even his offer of his daughter in marriage is double-edged, in that, as son-in-law, Achilles would rule *under* Agamemnon. Agamemnon's fixation on maintaining his authority most clearly intrudes at the end of his speech, when he demands that Achilles 'yield to me, inasmuch as I am more kingly' (160). Perceptively, Nestor remarks that no one could scorn Agamemnon's gifts, but says nothing about the sweet words he had also recommended.

In spite of his misgivings, Nestor takes command of the final preparations for the embassy. He spends most of the time coaching Odysseus, whose reputation as a persuasive speaker goes before him. With him are Ajax, the bulwark of the Achaeans in Achilles' absence, and Phoenix. Once ready, the three of them set off along the shoreline of the 'much-resounding sea' (182) – the same one walked by Chryses back in *Iliad* 1 (34) – to Achilles' tent. Here they find the hero playing the lyre and delighting his heart by singing 'the famous deeds of heroes' (*klea andrôn*)' (189) – a phrase that draws attention (again) to the *Iliad*'s innovating plot (the hero is singing about great deeds rather than doing them) and headlines the importance of the negotiations about to take place (*what* will Achilles be famous for?). Upon seeing them, Achilles immediately leaps up to receive them as his 'friends', the 'dearest of all the Achaeans' (197–8). Subsequently, the value of each ambassador becomes clear from the different speech that each man delivers. Where Odysseus delivers Agamemnon's offer, Phoenix makes an appeal based on his personal connection to Achilles; Ajax's speech is the bluntest and shortest, but appears to carry the greatest impact. Together, these entreaties and the responses they provoke help us not only understand Achilles' mindset, but also think through key issues about human endeavour, responsibility, worth, and, above all, friendship.

Odysseus demonstrates his ability as a speaker by using their situation to break the ice. Toasting Achilles, he draws a connection between the hospitality they receive at his hands and their earlier feasting with Agamemnon at the council, thereby putting the two occasions, and figures, on par with each other (225–8). At the same time, though, he notes the discord with their broader predicament. They are not there to feast, since the Achaeans are in dire straits. As Achilles does in *Iliad* 1, Odysseus installs himself as the people's spokesman: '*We* are afraid' (230), he bluntly admits. Like Nestor, he tries to redirect Achilles' wrath towards its proper target – that is, the Trojans and, in particular, Hector, through whom Odysseus focalises the threat both to the Achaeans' lives and to Achilles' fame (237–9). Most strikingly of all, Odysseus recalls Peleus's parting words of advice to his son to 'check the proud spirit / in his chest' (255–6). This (selective) memory allows Odysseus to make sense of Achilles' anger with Agamemnon and bring it under control (it was *expected*). Then Odysseus makes his gambit – 'Agamemnon offers you / worthy gifts if you change from your anger' (260–1) – and presents the proposal in full.

In what follows, Odysseus catalogues the gifts verbatim, with one notable change. He leaves out Agamemnon's demand for obedience. In fact, rather than lingering on the gifts, Odysseus concludes by playing upon Achilles' concerns for the group. Even if Agamemnon is still hateful to him *and all these gifts*, he says, 'at least take pity on all the other Achaeans / suffering in the army, who as a god / will honour you. You can win very great glory among them' (301–3). In the end, Odysseus shows that he at any rate understands that material gain is probably not going to be enough for Achilles. Yet nothing could have prepared him or us for how little value Achilles attaches to it, given that his quarrel with Agamemnon started over a single slave girl.

Achilles doesn't just reject Agamemnon's proposal as communicated by Odysseus; he chews over the carefully ordered catalogue and spits it back at him. Indeed, so incensed is Achilles that society itself seems to be in his sights. The political challenge is evident from his opening words: 'Hateful to me like the gates of Hades is that man / who keeps one thing hidden in his heart but says something else' (312–13). His remarks are ostensibly aimed at Agamemnon, as if he has seen through the catalogue to the king's latest clumsy attempt to assert authority. But the criticism is apt too for the messenger, Odysseus, known to the tradition for being duplicitous. Through Achilles, Homer asks us to see such 'double speak' – saying one thing while meaning another – as not only the fundamental cause of his grievance but also, perhaps, a central problem for political discourse. Clearly, speaking frankly has its dangers (perhaps Achilles should have hidden his feelings about Agamemnon in *Iliad* 1), and diplomacy depends on holding some things back. But, on the other hand, giving a speech in which one hides what one thinks also imperils open discussion. Previously critical while using the assembly as a place for debate, Achilles now begins to critique the nature of political discourse itself.

Achilles' directness manifests itself in two ways. First, he exposes the reward system, by which the individual is compensated for the effort he puts in, as a sham. As his quarrel with Agamemnon seems to show, he who does nothing (Agamemnon) gets the same as the one who does everything (him). This in turn undermines the very reasons why they're there, as he compares his conflict to the cause of the war itself. 'Are they alone among mortal men to love their wives / the sons of Atreus?' (340–1). Here Achilles makes explicit what Homer earlier had only implied, when he began the story of the Achaeans' war for Helen with internal strife over Briseis. According to Achilles (and Homer?), the whole of the Trojan War saga is implicated in the opening conflict between the greatest of the Achaeans. If Agamemnon behaves like the Trojans, then what is the point of fighting in the first place?

Second, Achilles abruptly announces that *he will return home*, the next day. This 'plan' contests the very essence of the traditional

Trojan War tale. But his startling declaration comes from the special insight that he has into his fate from his mother: 'if I stay to fight about the city of the Trojans, / my homecoming perishes, but my glory [*kleos*] will be imperishable; / but if I return home to my dear fatherland, / my noble glory is lost, but a long life / there will be for me, and my end in death will not come swiftly' (412–16). Unlike the other heroes at Troy, Achilles *knows* that if he stays and fights he will die; it is not just a risk, but an inevitability. In this light, Agamemnon's promises mean nothing to him – he won't live to enjoy any of those promised possessions. Significantly, too, Achilles' semi-divine nature helps only so far as to supply him with knowledge of his mortality. As the epic unfolds, mortality preoccupies the hero. Here, it provides him with the stimulus to reflect on the situation of all those who fought at Troy. Achilles not only ponders the fairness of Agamemnon's coalition and recognises the irony of their conflict over a girl within the context of the Trojan War, but he also questions the purpose of any of it. Why strive, why care about honour, why even fight, when everyone dies the same?

The power of Achilles' unique speech derives ironically from its universal potential. As he struggles with measuring a man's value in material terms or by arbitrary judgements, Achilles challenges his fellow Achaeans and Homer's audience. On this occasion, his questioning demands that we consider the very fundamentals of political relationships and behaviour. Just why should the Achaeans form a coalition against the Trojans? How should a man's worth be assessed? What can really compensate for death? Even though Achilles finds that his own thinking changes subsequently, the questions he raises linger on in the minds of the audience, for each person to resolve for him- or herself.

For a long time, Homer tells us, no one speaks (431–2). The silence that greets Achilles represents a communication break-down, the failure to anticipate these specific complaints, and, again, the distance between Achilles and the rest of the Achaeans. At length, Phoenix, Achilles' old tutor, speaks. He delivers the longest speech in the epic (434–605). Unlike Odysseus, Phoenix makes friendship the central part of his speech, not a passing concern. In important ways, the content of this speech offers some responses to Achilles' questions and anticipates what may make him return.

Phoenix immediately strikes a personal note by wondering how he could stay at Troy should Achilles depart. For Phoenix, Achilles is family. He was an exile taken in by Peleus, and treated like his son. In turn, Phoenix cared for Achilles, recalling the times when, as a baby, Achilles used to dribble food all over him. By offering a picture of the infant Achilles babbling childish things, Phoenix gently establishes himself as a father figure (where Odysseus, and Agamemnon, had so badly failed), and draws a subtle connection to the present crisis. Phoenix is here to reintegrate Achilles into society and teach him to speak a second time.

He does so by using two special kinds of speech, the parable and the story from myth. Both explicitly invite interpretation, which in turn encourages Achilles to take his first steps towards re-engagement. Phoenix's 'parable of the Prayers' exploits the theme of Achilles' near-divinity to show that even the gods can be turned aside from wrath when humans supplicate them. After this, Phoenix offers a tale from the heroic past, the Calydonian Boar Hunt (a tale that Peleus, Achilles' father, participated in, according to some accounts). Phoenix explicitly frames the story as an example to Achilles, objecting that Achilles' behaviour *does not* follow the lessons learned from 'the famous deeds of men' (*klea andrôn*)' (524), the very phrase used to describe Achilles' song when the embassy first arrived. The central story of the impetuous hero Meleager, moreover, appears to have been adapted by Phoenix to suit his context. Phoenix depicts a hero getting angry and refusing to fight for his people, and then receiving a series of entreaties, notably from *his friends*. In the end, Achilles' old tutor observes, the hero returns to fight, but too late to receive the gifts that had been offered.

The impact of Phoenix's speech is readily discernible. After silencing the embassy with his first response, Achilles is drawn back into dialogue. His first words, *atta* ('papa', 607), echo those of a baby to a father, as if he were learning to speak again. And Achilles is only too aware of the effect of Phoenix's words. He warns Phoenix not to 'confuse' his heart by holding Agamemnon dear for fear of becoming his enemy. But, even as he struggles to maintain distinctions between friend and foe, Achilles shifts position. He announces that in the morning he will 'think about' whether he should stay or go (619).

At this point, Achilles nods to Patroclus to prepare a bed for Phoenix (620–2). The discussion seems at an end. Then, even as he prepares to depart with Odysseus, Ajax speaks. This mighty warrior, upon whose shoulders now rests the defence of the Achaeans, is not renowned for his speaking. (In the gloomy underworld of *Odyssey* 10, he famously refuses to say anything to Odysseus, still burning with hatred at being cheated – as he sees it – out of inheriting Achilles' armour.) Here, his speech stands apart for its gruff frankness. He begins, taking his lead from Achilles' apparent farewell, by addressing Odysseus (624). The two of them should go home, since Achilles 'has made savage the proud spirit in his chest' and does not 'remember his companions' friendship' (629–30). Ajax gets right to the heart of the matter: friendship. Achilles greets the embassy as friends; Phoenix exploits his friendship to reopen negotiations; now Ajax turns the tables on Achilles by accusing him of not respecting those he has welcomed in under his roof, though they are, he acknowledges, the dearest to him (640–2). Ajax hits the mark. Achilles is forced to admit that he is right. Yet, still Achilles cannot bring himself to accept their petition. His heart still swells with anger (646). But he does make a final concession. He commits himself to *remaining at Troy*, and will even return to battle if and when Hector arrives at his ships (650–5).

Contrary to initial impressions, the embassy actually *succeeds*. It is true that Achilles does not yet give up his wrath and return to the fighting. In this sense, the embassy has come almost too soon. The next time we see Achilles, in *Iliad* 11, he's looking out over the battlefield, wondering when the Achaeans will come to him, still waiting for an embassy, it seems (609–10). But the embassy does succeed in committing Achilles to stay at Troy. And it does that because of his *relations* with his fellow men, not because – in fact, in spite of – the many and the great gifts that Agamemnon offers. Even as Achilles asserts his individuality, he feels bound by his friendships.

One friend remains with him throughout – Patroclus. He's there, silently listening to Achilles playing on the lyre and singing the deeds of great heroes, when the embassy arrives (190–1). He is the one to whom Achilles turns to make ready a bed for Phoenix. In *Iliad* 11, it is Patroclus whom Achilles sends to the Achaeans, to discover what's happening (611–12). All the while he remains silent – Horatio to Achilles' Hamlet, always by his side, always supportive. Only once does he criticise Achilles, when he returns at the beginning of *Iliad* 16 with news of the impending catastrophe – Hector is about to set fire to the Achaean ships. Achilles, still angry, refuses to fight himself, but concedes to his friend's desire to fight in his place.

The embassy scene extends the *Iliad*'s investigation into politics from institutional frameworks to language itself and basic relationships – the foundations for any political community. Achilles' refusal of Agamemnon's catalogue of gifts represents a rejection not only of the king's control but also of the subtly coercive manner of Odysseus's persuasion. His refusal, moreover, poses questions for the audience about the kind of speech that ought to be used in political situations. How frank, or how diplomatic, can or should you be? In their contrasting ways, Phoenix – by inviting Achilles to draw the lesson – and the blunt-talking Ajax manage to pull Achilles back from the brink and commit to staying. Nevertheless, he remains resolutely out of the fighting. His mind changes only once his best friend, Patroclus, lies dead.

Founding a political community

From the beginning of the epic through to the point when Achilles finally enters the fray, the public assembly has been *the* venue for the strife. The proem's announcement that the *Iliad* begins when godlike Achilles and Agamemnon lord of men stand apart in strife doesn't just offer another story set within the period of the race of heroes; it justifies their demise and sets out the central questions for establishing institutions and political standards in their wake. Rather than attempting to portray the realistic workings of an assembly or, more generally, the real-life political situation in the Greek world of the time, Homer composes a foundational narrative that can speak to the concerns of all Greek communities regardless of their specific political constitutions and allegiances. At the same time, the *Iliad* provides audiences with a past that they can recognise as transitional to their *present*, whether conservative oligarchs or radical democrats.

The quarrel between Achilles and Agamemnon is fundamental to the *Iliad*'s depiction of politics. It is not only that Homer depicts elite heroes (Achilles and Agamemnon) at odds with each other; he also shows an intense interest in the situation of the *people* who depend on their leaders for salvation (as epic narrative puts it). Accordingly, the quarrel plot, which extends through and motivates much of the *Iliad*'s action, provides a frame for considering questions of a political nature (who should be prominent, when, where, how, and why), the consequences of failing to resolve internal conflicts, and the strengths and weaknesses of man-made solutions, such as *ad hoc* compromises or even institutions. Its characters are not uncivilised heroes who do what they want, who go on quests, who reap the benefit of their individual labours. Instead, we find men who can only profit by working together in coalition politics and who suffer more if they cannot organise their co-operation effectively. In part, the epic provides what we might consider an explanatory myth for the origin of human political conventions within a dramatisation of *why* they are so crucially needed. In the wake of the death of the race of heroes, the *Iliad* traces out the need for and development of *institutions*.

From this perspective, Achilles' act of establishing an assembly in the first episode of the epic poses general questions important for any community. The drama of the *Iliad* resides not so much in an aristocratic argument over relative honour as in its fallout, in the continuing negotiations and renegotiations as men try to resolve and/or manage the consequences of conflict. It is in the aftermath of the strife introduced in its opening movement that the poem unfolds the business of governing. Indeed, ingeniously Homer's epics imitate the evolutionary nature of political institutions. Rarely are whole-scale political settlements created at a single stroke, as in the framing of the US Constitution. The United Kingdom, for example, lacks a written constitution. There is the *Magna Carta*, but how this thirteenth-century text relates to current parliamentary democracy, let alone the notion of the United Kingdom itself, is a moot point. Rather, political institutions tend to develop over time in reaction to cultural demands from the bottom up; they are not imposed top-down. The *Iliad*, we suggest, invites its audience to think about this process and get involved in making sense of its song of strife.

By posing serious challenges to the rule of one man, exposing flaws in the intense rivalry between competing heroes, and showing the predicament of the group at large, the *Iliad* responds to, engages in, and may even help *shape* contemporary political concerns. In fact, it is precisely by projecting these concerns on a previous age that Homer encourages his audience(s) to explore their own strife through the conflicts of prior mythical figures.

Most importantly, by posing difficult questions and providing no easy answers, the *Iliad* fosters political conversation, facilitating as many responses as there were different cities in the Greek world.

This political theatre, of course, also reflects deeply on its players. Achilles' meditations on the worth of heroism, the value of possessions, and the invaluable prize of friendship are not for naught. Such thoughts frame our reception of the political theme and invite us to consider the interdependency between the public and private. Achilles' personal resolve condemns the race of heroes to oblivion even as it acts as a catalyst for a new kind of politics to emerge, like a phoenix rising from the ashes. As we will find in the next chapter, the *Iliad* is also concerned with exploring how Hector struggles with his own questions of individual fame and social worth, as well as the fate of Troy itself.

3
Inside Troy

As much as the issue of politics is crucial for much of the *Iliad*'s force, it is doubtful whether the poem would have captured the imagination of so many audiences were that the only important element. To explain the poem's enduring emotional appeal we must enter Troy itself. As a poem set within the tradition of the conflict between the Achaeans and Trojans, the *Iliad* is remarkably even-handed in its treatment of both sides of the war. Where later Greek narratives draw a stark distinction between the civilised Greeks and the barbarous inhabitants of Asia – the 'other' against whom all that is good and 'natural' is defined – Homer's Trojans are basically like their Achaean counterparts. Greek and Trojan alike belong to an age of heroes. They pray to the same gods, speak the same language, and share many of the same beliefs about honour and fame. Homer even inverts the basic plot-based distinctions between the two sides. For the majority of the poem, with Achilles withdrawn from battle, Homer has the Trojans besiege the Achaeans behind their hastily constructed walls (*Iliad* 8–20). As a result of Zeus's plan to honour Achilles, heroes on both sides die, forcing all to face incredible loss.

A good deal of the power of the battle scenes in fact derives from Homer's balanced handling of both sides. Homer's sympathetic and sensitive depiction of the Trojans allows us to care for all the men who die, not just for the Achaeans. But, in addition, the *Iliad* is marked by its interest not just in representing the violence of war but also in exploring its wider impact on the family, women, and the home. It is among the Trojans that we find humanity's ebb and flow. From Hector's admirable bravery to Paris's self-confessed shirking, the Trojans stand for the many disparities in human potential. Since the Achaean families are at home across the sea, Homer uses Troy to evoke and explore universal themes raised by war. Where the Achaeans mention in passing those they left behind – their parents, wives, and children – the Trojan heroes have their families on stage with them to share their fates and await their doom. The *Iliad* makes a considerable impression by affording us a view of the war from the perspective of the Trojan women whose views and roles are by no means rote or simple. The audience are treated to the fears and affection of Trojan mothers and wives and even of the turncoat sister-in-law, as the wider experience of human life is brought into focus.

The *Iliad* is also interested in the political situation of the Trojans for its own sake and as a comparison to the state of affairs among the Achaeans. Indeed, one of the features often overlooked when assessing Homer's exploration of politics is the way that the epic deploys the same questions on three distinct fronts – the wrangling of the gods, the strife among the Achaeans, and the struggles of the Trojans in the face of certain doom. Thus, while the Trojan assembly lacks the intensity of the Achaean space, it does raise important issues that strike at the heart of Trojan society. More than anything, it serves to highlight the prominence of Hector, whose very name, meaning 'the defender', shows what he means to his people. But equally his dominance over debate exposes damaging fault lines underlying Troy's security, though Homer makes this a political failure of the Trojans at large. As for Hector, Homer focuses on his interaction with the women of Troy, thereby helping to cast the Trojan hero in a different light, as well rounded and likeable. So successful is Homer's portrayal that readers often find Hector more approachable and readily sympathetic than Achilles, and the true hero of the epic. No mean feat for the 'enemy's' lead warrior.

Trojan politics

If we flash forward to the fifth century BC, we can see how striking Homer's portrayal of the Trojans really is. When faced by a
similar cataclysmic struggle between East and West, the historian
Herodotus naturally turns to Homer to describe the Persian
invasion of Greece. But the way he frames this conflict is starkly
different: he wants to find out why Greeks came into conflict
with 'barbarians', a term which already had negative connota-
tions at this time. The experience of the Persian Wars must have
been formative – Xerxes' armies were packed with men from all
over the world with different dress, attitudes, and language. But it
is also the case that this experience belongs to an interpretative
framework that makes sense of the world in terms of oppositions.
Everything that the Greeks (believed they) were – manly, good at
fighting, free – the barbarians, and especially the Persians, were
not. Indeed, Herodotus's narrative stands out as a definitive
moment in our record of Greek cultural history where we first
find the people of Hellas defined as a unity. But this was by no
means the dominant strain of the post-Persian Wars world. In
political reality, all Greek cities, including (or especially?) Athens
and Sparta, fought *and* sought alliances with the 'barbarians'.
Meanwhile, Athenian artistic representations, both dramatic and
visual, constantly toy with casting the Greeks as the 'other', uncivilised, untrustworthy, and brutish.

In truth, Herodotus's *Histories* is too complex (and interesting) to be reduced to simple binary opposition. Even so, a Greek
in the classical period, accustomed to seeing the world in terms
of polarity, might have expected similar differences when coming
to Homer. For example, on the Athenian Parthenon (made
between 447 and 432 BC), Greeks line up alongside the Olympian
gods and Athenians in their respective struggles with Trojans,
Giants, and Amazons – a straight fight: the forces of order versus
disorder. Even in the *Odyssey*, the negative traits of other peoples

are consistently brought to bear on our understanding of Odysseus's return home. Yet, in the *Iliad*, such differences are difficult, if not impossible, to sustain. One famous passage at the beginning of *Iliad* 3 does draw a distinction between the sides in behavioural terms: as the armies form up to fight, Homer compares the sound of the Trojans babbling to the squawking of cranes and other foreign birds in flight (2–7), while the Achaean phalanxes advance resolutely in silence. But, apart from some other minor ethnographic distinctions, the Trojans appear to have the same beliefs, fears, and values as the Achaeans. Homer doesn't set the Trojans up as monsters or strangers to be hated. If anything, they are as sympathetically cast as the Achaeans themselves.

There does, however, appear to be one exception that proves the rule, especially because it is not an ethical criterion but rather *political*. The Trojans practise politics somewhat differently from the Achaeans. The difference is evident from Homer's representation of their institutions. Not only are there fewer Trojan assemblies, but those that do occur are either more perfunctory or else marked as peculiar. There can be little doubt that one reason for this is the fact that the poem focuses on the Achaeans and their political settlement. Nevertheless, Homer's emphasis does seem pointed: if he wanted to present the Trojan polity as similar or even superior to the Achaean coalition, he could. Instead, we find a troubled people with troubled institutions, which, importantly, fail to develop over the course of the poem. We needn't assume that Troy falls because of their poor political handling of the crisis – Troy *always* falls in the tradition. It may be the case, however, that, in this version of the tradition, the absence of an equivalent political settlement plays a role. Nor should we imagine that the problem develops *by virtue* of their being Trojan. Indeed, it is impossible to say whether Trojan politics are limited because they are a city under siege or whether they are under siege as a result of deficient and unresponsive politics. More productive is to reflect on *why* Homer would integrate such detail into his epic.

Thus, we must consider the *Iliad*'s political picture as a whole. What do the contrasting portrayals of the Achaeans and Trojans tell us about them?

The *Iliad* depicts the Trojans in three assembly scenes (compared with six for the Achaeans and two or three for the gods). Unlike the Achaean assemblies of *Iliad* 1, 2, 9, and 19, whose very establishment and performance is up for debate, each Trojan assembly emphasises deficient features of the city's political institutions. The first Trojan assembly passes almost without comment. Iris, the messenger of Zeus, finds the Trojans *already* assembled before *Priam's* gate. (The Achaean assembly, we learn in *Iliad* 11.806–8, occurs not by Agamemnon's tent but by Odysseus's ship in the *middle* of the camp, thereby illustrating the commonality of the space.) And the assembly only features the goddess and the royal family. In disguise Iris remarks on Priam's fondness for 'endless speeches'; as she turns to Hector, he dismisses the assembly. There is no debate. This assembly exists, it seems, solely for the purpose of watching *someone else's* performance (here, the gathering of the Achaean army).

The next Trojan assembly, in *Iliad* 7, strikes an even more incongruous note. An unruly assembly (345–6) gathers, again before Priam's house, to hear a proposal from Antenor. Antenor has credentials – he was part of the Trojan delegation who received the Achaeans' original embassy for Helen's return. (We learn this in *Iliad* 3.) Here, he recommends returning Helen. Unsurprisingly, Paris rejects this proposal and instead offers compensation in the form of material goods. Priam adjudicates and endorses his son's offer, which – equally unsurprisingly – is rejected by the Achaeans (voiced by Diomedes, in his first public performance). Throughout this assembly, we hear nothing from the Trojan people. They neither shout in acclaim nor do anything other than receive the instructions and 'hear and obey' (379). While the structure is reminiscent of the Achaean assemblies – two speeches offer rival plans followed by a third proposing some sort of compromise – the content and spirit radically differs. Furthermore, whereas the Achaeans admit contrasting views from their speakers only to have a third offer a middle way, the interests of the Trojan royal family remains paramount and is served by Priam's judgement. Such a deficiency is especially dire for the Trojans, since, after all, to return Helen would be to end the war.

So surprising is it that the Trojans do not return Helen that Herodotus maintains that she cannot have been in Troy in the first place (*Histories* 2.115–20)! Homer himself confronts the issue head-on in *Iliad* 3, just after we have been introduced to her for the first time. The Trojan elders sit by the Scaean gate (149), reflecting on whether Helen is really worth the pain. Their position by the walls symbolises their marginalisation from political power. Crucially, their deliberation does not take place within any institutional framework – the Trojans lack a council forum. In *Iliad* 10, when there is an opportunity for a council to discuss plans on spying (as the Achaeans have just done), Hector merely calls the leaders together to execute a plan he has already devised (299–312). Shortly afterwards, in *Iliad* 13, he is advised by the bird interpreter Polydamas to call together the best of the Trojans to aid in deliberation (740–1); Hector agrees, but continues to fight anyway. As the Trojan elders sit by the walls and reflect on what to do with Helen, Homer compares them to cicadas (3.151–352). Even though they are deliberating on the topic that could end the war, their voices appear like the distant hum of chirping insects, completely ineffectual and apolitical.

The final Trojan assembly in *Iliad* 18 (243–313) builds on and adds to these differences at a critical moment. Upon hearing of Patroclus's death, Achilles throws the battle into confusion with a deafening cry, which not only rallies the Achaeans to protect Patroclus's body but also heralds his return to the fray. The Trojans withdraw in panic and hold an assembly, then and there, on the battlefield. Their sense of desperation is heightened still by the fact that it is night and no one has eaten: they mill about standing, seized by terror at the prospect of Achilles' impending return (243–8). Polydamas, who acts as a special adviser to Hector in books 12 and 13, once more speaks up. Where in *Iliad* 13 his intelligence emerges through the good advice he offers Hector, here Homer himself emphasises Polydamas's credentials – he is as good with words as Hector is with the spear (251–2). It is then striking that Hector dismisses Polydamas's recommendation for immediate flight to the city, with a good deal of bluster about his willingness to face Achilles and win glory. But, when Hector orders them to set guards and wait in the plain, the Trojans cheer for him. At this point, in a highly unusual gesture, Homer enters the poem to condemn the Trojans as 'fools' (312), whose wits have been stolen by Athena.

Thus, Homer uses the critical moment of Achilles' return to imply that the suffering of the Trojans is in part due, not only to their leaders' desire for honour and the weakness of their political institutions, but also to their own self-deception. It paints a more complex picture of Troy, evoking the duties and responsibility of the assembly in general rather than the fault of one man or family. The Trojans *should* dissent at this point, but they do not. But this moment is also a testament to the psychological depth of Homer's portrayal of the Trojans. Over the course of the epic, Hector's fatalism becomes infectious. We know that Troy is doomed to fall; yet, the Trojan prince stands to face this destruction. If he is guilty of anything, he has perhaps allowed himself too great a faith in the delusion that Troy might survive. Ironically, it is this very faith that hastens his death and the fall of the city.

Hector, family man

While Hector comes across as a leader who remains largely deaf to others and overly self-reliant, the *Iliad* emphasises most his familial relationships. It must be remembered that nothing required Homer to present Hector in this way. His formulaic epithets, such as 'man-slaying', 'horse-taming', 'bronze-helmed', 'shining', 'strong', 'dread', etc., hardly anticipate a gentle, loving man. While our available evidence is limited, we meet a rather different Hector in the late fifth-century Greek tragedy *Rhesus* (attributed to Euripides), where he plays a hateful and diabolical killer. Homer's depiction of Hector constitutes a very different take on the Trojan hero and warrior who acts as a counterpoint to Achilles.

A crucial part of what makes the *Iliad* distinctive lies in Homer's ability to depict the heroes as fully rounded *men* not demigods. The Homeric hero is never just a killing machine who lives and dies by his sword. Rather, Homer's heroes live in communities, form and manage relationships just as the members of the audience do, and have loved ones for whom they care. So, Homer uses vignettes of life in Troy to incorporate into his heroic tale of strife and personal honour the effects of war on family and city. As the primary defender of this city and the enemy hero whose humanisation is part of what makes the *Iliad* exceptional, Hector appears in a series of scenes that depict him as brother, son, husband, and father. Through the figure of Hector, Homer looks forward to all that will be lost when he dies and the city falls.

The first time we witness Hector in a family context is as an exasperated older brother. At the beginning of *Iliad* 3, he abuses Paris for the trouble he has caused their city and cajoles him into facing Menelaus in a duel. At first sight, Hector comes out of this exchange badly. The ferocity of his attack is only barely justified by his brother's concession that he, Paris, deserves the criticism; in fact, the latter's feeble surrender makes Hector look a bit of a bully. At the end of the same book, however, even Helen insults Paris, when, after he loses his duel to Menelaus, Aphrodite whisks him from the battlefield so that he can have sex with Helen back in Troy. Worse: when Hector leaves the battle bloodied but unbowed in *Iliad* 6, he finds Paris still languishing with Helen in the women's quarters! This time Hector is more encouraging – it hurts his feelings that people say negative things about Paris. But, in *Iliad* 13, Hector explicitly blames Paris for the loss of Troy's leaders (769–73). The complex fraternal relationship points to a man wrestling with his emotions: Paris is the cause of the war, a reluctant and marginally effective warrior, but he is also Hector's brother. Thus, Hector wavers between venting his frustration, worrying about their reputations, and supporting Paris. It is not that Hector is a bad brother; it is just that he appears to be a real one. He loves his brother and it is his duty to support him, the man who sealed his doom and his city's.

The events of *Iliad* 6 overhaul the rather dim view of family life provided by the forced sex between Paris and Helen, and indelibly transform our view of Hector's character. His reasons for leaving the battle differ vastly from his brother's. He has been charged with the task of instructing the women of Troy to sacrifice to Athena. Already we are invited to regard Hector, not as a killer of men, but as a pious man of a beleaguered city. His passage inside Troy transports the audience from the blood, toil, and sweat of battle, to the perfumed domestic sphere of women and children. Not that the scene only serves as a break from the fighting. It also shows us what's at stake in the fighting – ordinary people's lives and livelihoods. In a similar break from the spectacle in the film version of Tolkien's *The Two Towers*, Peter Jackson takes the camera inside Helm's Deep, to pan across the civilians huddled together and trembling at the noise of the battle around them. We see the fragility of human existence, get a sense of the natural fear of those unaccustomed to and ill equipped for war, and achieve a better understanding of what motivates those who fight, who are brave because they have to be, in order to protect their families. So too Hector's mettle, forged in war, is tempered and cooled in his city. Homer announces his theme upon Hector's entry inside Troy, when all the Trojan wives gather about him for information about their fathers, husbands, sons, and brothers. During the course of *Iliad* 6, Hector plays all four roles, becoming the figure through whom Homer explores the ties of friendship and family that apply to all those fighting at, and for, Troy. Accordingly, the death of Hector in this story is far more than the loss of a warrior. It is the destruction of the family and the city through the severing of the bonds that make up a human life.

By setting Hector up as son, brother, father, and husband, the epic also makes room on its muscular and violent stage for the women who give the fight meaning. Hecuba represents a 'typical mother' (in the phrase of an ancient scholar). Andromache teaches us both about the pride and anxiety of a wife and the deep, gut-wrenching, and protective fear of a mother with an infant in her arms. Perhaps most intriguing of all there's Helen – here not so much a dangerous lover and cause of a terrible war, as a begrudgingly respected sister-in-law, wife of a lesser son, a woman unwanted by the family but given a home nevertheless. Homer is alert to these complexities. Perhaps ominously, Helen is eager for her man to fight, while Andromache longs to save hers from leaving her side.

Similarly, Hector's halting engagements serve both to characterise the man and deepen our understanding of the women around him. Hector's first close encounter depicts him as a son – but not in the way typically envisaged in epic. Hector has a patronymic epithet like the rest of the heroes: *Priamidēs*, 'son of Priam'. But only he and Achilles are ever seen with their mothers, by virtue of which we get to see a different side to these two heroes. Hecuba's first appearance in the epic highlights her concern for her son – he should take a break from the fighting and enjoy some wine. Hector firmly rebuffs her, even giving voice to the fantasy that his brother had died in infancy. As it is, he must fight, so he can't dally here and drink wine – he might lose courage; besides, he is too unclean from the battle to pour libations to the gods. For this reason, he insists, his mother should gather all the Trojan women to offer prayers to Athena. Hector emerges here as a loyal son, a conscientious leader, a pious man, but one who seems insulated or detached from those he protects. A picture emerges of a man struggling with his emotions, keeping duty foremost in his mind. Disarmingly, in a devastating passing comment, Homer notes the futility of the women's efforts – Athena turns away from their offering. We are never allowed to forget the dreadful fate that hangs over them, even as we may recognise Hector's courage and admire his fortitude.

Upon finding Paris in the women's quarters posing in his shining armour, Hector again chides him. Suitably chastised, Paris again promises to do his brother's bidding and hurries to ready himself for battle. It is Helen who delays Hector and presents the greatest threat to his swift return to battle. Famous as the face that launched a thousand ships, Helen generally has a poor press in surviving ancient Greek literature. The Chorus of Argive elders in Aeschylus's *Agamemnon* (458 BC) famously toy with her name, rendering Helen as 'Hell-en', aka 'the destroyer' – the destroyer of ships, the destroyer of men, the destroyer of Greece's youth. The *Iliad* is more ambiguous. Even when the Trojan elders directly address the problem of Helen, they refrain from condemning her. Instead, they judge that 'there is no blame to suffer pains on account of this woman', though they wish her gone (3.156–60). Homer further explores her ambiguity in the meeting with Hector. After Hector has chastised his brother, Helen breaks in. She refers to herself as a 'nasty bitch, scheming evil, hated by all', and wishes that she had died the day she was born or, at least, had 'been the wife of a better man than this' (344–51). All the other Trojan women are cruel to her, but Hector, she says, has always been kind. Her words Homer glosses as 'sweet', 'endearing'. Thus, the epic leaves us to contemplate the nature and extent of her seductive powers and to wonder whether, or how far, this son of Priam is also under her spell.

Perhaps part of Helen's fatal attraction is that she tells people –
specifically men – what they want to hear. (She does the same
with Priam in *Iliad* 3.) Even so, here Hector refuses her invitation
to rest awhile and hurries on. In part, this scene sets in relief
Hector's sense of duty. He will die because of *this* woman. Yet, he
treats her kindly and refuses to condemn her. If he is seduced by
her charms, the pull of his city and family are stronger.

For one reason why Hector hurries on is to take the opportunity to see his wife, Andromache. The problematic and somewhat lamentable relationship between Helen and Paris prepares
the audience for Hector's next role as a husband and father. In a
subtle departure from the pattern thus far established, when
Hector arrives at home, his wife isn't there. Instead, he finds her
at the Scaean Gate overlooking the battle, so concerned is she for
the defence and safety of the city. Their meeting is to be one of
the most memorable scenes of the entire poem.

In contrast to his dominant persona on the battlefield as Troy's
main warrior and bulwark, inside the city Hector comes across as
far more human. This is nicely demonstrated by the different
names his son has. While everyone else refers to him as Astyanax,
'lord of the city', Hector calls him Scamandrius, after the river
that flows by Troy. The two names point to the child's dual identities, as the future protector of Troy (for the people) and as
someone closely rooted to the land and family history (for
Hector). When Hector finally finds his wife and child, he doesn't
speak, but gazes smiling at his son. Memorably, a short while later,
as Hector reaches out to hold him, the baby cries – he doesn't
recognise his father in his bloody helmet with its plume nodding
fearsomely – and the parents together laugh at the misplaced fear.
But there is latent sorrow underlying the laughter. When Hector
prays to Zeus for his son to be a greater hero than he, Homer's
audience would know that Astyanax's true fate was to be hurled
from the walls of Troy. War with its dreadfully nodding plume
will claim Hector's son soon enough.

What then of Andromache? According to surviving fragments and summaries, the Trojan War tradition included the
myth of the Amazons. These were a famous group of warring
women, elsewhere depicted, for example, on the Parthenon in
Athens, whose very name points to their warrior-like nature:
'Amazon' derives from the Greek 'a-mazon' or 'without a breast'
for (in the imagination of Greek artists) how else could they
shoot a bow? The *Aethiopis* apparently told the story of how
Achilles fell in love with the Amazon Penthesilea as their eyes
made contact at the very moment he delivered the deathblow.
There is a distant echo of this mythical tradition here, when
Andromache (whose name means 'man fighting') starts talking
tactics from her vantage point overlooking the battlefield. The
point is that, unlike Helen or even Hecuba, Andromache comes
across as Hector's kind of woman. Just like them, however, she
tries to persuade him to stay out of the fighting – by directing the
war from the battlements. While the couple are finely matched,
there is incongruity in Andromache dictating terms. But she does
so because Hector means everything to her. Quite literally: 'You
are a father to me, and my honoured mother, and my brother, and
you are my young husband' (429–30). Just as the city, without its
hero, is doomed to fall, so too without her man Andromache will
be nothing. Achilles has already killed her father and all of her
brothers, when he sacked her home city of Thebe.

Hector's response is somehow heartfelt and tone-deaf at the
same time, showing tenderness to his wife, but incapable of heed-
ing her pleas. Crucially, Hector protests, he is responsible not to
Andromache alone but to the whole people. He feels shame
before both Trojans and Trojan women, and this compels him to
fight. But he also expresses desire to win glory (*kleos*). The tension
between fighting out of shame and/or fighting for fame spurs
Hector on, and makes his story so compelling for the audience.
He has the notion that 'there will come a day when sacred Ilion
will perish' (448) and his wife will be enslaved. But he frames

Andromache's enslavement in terms of his own fame. People will say: 'This is the wife of Hector, who was best at fighting / among the Trojans, breakers of horses, when they fought about Ilion' (460–1). Fame is the only thing with which Hector has to console himself as he looks forward to that fateful day. The paradox for Hector is that there really is no other way for him to behave. Unlike Achilles, Hector cannot withdraw from the conflict. He must always fight and he must always win. He, unlike Achilles, does not know he will die in this battle. Indeed, to carry on, he must believe he will prevail.

This position, however, is framed by what the audience know and what even Hector seems to be aware of: that he will die, the city will fall, and Andromache will be enslaved. There is a poetic futility that adds deeper meaning to his words and lends poignancy to his predicament. Thus, Homer puts flesh on Hector's bones as a warrior, imbuing his struggle with a latent sadness.

In this final scene in Troy, Hector's military responsibilities come to the fore. The only way that he can resolve the tension of the tug on his heart for his wife and child is to turn away completely. When Hector takes his helmet from his head to kiss his son, it is the final time in the epic that he is anything but a warrior and slayer of men. Rather than be distracted or weakened by his wife's conviction, Hector erects a boundary between them by sending her to the work of women, while, at the same time, establishing a clear sphere of influence for himself. 'War is a concern for all men / who are at Troy and me especially' (492–3), he pronounces. The remark becomes so famous that the Athenian comic playwright Aristophanes can quote the line in his sex comedy *Lysistrata* put on in 411 BC.

Just as quickly as we glimpse a tender Hector, the family man, Homer sends him back into battle to play out his role as Achilles' great adversary. In Aristophanes' *Lysistrata*, the joke is that a man who doesn't want to listen to his wife complaining about the war (between the Athenians and the Spartans) merely quotes Hector to shut her up (520). The scene in *Iliad* 6, however, has a very different effect. As Hector departs Troy, the women of his household mourn him, as if he is already dead. Hector will never see his wife or son (or mother) again. The next time his helmet comes off, he will be lying dead in the dust.

A glorious death?

In the hands of a lesser artist, Hector might have excelled as either a tragic hero or savage enemy. But, although *Iliad* 6 frames him as ultimately tragic, seemingly fully aware of his own doom, the episodes that follow show him wrestling with his fate. At times during this struggle, Hector ceases to be so sympathetic. Moreover, as the narrative unfolds, a gap steadily opens between what Hector expects and what actually happens, a distance brought out by the irony of his martial aggression and marked by his language. In the company of his men, he blusters, overreacts to criticism from his allies, and injects terror into the Achaean line. That Hector becomes one of the most persistent and insistent voices for immortal fame brings him closer to Achilles, even as he marches inexorably towards his enemy and his doom.

One irony of Hector's depiction in the *Iliad* has already surfaced. While the Trojan War tradition presents the Trojans as the people besieged, for the majority of the action in the *Iliad* Homer portrays Hector in the field as an aggressor trying to break through the Achaean fortifications. This radical inversion may well have come as a surprise for Homer's audience. Above, we mentioned that Hector's epithets paint a picture of a violent and brutal warrior. His name, however, 'the defender' (literally, 'the one who holds') seems to indicate that his established position, the one for which he would be famous in the tradition, was to *defend*. Indeed, defending the city from its walls is what Andromache countenances. Far from being outlandish advice from a woman, her strategy may well be more in tune with the tradition. Of course, no Homeric hero is defined by his name alone. But we can sense that the tension between Hector's expected military position as a defender and his Iliadic depiction as a man eager to lead his people in the rout of their enemy is meaningful. For it is not only Andromache who warns Hector off from fighting outside the walls. From the walls, in *Iliad* 22, his parents beg him to stay inside, while throughout the epic his special adviser, Polydamas, repeatedly insists that it is wiser for the Trojans – and especially for Hector, the 'defender' – to wage a defensive war.

However, Hector strains against such bounds, 'trusting in Zeus'. Indeed, for the majority of the epic, Hector has good reasons for his confidence. Achilles has withdrawn from battle. Not only that: at numerous points, the gods show clear signs of support for the Trojans. In *Iliad* 15, Hector even recovers from wounds that would normally prove fatal. What person wouldn't think that fortune was on his side, perhaps even that fortune favours the brave? Yet, the audience knows that Zeus's support of Hector is limited. He glorifies Hector only so long as Achilles sits out the battle. Indeed, Zeus makes it clear, when articulating his plan, that his honouring of Achilles entails Hector's death and, ultimately, the fall of Troy. Zeus's favouring of Hector is, if not deceptive, at any rate misleading. Hector dominates the majority of this epic because Zeus means to honour Achilles. Nevertheless, the hopeful heart that beats within Hector's chest and prevents him from giving up, his obstinacy that he may, against all the odds, win out, is part of what draws us to him.

But it is not only optimism and sheer force of will that keeps Hector fighting. If Hector knows that he is going to die, and fights on because there is nothing else that he can do, he consoles himself and others with the rhetoric of compensation – Hector, even more than Achilles, is the epic's spokesperson for fame (*kleos*). In *Iliad* 6, Helen imagines them both providing the subject matter for tales of the future; shortly afterwards, Hector eyes his future glory in his wife's captivity, almost seduced by the possibilities of living on in men's minds. When, in the next book, Hector challenges an Achaean hero to meet him in a duel, he fantasises that the grave of the man whom he kills will be a reminder of *his* glory for men to come. Yet, caught between having no choice but to fight in defence of his homeland and the (rather desperate) belief that he can defeat the Achaeans or at least win glory for himself, he frequently equivocates. When, in *Iliad* 8, he promises his troops that he will face Diomedes on the following day, he expresses uncertainty about who will triumph. After the mortally wounded Patroclus warns him of his own impending doom, Hector responds: 'Who knows whether it is Achilles, son of lovely-haired Thetis, / who might die struck by my spear and lose his life?' (16.860–1). Even when rallying his army in the light of Achilles' return, Hector prevaricates: 'but facing him / I shall stand to see whether he carries great power or I carry it. Enyalios [Ares] is even-handed, and he kills he who has killed' (18.308–9). Far from alienating the audience, Hector's equivocation takes the edge off his boasts and fills his character with very human doubt. He possesses a humility suggesting that he has surrendered himself to whatever will happen, while steeling himself to face it bravely.

What will happen is determined the moment he delivers the fatal blow to Patroclus. Achilles, in terrible wrath, seeks revenge and won't stop until he has killed Hector. For two whole books (*Iliad* 20–2), Achilles rages over the battlefield like a force of nature, killing so many Trojans that the river god Scamander rises up to complain that bodies are choking his waters. To Priam, watching the slaughter unfold from Troy's walls, Achilles appears like the baneful Dog Star, Sirius – brightly shining but deadly, a harbinger of doom heading straight towards his son. From his vantage point on the walls, Priam pleads with Hector. He is the city's last hope; he can't put all their lives at risk by facing Achilles;

he should retreat behind the city's walls to live to fight another day. Hecuba's gesture is more immediate and primordial. She bares her breast to her son, appealing to him not to turn away from the one who suckled him. But Hector remains steadfast, outside the walls, awaiting Achilles' ire.

Prominent in his mind again are the twin notions of shame and fame. At first he deliberates whether he should indeed retreat within Troy's walls. But Polydamas now returns as a figure haunting Hector's imagination with reproaches for ignoring his earlier advice. So Hector recognises too late that he has brought destruction upon his army 'through his own recklessness', and he can't stand the shame of facing his aggrieved people (22.99–110). Agamemnon too 'lost his people' because of his impetuosity and selfish desire for honour. The theme echoes with the larger poetic tradition as well. Throughout the *Odyssey*, we will hear of people who perish 'because of their own recklessness', men like the suitors who are courting a woman who is already married. Unlike either Agamemnon or the *Odyssey*'s suitors, however, Hector acknowledges his fault and shows himself ready to do what he must. As a result of his decisions, he realises, he must confront Achilles 'trusting in his own strength' – not any more, we should note, in Zeus.

Yet, as he faces Achilles, Hector remains full of contradictory emotions and thoughts. Even now he holds out the hope of prevailing, or of negotiating with mighty Achilles, putting down his weapons, surrendering Helen, and ending the war. At the same time, he seems almost resigned, as if after ten years of war (and twenty-one-odd books of the *Iliad*) he just wants the final moment of resolution to come. 'Better to bring on the fight with him as soon as possible: / We shall see to which one the Olympian grants the glory' (129–30), he tells himself. But, at the moment he spies Achilles, looking – as Homer tells us – like Ares the god of war himself, his resolve fails completely and he runs. The two heroes then race around the city of walls, as all of Troy's people look on in horror and the gods look down in pity – since 'swift-footed' Achilles is, it seems, not quite swift-footed enough to catch his quarry – until Athena steps in (disguised as Hector's brother Deiphobus) and halts Hector. Finally face-to-face with his doom, Hector regains his poise. When he tries to set some ground rules for the conflict, such as returning the vanquished hero's corpse, it is Achilles who transgresses human convention, who denies that there can be any oaths between lions and men. For his part, Hector recognises that the gods have deceived him and accepts his fate with equanimity: 'Now my evil death is close and not still far away, / nor can I escape it. For a long time it must have been pleasing / to Zeus and to Zeus's son, the far-striker [Apollo], who before now / defended me gladly' (300–3). His final thought turns towards accomplishing some fine task so that future generations will not forget his name. Achilles, still consumed with rage, cares nought for such aspirations. His only thought is to make Hector pay for Patroclus's death by killing him. But, even as Hector is despatched, we understand that this is not enough for Achilles. Homer leaves open the question of what Achilles will do with Hector's corpse and how this epic will end.

Homer demonstrates the significance of Hector's death by exploring the reactions of those dependent on him. The whole city fills with lamentation 'most like what would have happened, if the whole of / Ilion had been burning top to bottom in fire' (410–11). Priam collapses in lament, smearing his body with dung, before desperately appealing to be allowed to go and beg to Achilles for his son's corpse. Ripping off her veil, Hecuba laments that her son already had honour and glory from the city while he was alive. But Homer focuses on the reaction of Andromache. We first see her in blissful ignorance, preparing her man a bath for his return from battle. Then she hears wild wailing and, with growing unease, hurries to the walls in fear for her headstrong husband. When she finally spies her husband, he is dead and his corpse is being dragged behind Achilles' chariot.

It is almost all too much. She collapses and 'her spirit left her', as if she were dead herself. Upon recovering her (life) breath, she delivers one of the most extraordinary speeches in the epic. She laments not so much her own fate as the future of Astyanax whom, she imagines, will languish as an orphan driven away even from the tables of the men who were his father's friends (477–514). The pathos of this vivid image is increased by our knowledge that even this is a better fate than that which awaits Hector's son.

It is fitting that the monumental events of *Iliad* 22 are brought to a close through how others view Hector. Certainly, Homer does not make judging Hector easy (if it is something he asks us to do at all). In his final moments, Hector admits his weaknesses, runs from the fate he has been stubbornly pursuing, and dies with his eyes open to the world's inequities, in contrast to the man whose blind rage has wrought destruction on all. Furthermore, in death Hector provides a framework for thinking about the two Achaean leaders whose conflict had erupted so disastrously at the beginning of the *Iliad*. Like Agamemnon, Hector is a leader seemingly unpractised in the subtleties of co-ordinating a coalition and at times too concerned with his personal honour. Like Achilles, he struggles with the certainty of a short life, and gives voice to the epic's interest in fame (while also calling its worth into question). But, unlike both Achilles and Agamemnon, he ends up destroying his people by trying to *save* them. Where Agamemnon and Achilles doom their people because they pursue self-interest policies, Hector's selfishness is to refuse to believe that he cannot protect them.

The magnanimous spirit of the *Iliad* itself hinges on its depiction of Hector. In his flaws and his internal struggles to do what is right, we may see ourselves – the capacity for self-denial, the wilful misreading of signs, and the ultimate inability to surmount fate. Even though Hector is the 'enemy', Homer depicts him as one of the poem's most complex and sympathetic characters.

His depth comes from his connection to everything that is denied to the Achaeans – a home and a family beyond the fighting and battle for power and glory. Ending with his burial, rather than any outcome achieved by the Achaeans, Homer ultimately gives Hector the fame he so desperately hopes to safeguard right up to the end.

4
Ending the Troy story

Anger has been the watchword of the *Iliad* since the poem's beginning. It permeates the first episode from Apollo's anger for the mistreatment of his priest to Agamemnon's anger at being contradicted in the assembly and then, fatally, to Achilles who bristles at Agamemnon and condemns his comrades for standing silently by. The *Iliad* then charts the consequences of this anger, as Achilles' withdrawal and Zeus's plan bring death and destruction to the Achaeans. When the embassy comes to Achilles in book nine, his slighted spirit keeps him from rejoining his colleagues in battle. Similarly, in book sixteen, when his best friend appeals to him in tears, his anger remains, although he relents sufficiently to allow his friend to fight in his place.

This fateful decision sets a new direction for Achilles' wrath, as rage against Agamemnon gives way to rage at Hector for killing Patroclus (and at himself for failing to protect his friend). He hurriedly puts aside his quarrel with Agamemnon (in the assembly of *Iliad* 19) just so that he can enter battle as quickly as possible. For the next three books (*Iliad* 20–2), the 'best of all Achaeans' rages through the battle, cutting great swathes of Trojans down, until, finally, he despatches Hector's soul to Hades. But such is his wrath still that he ties Hector's body to his chariot and drags it over the Trojan plain, until Patroclus's ghost stirs him to bury his body. Then, after sacrificing twelve Trojan youths on the pyre, Achilles holds games in his friend's honour.

These games, which take up the whole of *Iliad* 23, are important: the Achaean heroes compete with each other for glory (prizes) before their peers, while Achilles acts as moderator. Thus, we find Achilles again setting up an institution, and one, moreover, that again legitimises conflict for the public good. It is not an easy or complete settlement – bickering and infighting among both contestants and spectators characterise the games. Nevertheless, under Achilles' guidance, the Achaeans experiment with a different kind of politics – one that requires mediation, negotiation, and concession. In this imaginary 'city', Achilles provides an abundance of gifts to ease the competing claims between the victors and those expected to win – much as the Achaeans must cope with the disjunction between expectation and events during the course of the narrative. Nor does the 'fantasy' aspect of this diminish its thematic significance or political impact. Through his stewardship of the games, Achilles explores many of the same issues that sent myriad Achaeans to their doom, and hits upon solutions that are worthy of reflection for all that they are complex and fleeting. Such resolutions as there are come through the community of the participative assembly, underpinned by persuasive speech.

But the poem does not end with the Achaeans' show of civic unity. When the games break up, and the Achaeans go off to eat, Achilles goes on with abusing Hector's body. The political theme is only a part of the *Iliad*'s story; its hero's personal narrative is still incomplete. Hector's death is clearly not enough to satisfy Achilles' appetite for destruction, which poses the question: just how will this epic of wrath end and what kind of epic will result? The central scene of this final act will in fact bring together two enemies, Achilles and Priam, face-to-face, under divine protection, leaving us to contemplate the wider significance of this episode for interpreting the poem as a whole.

Apollo calls an assembly

While the Achaeans dine as Achilles abuses Hector's body, one group does take notice – the gods. They look down on Achilles 'in his wrath' 'shaming' Hector, and 'pity' the fallen Trojan hero (22–3). Pity has been important before, when Zeus contemplates saving his son Sarpedon. Now the gods show pity collectively and for a mortal. They remain *interested* in human affairs right to the bitter end. Finally, 'on the twelfth day', Apollo can stand no more and calls an assembly.

The poem commences with Apollo's anger at Agamemnon for disrespecting his priest. As the *Iliad* draws to a close, we again see Apollo spoiling to get involved in human affairs, giving the epic a sense of formal closure, only to surprise us with variation. Apollo doesn't intervene directly. Instead, he takes up the case in an assembly of the gods (33–54). In it Apollo expresses disgust at Achilles' mistreatment of Hector's body. His anger is all the more because Hector was pious. Hector's willingness to burn sacrifices to them obligates them, in Apollo's mind, to 'save him, though a corpse'. Saving the dead may sound odd, but it serves to indicate the significance of the gods' care. They weren't able to save Hector, because that would have been contrary to fate. But they can 'save' his corpse and honour his final wishes to be returned to his parents for the rites that are due to the dead.

Equally striking is Apollo's accusation that Achilles has 'destroyed pity and lacks shame'. The case of Hector himself has shown the key role shame plays in sanctioning correct behaviour. Achilles' lack of shame underscores his separation from the world of men. More disturbing still is the idea that he has 'destroyed pity'. Though it is far from clear what Apollo means by use of this odd expression, Achilles has flouted acceptable behaviour since the death of Patroclus. In *Iliad* 21, before killing the Trojan Lycaon, he 'consoles' his enemy with the lesson that even Patroclus had to die. More explicit is his cruel response to Hector's appeal to respect the other's fallen body: 'there are no trustworthy oaths between lions and men' (22.262). Achilles has destroyed pity, because he no longer sees himself as human or, at any rate, governed by human rules. Apollo sums up the case against Achilles by saying that he 'shames the dumb earth in his wrath' (24.54). Since human standards of shame and empathy are no longer sufficient to curb him, only the gods remain to enforce proper codes of conduct. Apollo intervenes here *not* because of a personal tie (the insult suffered by *his* priest) but in defence of a *general* principle – the right to burial. This is the new covenant the *Iliad* offers. In the *Cypria*, Zeus (apparently) took pity on Earth and planned to rid her burden by destroying the race of heroes. Now the Olympian gods pity the Earth for the body of which it is deprived and intervene for the voiceless corpse.

Apollo's intervention to support a general principle – that all pious men deserve burial – raises an important objection from Hera. The heroes at Troy aren't all equal. Hector is mortal; Achilles, the child of a goddess: therefore, shouldn't the gods maintain a critical distinction between the two? Hera's opposition here consciously recalls a bygone era, in which the *Iliad* has its origins – namely the wedding of Peleus and Thetis, which Hera explicitly cites. But the *Iliad* has moved on since those times, as demonstrated by what happens next. Zeus intervenes to adjudicate. In previous times, the father of gods and men has himself been the catalyst for strife, such as when at the beginning of the *Iliad* his promise to Thetis (to honour her son) had almost returned the gods to war (the story of Hesiod's *Theogony*), which Zeus's rule was supposed to have brought to an end. Now he acts as an arbitrator. He categorically asserts that the honour between the two heroes 'won't be equal'; Achilles will always be more honoured than Hector (as this poem attests). Nevertheless, Hector is 'dearest' of mortals to the gods, because of the sacrifices he made or, as Zeus puts it, his altar 'was never lacking an equal share'. At the end of *Iliad* 1, strife on Olympus fails to break out because Zeus has already assigned each god his or her due, so that none 'was lacking an equal share' – this portioning out of honour takes place in the *Theogony* and *Homeric Hymns*. But here, in *Iliad* 24, we receive an important gloss on that equal share. While the gods no longer dine at our table, we may gain their favour by making due sacrifice.

We are now firmly in a world like our own, in which men can win favour from the gods through their piety alone.

After arbitrating on the matter of the gods versus Achilles, Zeus sends for Thetis. When she arrives on Olympus, she receives hospitality from all. Even Hera welcomes her with a drink, with none of the rancour that accompanies her earlier visit. Accordingly, the movement of the beginning of the poem, when Achilles persuades Thetis to go to Zeus, is now reversed, as Zeus sends Thetis to instruct Achilles to give up Hector's body for ransom. Through its very structure, the *Iliad* demonstrates the progression from a world in which gods and heroes interact continually to a world where gods, and particularly Zeus, operate from a distance and encourage men to show humanity towards each other. Yet these gods still have a significant engagement with the plot. Where the world went awry in *Iliad* 1, when Agamemnon rejected the offer from one father to ransom his child, it is set aright again in *Iliad* 24 when Achilles accepts the ransom from another father for his son.

Achilles, however, remains a problem. Thetis finds him still mourning, as his companions prepare a meal for themselves. How long will he go on 'eating' his heart out, she asks him, when he should remember to eat and have sex with a woman (128–31)? By not eating and not having sex, in short by not engaging in the basic activities of human life, Achilles flouts his human nature and denies his inevitable death. This is Thetis's point. Since Achilles is now soon to die, he should embrace mortality and live; instead, though alive, he chooses not to live, depriving himself of the little pleasure life still has to offer. In any case, Thetis concludes, Achilles will have to release Hector, or else fear incurring the gods' wrath.

Achilles' response is pointed, but difficult to read: 'So be it. He can bring the ransom and take the body, / if the Olympian himself so keenly orders it' (139–40). Is his tone one of defiance, contemplation, or resignation? The ground has been prepared, but questions remain. How will Achilles receive Priam? And what does it mean when he does?

The meeting of Achilles and Priam

While Thetis visits her son, Zeus sends his messenger Iris to ready Priam for the task ahead. She finds him in desperate lamentation, his clothes smeared with animal dung, his mind unhinged by sorrow as he curses his remaining sons as useless. When he tells Hecuba that he's going to Achilles to ask for their son's body back, his wife thinks he's lost it. Who on Earth could conceive of entreating their son's killer for pity? (So consumed with hatred is she, that she longs to sink her teeth into Achilles' liver.) Nevertheless, in spite of opposition from his wife, daughters, and sons, Priam is prepared to take a massive leap of faith. When he asks for a message from Zeus and an eagle flies by, he takes that as a sign of the gods' trust and departs.

Homer increases the sense of foreboding with imagery suggestive of Priam going to his death. Hermes, in disguise as one of Achilles' men, meets Priam to guide him across no-man's land, just as he accompanies the souls of dead men to Hades. Adding to the gloom is the fact that Priam's endeavour resonates with other journeys to Achilles' tent. In *Iliad* 1, the two heralds sent by Agamemnon take Briseis away from Achilles; the embassy of *Iliad* 9 fails to persuade Achilles to return; on coming back to Achilles in *Iliad* 16, Patroclus succeeds in winning over his friend, but condemns himself to death. But the scene reverberating most strongly with Priam's journey is the opening of the *Iliad*, when another old man sets out for the Achaean camp to plead for his daughter's return. The fallout from that episode, which sets the tone of the epic, accounts for all the suffering in the *Iliad* up to this point – Achilles' anger, his withdrawal from battle, Patroclus's death, and his revenge against Hector.

The gods set up this meeting between vanquisher and vanquished. But the actual communication between the two takes place without the gods' interference or even presence. Revealing his true identity to Priam, Hermes states that the gods must remain untouched by death, before duly departing. From this point on, the poem's action and perspective will be all about humanity.

The scene is set for Priam's grand entrance (477–84). To begin with, Homer compares Priam to an exile accused of murder in his own land who goes to a powerful man for help – a simile that seems hardly appropriate for Priam's circumstances, given that he has committed no crime. Yet, ancient Greek myth is full of examples of exiled murderers, who escape the stigma of their crime by fleeing their homeland to receive a second chance in a new home – heroes such as Jason or Perseus. We have seen this too in the *Iliad*: both Phoenix (9.478–84) and Patroclus (23.83–90), though fugitives, were welcomed by no other than Achilles' father, Peleus. The simile turns out to be highly pertinent and increases the tension still further. Will Achilles turn out to be like his father and accept Priam's appeal?

Homer describes the old man falling to the floor to embrace Achilles' knees in supplication – the ritual act when one figure puts him- or herself at the mercy of another. It is an act so steeped in ritual significance that Zeus himself presides over it to make sure that it is respected. And, yet, up until this point in the poem no supplication has succeeded except for Thetis's gesture in book one, which ironically leads to the slaughter of many. Finally, Homer focuses on the harrowing gesture of Priam kissing 'the hands, / terrible and man-slaughtering, which had killed so many of his sons' (479). This is only the second kiss of the entire epic – the first was when Hector bent down to kiss Astyanax, in his farewell to his son and wife. That startling epithet 'man-slaughtering' is significant too. It was previously used only of Hector himself (and the first time just after he kissed his son). The transfer of the epithet from

Hector, the man who killed Patroclus, to his killer encapsulates the stakes for both men in this highly charged moment.

With his opening words, 'remember your father', Priam immediately and directly appeal to Achilles' memory of Peleus (486). In inviting Achilles to remember his father, Priam joins those who have evoked the figure of Peleus to exert influence over Achilles, as in the embassy scene. There, Agamemnon's impressive catalogue sought to bring Achilles to heel; Odysseus selectively remembers Peleus's advice to his son in order to win Achilles over; Phoenix points to his service as Achilles' surrogate father as proof that he has Achilles' best interests at heart. Peleus, whose importance as Achilles' father (and, thus, for cosmic order) is cued in the very first line of the *Iliad*, is the poem's great absent presence. In recalling Peleus, Priam first draws attention to their similarity. Both he and Peleus are old, alone, and bereft of sons to care for them. To make their resemblance greater, Priam exaggerates his loss by claiming to be in mourning for 'my only son, [who] guarded the city and its inhabitants, / the one you killed a few days ago as he fought in defence of his fatherland, / Hector' (499–501). Strictly speaking, Hector isn't Priam's only son – indeed, Priam has sons by the legion. But, given that Hector was the bulwark for all Trojans, Priam's loss is as great *as if* he had no sons left alive. It is now that Priam looks to draw a critical distinction between them – Peleus's loneliness is only temporary since he has hope of seeing his son alive. The truth is that Priam's connection to Peleus ironically goes much deeper than he implies or could ever suppose. Peleus too is now doomed to live out his life alone, for he will never see his son again. Priam does not know this, but we do, and so does Achilles. So, serendipitously, just when Priam distances himself from Peleus, Achilles may be seeing himself in Hector – the corpse denied to a defenceless father.

After invoking Peleus, Priam announces his purpose to offer ransom for his son. His proposal echoes the first spoken words of the epic, when Chryses appeals for his daughter's return. But, whereas Chryses appeals for the release of a living daughter, Priam simply wants his son's body back. He concludes in starkly affecting terms: 'Respect the gods, Achilles, and pity me, / remembering your father: but I am still more pitiful, / since I dare do the things which no other mortal man on this earth could do: / I put my lips to the hands of the man who has murdered my son' (503–4). Respect and pity are the two qualities that, earlier, Apollo says Achilles lacks. But Priam also identifies two crucial aspects that facilitate pity. First is respecting the gods (and Achilles has already received a reminder about this from his mother). But memory too plays a key role, as Homer hints at in the description following Priam's speech. The two men weep together, remembering different people. Priam weeps in memory of 'man-slaughtering' Hector – that epithet again revealing what's at stake, by not allowing us to forget that Hector killed Patroclus. For his part, Achilles weeps in memory of both his father (showing the success of Priam's appeal) and Patroclus. Sorrow draws them together and keeps them apart.

Achilles' reply to Priam reveals characteristic assurance tempered by sensitivity. He begins by recognising the unique suffering that 'unlucky' Priam has had to endure. Even daring to be there before him impresses Achilles, such is the courage Priam has shown. Following Priam's lead, Achilles reinforces the connection between them and announces, finally, that he is ready to put away his anger. The coming together of their fates in fact prompts Achilles to ponder the human condition more generally. All men, Achilles maintains, are 'unlucky', while the gods live a life free from care. The cause is Zeus himself, from whom some men get blessings mixed with ills, others just the bad stuff. The proof is before them both. His own father, Peleus, appeared to be so blessed by divine favour that he had a goddess for a wife. But now he will never see his son again and will die alone, surrounded by enemies. So too Priam was called happy, until now.

Achilles' consolation is the mark of a character who is now able to look beyond his own situation and appreciate the circumstances of another. By seeing beyond himself, he shows empathy and confirms that he is no longer the hotheaded young rebel from the poem's beginning. Up to a point.

Thus far, Achilles has answered Priam's fortitude and bravery with consolation for his woes, thereby recognising his own place in a human world of suffering and loss. A ransom for a loved one is, finally, accepted; boundless gifts are, finally, bestowed. Achilles' advice to Priam is to bear up, 'for you will not gain anything by grieving for your son. / You won't bring him back; sooner you would suffer some other evil' (550–1). To accept Priam's appeal, Achilles has had to accept Patroclus's death and his own impending doom. Priam, however, does not appear to have achieved the same peace. Instead, he impatiently asks Achilles to accept the ransom and release the body for him to take home. Priam's haste provokes a response that sounds ominously familiar (559–70). 'Looking darkly at him', Achilles sternly rebukes Priam. This speech introduction, 'looking darkly at him', takes us back to the beginning of the epic, when Achilles first responds angrily to Agamemnon's greed. Similarly, Achilles' opening words to Priam, 'no longer rile me old man', echo Agamemnon's rejection of Chryses' ransom. Pointedly, Homer marks the moment of crisis by describing Priam cowering in fear in the exact same terms he used of Chryses cowering in fear before Agamemnon. Just when we thought that the challenges of the poem's beginning had been resolved, Priam's haste and Achilles' anger threaten to plunge us back into strife and conflict.

There is another important point here. Now that Priam has disrupted the moment of shared understanding by prematurely seeking his goal, Achilles makes an important admission. Retracting his previous consolation, when he wondered how Priam could 'dare come' (519) all alone to his tent, now Achilles asserts that 'no mortal would dare to have come' (565) without divine aid. Here Achilles shows himself to be well aware of Zeus's hand behind Priam's journey – after all, his mother gave him advance notice that this would happen. And he threatens to defy Zeus's orders should Priam fail to show sufficient respect. The resonant language suggests that the cycle of violence cannot be so easily broken. At no point is the audience allowed to forget just how much each figure must give up in negotiating a settlement of sorts. On the other hand, the fact that Achilles *is* fully aware that the gods are behind Priam's visit, but that he will do as *he* sees fit regardless, emphasises his personal responsibility and will. It is his *choice* to return Hector, a choice that in turn reveals his humanity. Thus, when – after his speech has the old man cowering – he 'leaps up like a lion' (572), it is not to strike down his adversary – as the lion motif usually expresses (in battle) – but to prepare Hector's body for return.

Instead of hostilities renewed, Achilles reaffirms his commitment to accept Priam's ransom for Hector's body and reconciles himself with his own mortality. Significantly, he tells Priam that they should eat. Eating in the heroic world is always an important event. Throughout the *Iliad*, the consumption of food occurs at critical moments: in *Iliad* 9, Nestor instructs the Achaeans to eat, while he ushers the leaders into council with Agamemnon (where they also eat) to organise an embassy to Achilles; that embassy is greeted with an invitation to dine; Odysseus resists Achilles' immediate call-to-arms with a reminder that the troops need to eat (*Iliad* 19); after Patroclus's funeral games, the people go off to eat. The *Odyssey* describes the ritual of eating being transgressed – how guests (the suitors) eat a host (Telemachus) out of house and home, or how a monster (Cyclops) eats his guests (Odysseus's men). Since Patroclus's death, Achilles has refused food. He has lasted this long only because of divine sustenance from his mother. The fact that Achilles now recommends that the two of them should eat demonstrates his acceptance of his mortality and his full (and willing) return to the realm of men.

Thus, the two men together, finally, eat. And, as they sit opposite each other, they gaze in wonder at each other. Priam wonders at Achilles, who appears like the gods. But Achilles' 'godlike'
quality is arguably not now his divine parentage, but a reflection
of what he has *done* – his achievements in battle and, especially,
his actions and choices outside of it. In turn, Achilles wonders at
Priam, at his noble bearing, at the words he speaks. What exactly
those words are, we are not told. Homer leaves us wondering at
the reconciliation between these two men, so different in nature,
experience and fate, but joined together in loss and mutual
respect.

The burial of Hector, tamer of horses

After listening to Priam in wonder, Achilles raises a practical
concern: how many days would Priam need to bury his son?
Upon learning that the Trojans would need eleven days, Achilles
promises to hold the Achaeans off from attacking until eleven
days have passed. Then both men go off to sleep, Priam in the
porch of the tent, Achilles with Briseis. In his last appearance of
the epic, we finally see Achilles asleep in the arms of his mortal
woman – the prize over which he had fought with Agamemnon,
the slave because of whom countless Achaeans have died. As his
mother recommends, Achilles, with his life now almost over,
enjoys one of life's simple pleasures.

Such quiet repose is not for Priam, however. Hermes wakes
him to warn him to depart quickly, lest Agamemnon should find
him and do him harm. (Agamemnon's final appearance is as the
potential threat to the scene of reconciliation and understanding.)
But Hermes' warning also reminds us that the scene between
Priam and Achilles was, for all of its monumentality, just momen-
tary and personal, an agreement arrived at only by private contract
(and a temporary one at that) and the help of the gods.

Thus, we follow Priam, carrying his heavy load on the back of a mule cart, back to Troy, where he will bury his son. As the poem's last event, Hector's burial may appear initially surprising. The *Iliad* ends with no great last hurrah from the Achaeans; Troy hasn't even been sacked. But it is a fitting ending for several reasons. It brings Achilles' wrath to a tangible conclusion, as the last object of his anger is laid to rest. The burial rites also lay to rest the *Iliad*'s concern with human mortality: in this final chapter, we find both gods and men equally concerned with the right of a pious man to burial. Furthermore, Hector's burial represents the kind of funerary monument that he wishes for in *Iliad* 7 (though, in his poetic fiction, Hector imagines such a monument to belong to his fallen enemy). Lastly, the laments performed by the women of Troy echo the formation of memory that gives the vanquished life after death in the world outside the poem, while simultaneously initiating the creation of Hector's fame through and within the epic itself. In this way, the end of the epic brings closure to Hector's mortal life and some kind of answer to his prayers for eternal fame.

The three women whom Hector meets in Troy in *Iliad* 6, Helen, Hecuba, and Andromache, deliver the lament. Each one articulates what Hector meant to them and highlights different aspects of his character. First to speak is his wife Andromache (24.724–45). In her speech, she laments the fate of their child and of all the women and children of Troy who are sure to suffer now that they have lost their protector. She vividly predicts that Hector's son, Astyanax, will either spend a wretched life as a slave or else be thrown by some Achaean from the towers of Troy in revenge for his father's reputation; Homer's audience would know that Astyanax is doomed to the latter fate, widely depicted in both visual arts and other literary accounts (such as Euripides's *Trojan Women*). As for herself, Andromache's concerns are simple. She regrets that she did not receive some last 'close word' from her husband to remember as she mourns him the rest of her life (744). At the beginning of this final book, Zeus gives a 'close word' to Thetis (75), which sets in motion the (remarkable) series of events that have seen Priam journey to Achilles' tent and return with his son's body. Andromache's 'close word', which brings to an end the events that Zeus's edict initiates, is far more fragile, fleeting, and painful. In her mouth it signifies loss. It represents what she didn't get from her husband to lessen her pain or to give her something to contemplate, some solace as she continues life without him – as if any word could achieve that anyway.

For Andromache, Hector is the lost protector of the Trojans, the lost bulwark for her child, and the lost intimacy of a husband gone too soon. For Hecuba, Hector is the 'dearest' of all her children. Others Achilles has already sold as slaves. In fact, Hecuba counts Hector as lucky and blessed by the gods, for how else could she explain that Achilles returns him and that his corpse appears fresh? Thus, Hecuba expresses gratitude to the gods and also reflects the type of pragmatism in death that often overcomes mourners. Hecuba, who has seen so much death and the loss of so many children, counts herself lucky for a body she can bury.

Oddly, the last word on Hector, and the last speech in the *Iliad*, goes to Helen. The cause of the war, Helen takes this final opportunity to wish that she had died before ever leaving Sparta, before all these tragic events had been set in motion. Importantly, her plea for death echoes the sentiment expressed by Achilles in the assembly of *Iliad* 19, when he wishes that Briseis had died before he won her so that they all could have avoided the disastrous conflict. In both cases, the two protagonists of the Trojan War admit after the fact that the strife, of which they were a part or the cause, was not worth the trouble. She ends by recalling Hector's gentleness and predicting that now everyone in Troy will hate her. The tradition suggests that she is right.

After this triad of views on what Hector meant for different people – for a wife, mother, and outsider – the *Iliad* concludes with the burial itself. The scene of burial marks a moment of quiet repose and remembrance. But, even here, conflict intrudes. The Trojans – in spite of Achilles' assurances – post guards *just in case* the Achaeans should attack prematurely. The *Iliad* provides no lasting sense of comfort. The peace is only (ever going to be) a temporary respite from war. Like the plaintiffs and judges frozen in time on Achilles' shield (*Iliad* 18), the poem points to the continuation of conflict even after it has drawn formally to a close.

Back in *Iliad* 7, Hector challenges the 'best of the Achaeans' to a duel. There he imagines that, once he wins the contest, the dead hero's tomb would be a monument to, and symbol of, his ever-lasting glory. Ironically, the dead hero's tomb turns out to be his. But what kind of *symbol* is it? Homer describes how the Trojans' burial-mound for Hector leaves 'a mark' (799). The word here is *sēma*, which also means 'sign' or 'symbol'. (It's the origin of our words 'semantics' or 'semiotics'.) At its end, the *Iliad* leaves us with a sign of some kind to interpret. Ostensibly, that sign is Hector's burial mound, a physical marker of his fame. Yet, Homer glosses that burial mound as a 'hollow grave' (797). 'Hollow' – an adjective that also describes the Achaean ships – could indicate a vessel defined by its capacity to hold and transport, to retain and transcend. Simultaneously, this hollowness could indicate empti-ness, as if questioning whether any sign or token, such as a burial mound, could really make up for death or overcome loss.

These rival interpretations do not exhaust the game of signs. For, as well as Hector's grave, the sign may also refer to the *Iliad* itself, the ultimate symbol of Hector's 'hollow' grave, both as the marker of his absence and the vessel of his continued presence in men's minds. After all, this poem is *also* a transformative and tran-scendent symbol of some kind. On the one hand, it marks the transition from the heroic age to the present day. The *Iliad*, Homer's poem of rage, explores the issues thrown up by the ten-year Trojan War from the perspective of little more than a few days' worth of arguments, armed conflict, divine concern and human suffering. Its setting may be the plain in front of Troy, but the epic is far less focused on who wins and loses the conflict over Helen – a fact already determined by the poetic tradition – than with depicting and exploring the bitter political struggles among Achaeans and the intense sufferings of the Trojans whose survival rests with Hector. Indeed, the *Iliad* finds the death of Hector a suitable end point for its story of Achilles' godlike wrath, for by this point Achilles has come to terms with his own mortality, the fate of the race of heroes has been sealed, and institutions (not only the assembly and council but also the games and even the law court depicted on Achilles' shield) have been established which will provide man with the kind of security that was once dependent on individual heroic action.

For us (if not for ancient audiences too), Homer's *Iliad* also acts as a grave marker of an entire tradition of epic poetry singing about the wars at Troy and Thebes. 'So they buried Hector, tamer of horses' (804) goes our last line of the poem. While testimony from the 'Epic Cycle' suggests that the song about Troy continues after this point – the *Aethiopis* apparently even picked up the tale from this cue – not one of these other poems gets written down to survive the test of time. (Indeed, there is good reason to suppose that the very basis of the 'Epic Cycle' as we have it has been constructed to make sense of the *Iliad*.) There is only one other epic poem about the age of heroes that comes down to us, and this tells the story of the return home from Troy. This is the *Odyssey*, the subject of our next three chapters.

The *Odyssey*: a poem of many turns

In many ways, the *Odyssey* is everything that the *Iliad* is not. Where the *Iliad* is about the war, the *Odyssey* is about the return home. Where the *Iliad* resolutely fixes on a handful of days (in a ten-year conflict) and a narrow strip of land (between Troy and the Achaean camp), the *Odyssey* ranges over decades (primarily Odysseus's ten years of further striving) and over both known and unknown lands. Where the *Iliad* looks unswervingly at human relationships in a war footing, the *Odyssey*'s gaze takes in various fantasy folk-tale elements alongside one-eyed monsters, witches and the ungrateful dead. Fundamentally, where Achilles is known for his strength and might, Odysseus is known for his endurance and cleverness.

Of course, it is easy to exaggerate the differences – Odysseus can fight as well as the next man, while even the *Iliad* allows glimpses of his trickiness (particularly in the *Odyssey*-like book ten, when he leads a night-time raid on the Trojan camp). Perhaps it is better, like Aristotle, to think of the two poems as complementing each other, which allows them together to communicate not just the full experience of the Trojan War story but also the broadest range of human experience in general. While the *Odyssey* is not a sequel to the *Iliad* in the way one might expect from modern cinema (it doesn't pick up from where the *Iliad* leaves off), there is a great deal of crossover in terms of characters (Odysseus, Agamemnon, Achilles), plot (war and the return), and theme (what it means to be human). The *Odyssey* is even careful to keep off the *Iliad*'s turf and avoid any events narrated in that other poem.

Nevertheless, the style and tone of the two epics differ markedly, to the extent that the author of *On the Sublime* put the *Odyssey*'s wanderings down to Homer's old age, while the critical consensus ever since the nineteenth century has tended to see the two poems as having been composed by different authors. The difference can also be expressed in terms of the *Iliad* being a forerunner to tragedy whose actors must face up to the mortal condition of loss and suffering, while the *Odyssey* reads something like a comedy or novel, with its protagonist's journey from dangerous isolation to celebratory reunion with his family at home. Again, however, this is too simplistic. The *Odyssey* can be funny, such as when the witch Circe turns Odysseus's men into pigs. But it can also be deadly serious (as with Odysseus's slaughter of the suitors). Perhaps it is more accurate to say that the *Odyssey* is far more aware of itself as a poem and obsessively interrogates poetic authority and skill. Events are narrated out of order. Poets and storytelling come under scrutiny. The hero himself takes over the telling of his tale for three whole books. Even the restricted access to Olympus (limited to the beginning and end of the poem) make the gods appear as a formal framing device of the kind seen later in Athenian tragedy when a 'god' descends from a crane (the *deus ex machina*) to bring a play to an end. In fact, when Homer asks the Muse to start the tale 'from some point' (1.9), it is as if we are being asked to view the opening sequence as one arbitrarily chosen from any number of possible beginnings – for any story has any number of ways of starting (and ending). No wonder that the *Odyssey* was the primary inspiration and model for James Joyce's modernist classic *Ulysses* and continues to appeal to postmodern sensibilities in creations such as Daniel Wallace's *Big Fish* or Bryan Singer's *Usual Suspects*.

The differences are evident from the beginning of the *Odyssey*. Homer toys with his audience about what this epic will be about. Zeus appears to suggest that it will be one thing – a morality tale plain and simple – while Athena denies the relevance of this analysis to Odysseus's story. Odysseus isn't even featured for the first four books. Instead, Homer focuses attention on the dire situation back home on Ithaca, and on the hero's son, Telemachus. Through his own odyssey in search of his father, Telemachus undergoes a journey of self-discovery: he learns about his father, specifically how to become more like him. Importantly, we – the audience of the poem – also learn about Odysseus and the fates of the other Achaean heroes from Troy. And, through the journey that Telemachus takes, we learn about the superiority of Odysseus in relation to those other Trojan War veterans and, crucially, how to 'read' this poem.

The beginning(s) of the *Odyssey*

The *Odyssey* distinguishes itself from the *Iliad* in its opening lines:

> Tell me, Muse, of the man of many ways, who most especially
> Wandered much, after he sacked Troy's sacred citadel.
> Many were they whose cities he saw, whose minds he learned of,
> Many the pains he suffered in his spirit at sea,
> Struggling for his life and the homecoming of his companions.
> But even so he could not save his companions, though he tried
> For they were destroyed by their own recklessness,
> The fools, who devoured the oxen of Helios, the Sun god,
> And he took away their homecoming day. From some point
> Begin, goddess, daughter of Zeus, and speak to us.
>
> (1.1–10)

Where the *Iliad* begins in 'wrath', the *Odyssey* begins with 'man' (*andra*). And, just as 'wrath' sets the subject and tone for the *Iliad*, so 'man' epitomises the story of this return poem. 'Andra' invites us to think about *the* man in question, Odysseus, who is identified here only by the epithet *polytropos* (meaning 'of many turns'). The absence of a name anticipates many occasions when withholding it proves critical for Odysseus to survive (in Cyclops's cave or at home among the suitors) and foreshadows the task our hero faces to (re)discover and (re)claim his identity. Moreover, the elusive manner in which the poem announces its agenda hints at the slippery quality of its hero, as encapsulated by this epithet 'of many turns'. Just when you think you've got Odysseus (and/or the *Odyssey*), the hero (/the poem) slips through your grasp.

This first word also signifies a cosmological distinction. For *andra* can be translated simply as *man* (as opposed to the *heroes* and *demigods* of earlier generations). We have already seen the *Iliad* position Achilles as a kind of paradigm for men, as he confronts his own mortality (though he's advertised as 'godlike'). The *Odyssey* is a good deal more explicit, as it explores the tension between Odysseus as an individual hero and as a representative of man generally. The focus on 'man' also positions the *Odyssey* at a stage further on from the *Iliad* towards the world of men, with the divine apparatus all but stripped away in favour of human responsibility.

But *andra* can also mean 'husband', which sets up the key problematic of this poem – Odysseus as *Penelope's* man. In part, *andra* as 'husband' indicates the peril involved when Odysseus gets waylaid in an erotic encounter here and there: all spell danger to his return home, however innocent they may at first appear (such as Nausicaa). Additionally, it serves to draw up the battle-lines, for the suitors on Ithaca represent would-be husbands of Penelope. Suitoring is not intrinsically a malevolent activity or even intrinsically un-epic. In the fragmentary epic poem the

Catalogue of Women, ascribed to Hesiod, an impressive roll call of suitors lines up to marry Helen – only for the rather unimpressive Menelaus to win out (a surprise that perhaps partly explains Helen's elopement with Paris). Suitoring *can* be the subject of epic song. Unfortunately for the suitors back on Ithaca, endeavouring to win Penelope's hand, this woman *already* has a man.

Thus, the proem introduces Odysseus without naming him, struggling all the while to get a grip on the man. Something of that struggle surfaces in the repetition of the modifier 'many/ much' that defines the man 'of many turns'. This man wandered *much*, saw the cities and knew the minds of *many* men, suffered *many* pains. The 'manyness' indicates the range and extent of Odysseus's fame. He is the wanderer who was responsible for the sack of Troy (2). He excels in practical intelligence, based on an implicit connection between his travelling (seeing the cities of many men) and knowledge (coming to understand their minds (3)). Above all he suffers, struggling not only for his own life but also for his companions (4–5) – *this* Odysseus does labour to bring his men home. Barely contained by his epithets, Odysseus's remarkable multidimensionality makes him a man for all seasons. This poem isn't just about a war veteran endeavouring to get home and reintegrate with those he left behind – the son now grown up, the wife who may have forgotten him, the parents who may have perished in the meantime. It's about anyone's struggle to (re)discover who they are.

The rest of the proem (5–9) turns from Odysseus to his companions. This shift in itself reveals a certain slipperiness – the 'man' is no sooner mentioned than left to one side. This slipperiness continues even once the poem is underway 'from some point'. We turn first to Odysseus, still in exile, 'longing for his wife and his homecoming' (13) but held captive by the nymph Calypso. We learn that Poseidon, who up until now has stood in the way of Odysseus's return, is absent (away feasting with the Ethiopians). Expectations are raised of Odysseus's immediate return. Instead, Homer takes us to Olympus.

Zeus, the first speaker of the *Odyssey*, at first seems to be watching a different drama. We find him pronouncing on the story of Aegisthus, who murdered his cousin Agamemnon (and married his wife, Clytemnestra), and who is killed in revenge by Orestes, Agamemnon's son. According to Zeus, he continually warned Aegisthus that he would be punished were he to kill Agamemnon. His flouting of divine advice prompts Zeus to exclaim: 'Oh for shame, how mortals put the blame upon us gods, / for they say that it is from us that evils come, but it is they, rather, / who by their own recklessness gain sorrows beyond what is fated' (32–4). This opening scene fulfils two important tasks. First, it establishes the failed homecoming of Agamemnon as a counterpoint to Odysseus's – Telemachus is constantly being reminded of Orestes' brave action, while Agamemnon's ghost warns Odysseus about the dangers of the wife waiting at home. Second, it puts the audience on notice that this epic is going to be very different from the *Iliad*.

At the end of the *Iliad*, Achilles consoles Priam by blaming Zeus for mankind's woes – some men receive blessings mixed with ills, whereas the less fortunate only receive the bad stuff. Zeus's opening speech here in the *Odyssey* appears to 'correct' Achilles by emphasising that men are to blame for their own troubles. Where the *Iliad* takes pains to establish its plot as part of Zeus's will, the *Odyssey* makes men responsible for what happens. The idea of mankind suffering 'because of their own recklessness' becomes something of the *Odyssey*'s refrain, applied here by Zeus to Aegisthus, and elsewhere by Homer to Odysseus's companions (already in the proem) and especially to the suitors. The shift in theological perspective reinforces the *Odyssey*'s position in the epic cosmos, as a poem both looking back to the *Iliad*'s world of heroes and forward to Hesiod's vision of human existence in his

Works and Days, where man is solely responsible for his actions, while one god, Zeus, presides from afar.

The *Odyssey*'s Zeus has in mind all mankind when he pronounces that men are to blame for their troubles. Athena (the only other god to speak in the poem's divine assemblies) objects to its application to Odysseus. Punning on his name, Athena asks Zeus why Odysseus is so 'odious' (*ôdusao*, 62) to him. Did he not burn many sacrifices to the gods? The sentiment recalls the reason why the gods in the *Iliad* agree to salvage Hector's body, as if the *Odyssey* were picking up the theme of the other epic, if not the plot. But there is also a critical difference between the two poems. Where men in the *Iliad* suffer almost inexplicably as a result of Achilles' wrath and Zeus's will, the causality of suffering in the *Odyssey* is more plainly expressed.

The 'bad' guys of the *Odyssey* – the suitors, the companions, etc. – suffer because they do wrong. Even Odysseus's suffering is explained in these terms – by blinding Cyclops, Poseidon's son, he condemned himself to more years of wandering. And yet, even as the *Odyssey* draws up the battle lines between those with Odysseus and those against him, the poem makes it clear how the deck is stacked. If moral judgements are more explicit and frequent in this poem, the audience cannot avoid being implicated in judging Odysseus's treatment of his companions from Troy (all of whom he loses) and of the suitors (all of whom he kills). Significantly, Odysseus's name derives from the verb *odussomai*, which has both a passive meaning ('the one who is hated') and an active one ('the one who is wrathful'). Homer's poem explores this essential ambiguity and exploits the tension between the two senses to prompt us to reflect on which connotation best suits Odysseus. Is Odysseus victim, or aggressor, or both?

We learn from Athena that Odysseus presently languishes on a desert island, where the goddess Calypso 'detains the grieving, unhappy man, / and continually with words that are gentle and wheedling / enchants him to forget Ithaca' (1.55–7). Once Zeus agrees to Odysseus's return, Athena advises him to send Hermes to deliver the message: she herself will go to Odysseus's son in Ithaca. After stalling with Zeus's rant against mankind, the poem is kick-started by Athena, and we ready ourselves to be reacquainted with Odysseus. Instead, Odysseus remains 'hidden' by Calypso (whose name means 'the one who hides') for the next four books. The beginning of the *Odyssey* sets up expectation of Odysseus's homecoming and provides an explanation for its delay – only to delay it further. For, rather than rejoining Odysseus right away, we arrive where *he* wants to be (Ithaca), to do what *he* wants to do (meet his son and wife). Homer reminds us that this is a poem about life outside of war, about the kind of home to which Odysseus returns. So, we start by learning what has been happening on Ithaca in Odysseus's long absence, and in particular about his son, Telemachus.

Meanwhile, back on Ithaca...

The beginning of the *Odyssey* has prompted much scholarly criticism. No sooner is Odysseus mentioned than he goes AWOL for four whole books. At the beginning of book five, we even get the same meeting between Zeus and Athena, the same question (where's Odysseus?), the same decision (to release Odysseus), and the same action (to send Hermes to Calypso). According to the 'Analyst' critics of the nineteenth century, these first four books amounted to a 'Telemachy', a later insertion aimed at filling out Telemachus's biography.

We should recall, however, that the poem has already set out its allusive *and elusive* approach to Odysseus, when refusing to name 'the man of many turns'. We should be expecting twists and turns. We might recall too that the *Iliad* similarly removes its hero from the action (from halfway through book one through to book nine). If the *Odyssey* does so more explicitly, that is another manifestation of its greater self-reflexivity – it revels in drawing attention to its composition. One effect here, as in the *Iliad*, is to create suspense for the hero's return. But that is not all. It also re-creates the trickiness of its hero, just as Achilles' absence draws attention to his stubborn anger and social marginality. Furthermore, by beginning Odysseus's homecoming with a picture of home, the *Odyssey* addresses what home *means* to the hero and unpacks how his identity is bound up with his family, who in his continued absence suffer greatly too. These explorations pave the way for Odysseus's long-awaited appearance and serve to set into relief his exceptional return.

When we first meet Telemachus, he is shedding tears at his father's (lost) homecoming, just like Odysseus is doing on the shore of Calypso's island – already son is like father, even if neither knows it yet. Suitors besiege his house, clamouring for his mother's hand in marriage. Every day they lounge about, consuming his father's wealth, his inheritance. When Telemachus first speaks to Athena (in disguise as the loyal servant Mentes), he imagines his father dead and unburied: 'he has died by an evil fate...and his homecoming day has been lost' (166, 168). Though Athena assures him that Odysseus is 'alive somewhere, held captive on the wide sea' (197), and notes the striking resemblance between father and son, Telemachus expresses doubt. 'My mother says that indeed I am, but I for my part / do not know. Nobody really knows his own father' (215–16). The Telemachus we first meet is so disillusioned, so far separated from his father, that he doubts his own paternity.

In addition to posing the question of identity, Homer introduces the theme of hospitality. Throughout Greek culture the foremost indicators of good *economy* (from the Greek *oikos*, 'household', and *nomia*, 'proper management') are the treatment of guests, their behaviour, and proper gift exchange. Telemachus proves himself a consummate host, to a fault. He welcomes

Athena, offers her food, entertainment, and rest, before enquiring who she ('Mentes') is. When the goddess remarks that any decent man would be outraged to see the behaviour of the suitors, Telemachus takes this as his cue to lament his fate – things would have been different were his father certainly dead and buried with honour. Instead, the so-called nobles of the nearby islands and the prominent men of Ithaca have come courting his mother. While so far she has rejected these marriage proposals, he expects to be killed by one of them any day. Where Telemachus verges on being a perfect host, the suitors pervert the relationship by being parasitic, even violently voracious, guests. Athena's subsequent anger confirms their behaviour to be antisocial and illegitimate, and underlines the suffering of Odysseus's wife and son.

Her advice for Telemachus is this: he should call an assembly and travel abroad to enquire about his father. Bluntly, she adds: 'you should not go on / clinging to your childhood, since you are no longer a youth. / Or have you not heard what glory godlike Orestes won / from all men, when he killed the murderer of his father?' (296–9). Athena balances the accusation of immaturity by providing a new role model: Orestes grew up without his father but learned how to be a man. In the wake of Athena's criticism and encouragement – she reminds him that he is 'big and splendid' and must 'be bold also, so that in generations to come they will speak well of you' (301–2) – Telemachus begins his process of growing up.

Evidence of his newfound maturity follows swiftly, as his mother, Penelope, makes her first appearance. She has entered the hall to stop the bard Phemius from singing about the Achaeans' 'difficult homecomings' – unsurprisingly, a popular number for the suitors, but one particularly painful for her. Telemachus defends the singer and sends his mother back upstairs. Three points are worthy of note. First, while Telemachus is clearly not the master of a house yet, his outburst does show his willingness to speak up, and one person at least accepts his authority – Penelope, stunned, obeys her son. Second, he defends the bard on the basis that 'men always praise more that song / which is the latest to circulate among the listeners' (351–2), which gestures slyly to the very poem we are listening to, the *Odyssey*, the latest song on the block. Both points merge in Telemachus's echo of Hector. When that hero put his wife in her place in *Iliad* 6, he famously declared 'war is the concern for / all men but especially for me' (6.492–3). Here Telemachus sends his mother away with the words: 'speech is the concern for / all men but especially for me' (358–9). Telemachus *already* sounds like Hector, but he also articulates a crucial departure from that epic. While war was the concern of Hector and the *Iliad*, *speech* is the concern of Telemachus and the *Odyssey*, particularly *epic poetry itself* – that special kind of speech that is the context for Telemachus's remarks here.

The difference between the two epics is encapsulated by the next episode. As the suitors laugh heartily at Penelope's dismissal (365), Telemachus puts them on notice of his intention to change the situation in his household (and Ithaca) by calling an assembly for the following day. We have seen that the assembly was critical in the *Iliad*'s formation of a political community in the wake of Achilles' challenge to Agamemnon. The assembly is important in the *Odyssey* too, but for very different reasons. An old man called Aegyptius opens proceedings by remarking that the Ithacans have held neither assembly nor council all the time Odysseus has been absent. By calling an assembly, Telemachus mimics Achilles' achievement and re-establishes a public forum for discussion lacking since his father's departure. But how far does this newly revived openness go? Homer hints at the potential shockwaves of such an action in his introduction to Aegyptius (2.15–25). Aegyptius has three sons. One followed Odysseus and was eaten by Cyclops. One joined the suitors and will be dead by the poem's end. The third has retreated from society to live as a recluse. The three sons and their three paths point to the near impossibility of stable and civilised human relationships on Ithaca in Odysseus's absence and, more tellingly, in his *presence*. Their miserable fates foreshadow the civil strife that will consume Ithaca at the end of the epic. But, in spite of sufficient cause to speak up against Odysseus, Aegyptius remains silent. He doesn't know the fate of his sons. The *Odyssey* gestures towards openness – including an early challenge to Odysseus – only simultaneously to shut out the person with due cause from knowledge of it. Aegyptius simply asks why the assembly has been called. His work here is done.

Instead of a challenge to Odysseus, we hear his son. And the prospects for open debate don't look good. It is true that, by criticising the suitors for harrying his mother and consuming his wealth, Telemachus makes public the words he used earlier in the comfort of his own home. But, after appealing over the heads of the suitors to the Ithacan public to help him right the situation, he ends by hurling down the sceptre (80–1). So much for calling an assembly – by his actions, Telemachus reveals little faith in this institution to resolve the crisis. Of course, his actions also replay Achilles' sceptred ire with his community (*Iliad* 1.245) and, for a brief moment, Odysseus's son ranks alongside the hero of the *Iliad*. Then he *cries* – it is, after all, still early in his maturation. But his speech sets the tone. You're either with us or against us.

Unlike the Achaean assembly in the *Iliad*, the Ithacan assembly has little interest in social formation. It simply presents an opportunity for the battle lines to be drawn, as three suitors abuse Telemachus's household and two others defend it. First to react is the suitor Antinous, whose name, 'Mr Contrary-mind', already suggests a rebel with(out) a cause. Indeed, he immediately attempts to cast the events at Ithaca in a different light. It is all Penelope's fault for stringing them along. She promised to choose a husband upon completing a death shroud for Odysseus's decrepit father, Laertes: but every evening she has been unpicking her weaving, and has avoided making a decision. A second suitor, Eurymachus ('broad in battle'), takes up this alternative version by urging Telemachus to make his mother decide now. Tellingly, these two suitors claim for themselves as a group the title of *Achaeans*, using the formula 'sons of the Achaeans' so resonant with the *Iliad*. Eurymachus even attempts to reinvent the suitors in terms that evoke Agamemnon's heroic coalition at Troy: they won't give up on their '*harsh* courtship' (199), but will 'strive for the sake of her [Penelope's] excellence' (206). Just as those 'sons of the Achaeans' fought over Helen, so these 'sons of Achaeans' strive for Penelope. Helen, we know, was indeed the object of assembled suitors striving for her hand (in the Hesiodic *Catalogue of Women*). There is an early hint of this strategy in Antinous's denunciation of Penelope – '*the suitors* of the Achaeans' are not to blame (87), he asserts. The problem is that the *Odyssey*, from its very first word ('andra'), has advertised its story as being about a returning *husband*. These suitors are in the wrong poem. The bird interpreter Halitherses confirms this impression with an unusually unambiguous reading of a bird omen sent by Zeus: Odysseus will return, the suitors should mend their ways, the rest of the Ithacans should stop them.

Most significantly, by the time that the aptly named suitor Leocritus ('judgement of the people') dissolves the assembly, Telemachus has already indicated that he seeks resolution elsewhere. 'But come now,' he announces, 'give me a swift ship and twenty companions...I am going to Sparta and sandy Pylos / to find out about the homecoming of my father' (212, 214–15). Frustrated by the public, and highly destructive, opposition of the suitors, Telemachus gives up on the assembly entirely and seeks a very different path – to go boldly in search of his father. Unlike the *Iliad*, the solution to the community's crisis is not to be found in its political institutions. Instead, we are to go on a journey, where, together with Telemachus, we learn about Odysseus's homecoming. With the taunts and the threats of the suitors ringing in his ears, Telemachus manages to slip away unnoticed (with Athena's help) and sets sail for Pylos.

In search of Odysseus

Telemachus's journey is significant as the means by which he will find out about his father; but, by going on his own odyssey, Telemachus also learns to become *like his father*. For the stories about his father educate him about what kind of hero Odysseus is, and what kind of son he needs to be. And it is not only Telemachus who is learning about this 'man of many turns'. Telemachus's receptions in Pylos and Sparta provide a framework for us, Homer's audience, to understand the behaviour of the suitors in Ithaca and the experiences of Odysseus himself.

Telemachus arrives in Pylos during a wedding feast presided over by Nestor, the figure established in the *Iliad* as wise and fair (he is the one Achaean to try to stop the quarrel between Agamemnon and Achilles). Here he immediately demonstrates norms of hospitality by serving Telemachus food before knowing who he is, since 'it is better to inquire about and ask / guests who they are, once they have had the pleasure of eating' (3.69–70). Nor should we overlook the thematic importance of the wedding feast, which both underscores the impropriety of the suitors' endless, and antisocial, feasting and highlights, again, how far removed they are from the impulse of the poem – they will enjoy no marriage feast with Penelope for she is already married. Nestor's gracious hospitality extends to offering Telemachus a bed at night, a bath the next morning, a fresh horse, and a travelling companion (his son, Peisistratus). Upon arriving at the palace of Menelaus, such is the wealth that greets him that Telemachus likens the scene to the halls of the gods. Telemachus and Peisistratus are bathed, clothed, and put before a sumptuous feast; again, it is not until after dinner that the guests are questioned about the purpose of their visit.

The composition of each household provides the young man and the audience with points of comparison for life back on Ithaca. Nestor's household presents a full family to contrast with the single son and husbandless wife of Odysseus's home, a feeling that is particularly acute since Telemachus arrives during a wedding celebration. This family feasts, entertains, and propitiates the gods together − a world apart from Telemachus's predicament, whose house is fast being consumed by the suitors (with no thought to the gods or their host), and whose mother is besieged by marriage demands. For their part, Menelaus and Helen play the perfect host and hostess with the mostess, royally entertaining their guests with food, wine, and stories.

However, poke a little beneath the surface and one finds less the ideal home than examples to be avoided. For one thing, if Nestor was already old in the *Iliad* (the one figure who has witnessed the deeds of a prior generation of heroes), he is positively ancient in the *Odyssey*, a further ten years down the line. And, if before he used to recall the past to negotiate present crises, now he seems to be living in it, with countless stories of Troy, and especially the death of his son, Antilochus, preying on his mind. Nor is all well in the state of Sparta. Menelaus's doorman reveals underlying troubles when he asks whether or not strangers should even be let in! Though Menelaus responds angrily, the question implies that hospitality in his household is not what it should be. There is too a marked absence of children − their long-abandoned daughter Hermione barely appears.

The elephant in the room is the relationship of the married couple itself. Although it was her elopement with Paris that caused the Trojan War (and the *Iliad*), Helen is now back in Sparta living with her husband, Menelaus, as if nothing had happened. In fact, such is the scene of domestic harmony represented here that it may well have been Homer's *Odyssey* which gave rise to the story that Helen didn't go to Troy after all but an image produced by the gods. (This is the story told, for example, in Euripides's play *Helen*, which also stars a grumpy doorman.) But this married bliss is counterfeit. When Menelaus grows morose, Helen mixes into his wine a drug whose power would prevent sadness even in a man who has just lost his mother or father (4.219–32). When the thorny issue of Troy comes up, Helen insists it was Aphrodite who struck her with an infatuation that made her leave her child and husband. Most telling are the rival stories the loving couple relate to illustrate Odysseus's cleverness. Helen tells a story of how she alone recognised Odysseus when he penetrated Troy's defences in disguise – but his secret was safe with her (235–64). Menelaus counters with his own story of Odysseus's cleverness. As the Achaean warriors lie hidden in the Trojan horse, Helen calls out in the voices of their wives in an effort to expose them – and would have succeeded too had not Odysseus prevented them (266–89). Oh, and accompanying Helen at that time was her *third* husband, Deiphobus, Menelaus pointedly adds (another of Priam's sons, whom she married after Paris's death). The surface impression may be of a marriage made in heaven – and tradition has it that Menelaus is the one hero to live in the Isles of the Blessed after his death – but beneath the glossy image one finds a far less rosy picture.

As we (Telemachus and the audience) learn about these other homes, so we also find out about Odysseus through the stories of his former comrades. For Telemachus, these stories present the paternal role model he has been sorely lacking. When Nestor looks at Telemachus, he notes his good looks and size – qualities that should make him brave, strong, and capable of winning glory. But he also singles out Odysseus for his cunning and strategy; indeed, Nestor, no fool himself, was always of a single mind with Odysseus in assembly and council. The lesson for Telemachus is clear: to be his father's son, he must not only look like him but also act like him, which means precisely going beyond surface characteristics. Like saying one thing but keeping another in the heart, for example – precisely the accusation that the blunt-speaking Achilles had levelled at Odysseus in the *Iliad*. In Sparta, Telemachus receives rival perspectives on his father. Menelaus emphasises Odysseus's endurance as his defining characteristic – his story demonstrates Odysseus's resolve as the man who restrained the Achaeans from falling for Helen's deceitful imitations. In contrast, Helen's story highlights Odysseus's trickery in being able to penetrate Troy's defences in disguise.

These distinct views on Odysseus, each of which draws attention to different aspects of his character – his strategic cunning, steely endurance, trickiness – provide his son with a set of qualities to emulate. At the same time as supplying Telemachus with a role model, however, these tales within the tale also serve to prepare us, Homer's audience, for Odysseus's role in this poem. For all these qualities, particularly his ability to carry off a disguise, will play a crucial role in his returning home successfully. In fact, these stories about Odysseus are in and of themselves a demonstration of his epic fame (*kleos*). Since *kleos* literally means 'that which is heard', the *Odyssey*'s retelling of these stories through books three and four represents a *performance* of Odysseus's fame, even before the hero makes his grand entrance.

The accounts of Nestor, Menelaus, and Helen about Odysseus also furnish Homer with the opportunity to reflect on the Trojan War in general and compare the homecomings of the other heroes. Nestor's first response to Telemachus is to lament the loss of men like Ajax, Achilles, and Patroclus, while Menelaus wishes that he could swap his wealth for the lives of the Achaeans who fell at Troy. As for those who actually survive the war to head for home, Nestor records Athena's fatal wrath (for excesses committed by the Achaeans when sacking Troy), and the disastrous returns of most of the heroes. Menelaus himself returned home via Egypt, where he found out that Odysseus still lives – crucial news that Telemachus can take away. But the surviving Trojan War veterans are few and far between, and for none has the suffering been worth it. Indeed, Agamemnon's classic failed homecoming continues to haunt the poem. While Nestor promotes Orestes as the model son whose vengeance upon his father's killers wins enduring fame, Menelaus emphasises not the glory of Orestes but the suffering of the man who returns to a broken home – a fate that may yet await Odysseus. Oddly, neither hero offers Telemachus help. Yet, as we have learned during these two books, Telemachus is big and strong on his own, his family is already the topic of stories men will remember, and the task to defend the household is his. Besides, it won't be strength of arms that will win the day, but deceit, endurance, trickery, and disguise – all those aspects so dear to Odysseus.

Finally, after hearing so much about Odysseus, we return to him in *Odyssey* 5. We find him still languishing on an island, suspended between the world of gods and humans. Calypso promises Odysseus immortality, using a quasi-magical formula 'immortal and ageless' (136) that evokes a world where men *could* become gods. But the *Odyssey*, through its hero, rejects this world. Even though Penelope 'is mortal and you [Calypso] are immortal and ageless' (218), Odysseus longs for his homecoming and his mortal wife. As such, he affirms his status as a man, defined by growing old and suffering. As for his immortality, now that he has gained release from Calypso, 'the one who hides' (him from men's thoughts and esteem), this will take the form of epic fame – this poem.

However, first, Odysseus must make his first painful steps on the road to rebuilding his shattered humanity piece by piece, just as carefully and painstakingly as he builds the ship that takes him off his desert island. His journey will not be easy. Poseidon returns to the scene long enough to break his ship up and almost drown him. *Odyssey* 5 ends with our hero washed up on the shore of an unknown island, alive, barely, wrapped in a bush like the embers of a fire saved against the cold and darkness. Literally naked, metaphorically reborn into the society of men, Odysseus's challenge is how to get home from here.

Odysseus, singer of tales

At long last we come to Odysseus and his return home. And, as we do so, the theme of storytelling looms ever larger. For the *Odyssey* is not just about the story of Odysseus's homecoming: it also makes storytelling itself part of that story and the means by which Odysseus makes it home successfully. We have already seen glimpses of this interest in the stories that the other Trojan War veterans tell about Odysseus, which help prepare us for his homecoming and portray Odysseus's epic fame in production. Now, on the margins of human society, in the company of the golden-age Phaeacians, Odysseus himself will use stories about himself to help him achieve his journey home to his house and family. Nowhere is that clearer than when the hero himself takes up the telling of the tale (*Odyssey* 9–12).

From his marginal position on the shores of Scheria, Odysseus begins the final stage of his journey back to Ithaca. After thoughts of marriage are put in her mind by Athena, Nausicaa, the king's daughter, comes upon the naked Odysseus, with only a bush to cover his pride. Homer describes Odysseus's quandary – whether to rush forward and embrace Nausicaa's legs in the ritual act of supplication, or else make his appeal from where he sits. Strikingly, Homer uses a lion simile, common in the *Iliad* for describing battlefield action – supplicating Nausicaa in his state of undress, particularly when she's thinking of marriage, is as dangerous to Odysseus's return as any battle is to a hero from the *Iliad*. But, even as they flirt with danger, their encounter remains circumspectly proper. Odysseus even prays that the gods will grant her 'like-mindedness' with her future husband, since 'nothing is better than this and more steadfast / than when two people, thinking the same in their mind maintain a house, / a man and wife' (6.182–4). *This* is not the Odysseus who tarries with a foreign princess and has children, as other versions of Odysseus's homecoming apparently spun it. Instead, through Nausicaa's help, Odysseus gains access to the Phaeacian court and the ear of the king, Alcinous. In doing so, Odysseus establishes a matrix of themes around disguise, hospitality, and recognition that anticipates events back on Ithaca, even as it helps pave the way for that homecoming.

The primary means by which Odysseus manufactures a safe route home is through the medium of song. The ultra-civilised Phaeacians enjoy the good life – games, feasting, and, naturally, listening to poetry. Their bard, Demodocus, sings three songs that relate to Odysseus's situation in various ways, all of which continue the poem's self-conscious interest in constructing its hero's fame (and identity) before our eyes. The first is an account of the 'famous' strife between the best of the Achaeans – only, this time the two heroes in question are Achilles and Odysseus, while Agamemnon happily looks on, under the mistaken belief that this quarrel fulfils the prophecy that Troy will fall when the best of the Achaeans fall out. That quarrel is, of course, the story told by the *Iliad*, the 'best' of the Achaeans himself and Achilles. By inserting Odysseus as the best of the Achaeans to rival Achilles, Demodocus's alternative 'Iliad' makes a sly nod to this very poem, the clash between the two heroes symbolising the rivalry between the two Homeric poems.

Demodocus's next song takes us to Olympus, where the lame Hephaestus, suspicious that his wife, Aphrodite, is having an affair, sets an elaborate trap. (Among other things Hephaestus is the craftsman god.) His trick works and he catches Aphrodite with her lover, Ares, *in flagrante*. As in the *Iliad*, the consequences for the gods are not serious – the watching Hermes fantasises about being caught in bed with Aphrodite (8.339–42)! The story has a clear point for Odysseus, though, that is altogether more serious. That is, the righteous punishment of the illegitimate suitors, and their death – though the question of Penelope's faithfulness (or otherwise) remains undetermined. There may even be a hint at the composition-in-performance of an epic bard. Demodocus has just heard about the weak-legged Odysseus's victory in the discus: his story champions the lame but cunning god who gets one over on his physically superior rival, just as Odysseus shows up the younger and more agile Phaeacians. Of course, we don't know whether Homer operated like this. But it is noteworthy that we see a bard engage with his audience, just before Odysseus himself takes up the song.

Odysseus himself requests Demodocus's final song. He wants to hear the one about the Trojan horse. Demodocus obliges and describes how Odysseus's famous trick brought about the city's ultimate fall. But, upon hearing this tale, Odysseus weeps. Indeed, he weeps like a woman whose husband has been killed and her city sacked (523–30) – that is, he cries like a victim of his own ruse. Odysseus's response acts out his identity as a man who simultaneously suffers and who causes suffering. Homer explores this precarious balance through the rest of the poem, starting here with Odysseus's hijacking of the story.

'My fame reaches heaven'

All this time, since arriving naked on Scheria at the end of *Odyssey* 5, Odysseus has been the man with no name. As the ideal host, Alcinous has fed and entertained his guest without enquiring further. At long last, after noticing his guest in tears again (over a tale the man had requested), Alcinous can hold back no longer and asks who he is. The answer will extend over the next three books (*Odyssey* 9–12), as Odysseus takes up the reins of the poem. Here is one more example of Homer pushing the boundaries of what his epic can do – first denying the audience a view of the hero, next having the hero pass incognito in a world between men and gods, now handing him the telling of the tale itself. The central task facing Odysseus is twofold: to explain who he is and how he comes to be before the Phaeacians, and, by doing so, to enable his return home. As Homer recedes from view, the distance between Homer's audience and the Phaeacians collapses, leaving us to judge Odysseus's story alongside Alcinous and his court.

Odysseus immediately addresses the kind of song that he will be singing. Taking his cue from the hospitality that he is enjoying (as he did in Achilles' tent in *Iliad* 9), Odysseus toasts Alcinous, praises the bard Demodocus, and waxes lyrical about the pleasant circumstances in which he finds himself (2–10). The occasion that Odysseus describes is the symposium (literally in Greek 'drinking together'). Symposia (plural) were popular throughout ancient Greece as venues where society's elites could gather, party, enjoy poetry, and learn how to practise politics. But Odysseus draws a distinction between the kind of song that delights the Phaeacians and the story he is about to tell. Unlike a party piece, his (epic) song will be about (his) suffering. And his suffering comes about because of his lengthy absence from home. From the very beginning, Odysseus leaves the Phaeacians in no doubt what he wants.

Having made clear his (continuing) suffering, the hero finally reveals his name. 'I am Odysseus, son of Laertes, renowned by all men / for trickery, and my fame reaches heaven' (19–20). Odysseus immediately advertises his cunning as his defining feature and acknowledges his fame. We have already heard his praises being sung by both his former comrades-at-arms and the Phaeacian bard. Yet, Odysseus talks about his fame in an odd way: 'and my fame (*kleos*) *reaches* heaven'. While this may strike a modern audience as boastful, the oddity for Homer's audience derives rather from the tense of the verb. In all other instances of a hero claiming renown for their deeds, they imagine their fame circulating at some undisclosed point in the future. Odysseus's use of the present tense points to his uniqueness. Unlike fame derived from prowess in battle, Odysseus's fame comes as much from his ability to spin a story. *His* glory is in the here and now, in part produced through this very account that he begins to present to us.

The first episode in Odysseus's account sets out his degree of investment in this tale-telling. Odysseus picks up the story from the fall of Troy and still very much in the world of the *Iliad* – as Homer's audience may have expected from the *Odyssey*. From Troy (or Ilion, as Odysseus calls it here) the wind carried them to the Ciconians, whose city he sacked and whose possessions he and his men shared out, 'so that none might go deprived of his proper share' (42). With this account, it is as if Odysseus has learned the harsh lessons of leadership from the *Iliad*, noted Achilles' complaints against Agamemnon, and shows himself to be the model leader, sharing out the booty among his men fairly and, of course, sacking the city. But what happens next marks the departure from the *Iliad*. Odysseus gives the order to flee; his men disobey and party instead. As a result, they are surprised by Ciconian reinforcements, a battle ensues, and they 'suffer many pains' (53). Flight, a dirty word in the *Iliad*, here comes across as sound military strategy. Moreover, while he shows himself to be a good leader, his men disobey and perish because of their own recklessness. Odysseus's story pointedly allies to the *Odyssey*'s proem and underlines the undeserved nature of his own suffering.

The scene is more complex and complicated, however. Slippage in Odysseus's narration indicates problems with the protagonist hero being an epic narrator. Up until this point,

Odysseus has talked in terms of us (he and his men) versus them (those Ciconians). Now, with battle joined, Odysseus narrates:

> Both sides stood and fought their battle there by the swift ships,
> And they cast bronze-headed spears at each other,
> And, for as long as it was early and the sacred day was increasing,
> For that length of time we stood and fought them off, though they were more.
> But when the sun passed the time for unyoking the cattle,
> Then at last the Ciconians conquered the Achaeans and turned them.
> Out of each ship six of my strong-greaved companions
> Were lost; the rest of us fled from death and doom.
>
> (9.54–61)

At one point, Odysseus sounds 'Homeric' in his description of the two warring parties, particularly in his use of the third-person ('they cast spears', 'the Ciconians turned them'), the highly charged 'Achaeans' or the use of a temporal marker from the everyday world (unyoking the cattle). Yet, in the same breath his objectivity breaks down, as he slips into a first-person account – 'we stood', 'we others fled'. How Odysseus can, or rather *cannot*, keep the two aspects of narration apart is a revealing feature of his tale. His identity as a storyteller is undermined repeatedly and compromised by his responsibility as an agent within his story. Similarly, Odysseus is at once the leader of men who die and the figure who provides the account. It is as if Achilles or Agamemnon were able to give their version of events in the *Iliad*.

Many of these issues come into sharpest relief in the *pièce de résistance* of Odysseus's tale: his account of his meeting with Cyclops and the daring escape from the monster's cave.

Odysseus and Cyclops

The *Odyssey* has come to a crucial point in its narrative. Not only is Odysseus finally centre stage: but also he has taken over the telling of the tale. The *Iliad* shows awareness of his verbal dexterity on many occasions. The Trojan ambassador, Antenor, remembers Odysseus's words falling like snow, such was their (soft) power. Odysseus re-establishes order in the Achaean assembly through his use of words (and a stick with which to beat dissenters). He is the go-to man to deliver Agamemnon's offer to Achilles. In later representations, Odysseus remains famous for speaking persuasively – hence the anxiety with which his appearances are greeted on Athens's democratic stage, where words are everything. The *Odyssey* expands on the *Iliad*'s testimony by exploring Odysseus's trickiness in the light of his *storytelling*, with no narrator to help the audience negotiate his wiles. The first episode reveals, and revels in, the tension as Odysseus the narrator struggles to remain detached from Odysseus the actor. If the encounter with the Ciconians happens in a familiar post-Iliadic world, very soon we find ourselves in totally unfamiliar territory.

This world encompasses fearsome giant-like peoples known as the Laestrygonians, who assault Odysseus and his men, and the Lotus-Eaters, who spend their days in a drug-induced haze free from care. In the former case, Odysseus barely escapes with twelve of his ships, losing many to the monstrous cannibals. In the latter, Odysseus struggles to rouse his men, who forget their homecoming after consuming the Lotus flower. Emphasis falls on Odysseus's leadership, his care for his men, and his even greater desire to return home. Then he comes face-to-face with a one-eyed monster familiar from pots from around the Greek world – Polyphemus, Cyclops.

The episode begins familiarly enough. Odysseus spies an island, 'occupied by neither flocks nor ploughed fields, / but every day unsown and unploughed / it is deprived of men, but nourishes bleating goats' (9.122–4). Further details require Odysseus the narrator to import knowledge from the yet-to-be-told encounter: so, he continues, the reason for the lack of cultivation is due to the fact that 'the Cyclopes [plural of Cyclops] have no ships' (125). Lacking ships, the Cyclopes have nothing to do with men, 'who cross the sea on ships to each other / and who could have made the island a strong settlement for them' (129–30). His description of the possibilities for cultivation marks Odysseus out as a man of Homer's day. The early classical Greek world (c. seventh century BC), when the Homeric poems were probably coming into being, was the age of settlement and adventure. Greek communities were springing up all over the Mediterranean, as Greeks took to the seas and exchanged their wares with other trading peoples (like the Phoenicians). And everything that Odysseus is – inquisitive, modern, *civilised* – the Cyclopes are not, as we shall see.

The so-called 'Eleusis Amphora' by the Polyphemus Painter, c. 660 BC, Archaeological Museum of Eleusis, Greece

> Odysseus, marked out in a different colour to the rest of his men, takes the lead in blinding Cyclops. The painter captures the forceful moment in the depiction of Odysseus's forward thrust of his left leg. At the same time, he collapses two moments in one, as Cyclops is pictured with one hand still holding the cup of wine as he tries to prevent the stake from going into his eye.

After anchoring opposite this island, Odysseus takes one ship to explore it. After coming across a cave, he leads his men in to find a store rich with (unrefined) dairy products of all kinds. Helping themselves, they tuck into the feast. Though his men soon wish to be on their way, Odysseus insists on hanging around to meet the host. For, not content with these goods, Odysseus wants to receive 'guest-gifts' (229). Gifts were customarily exchanged between host and guest: so much part of the Greek world it was that, in *Iliad* 6, when opposing warriors Diomedes and Glaucus, meet they recognise their ancestral friendship and exchange gifts, there and then in the field of battle. Here, in Cyclops's cave, it is a fatal mistake, as Odysseus readily admits: 'I would not listen to them: it would have been better their way' (228). For at that moment a monster appears with his flock of sheep, rolls the boulder back to block the cave, and then, with his one eye, spies the intruders. Polyphemus the Cyclops makes his grand entrance in to Odysseus's tale.

This episode must have delighted audiences with its folktale elements. The giant defeated by a special weapon (a wooden stake) crafted by the trickster hero, Odysseus – the scene that is popularised on Greek pots features prominently in Homer's tale. But the *Odyssey*'s portrait is much richer in detail and significance. Once he has laid his eye on Odysseus and his men, Polyphemus asks who they are and what their business is. Although Odysseus (as the narrator) admits that deep fear struck them all, even so he (Odysseus the actor) speaks up (259–71). In the act of replying, Odysseus demonstrates the courage and the intellect needed to compose an argument in the face of terror. He makes two opening gambits. First, he proclaims that they are 'Achaeans come from Troy', whose sack means that Agamemnon, their leader, currently enjoys the greatest fame (*kleos*) under heaven. As if these credentials weren't enough, Odysseus also points to their status as suppliants, owed a gift of hospitality and safeguarded by Zeus who looks after the safety of strangers. This claim to hospitality distorts the events somewhat, given the fact that he and his men had simply helped themselves to Cyclops's food. Since they do not seem to respect the customary rules of hospitality themselves, one might wonder about Odysseus's obsession with guest-gifts. (More on this below.)

Polyphemus dismisses both claims. The Cyclopes 'do not concern themselves over Zeus of the aegis, / nor any of the rest of the blessed gods, since we are far mightier' (275–6). As for Agamemnon and Troy – Polyphemus simply passes them over. Cyclops doesn't know his *Iliad* and cares even less. It is with some irony then that his words echo Achilles' angry rejection of Priam's premature request for his son's body: 'and for not out of fear for Zeus's enmity would I spare / either you or your companions, unless my spirit instructed me' (277–8). But, whereas Achilles only briefly contemplates disobeying Zeus, Cyclops really means it. Whether the *Odyssey*'s revisionist take on Achilles is casting him as a monster akin to Cyclops is open to question. But one thing is clear: we are no longer in the world of the *Iliad*. The name of the game has changed and Odysseus must change too.

So, when Polyphemus asks his sly follow-up question, 'but come, tell me, where did you keep your well-made ship when you came? / Far away or near?' (279–80), we receive a lesson in storytelling and a justification for Odysseus's lies. If our hero tells the truth, Cyclops could trap Odysseus's other men. Instead,

Odysseus misinforms Polyphemus that their ship was the only one to make it to this land. Just as well – for, showing little interest in the answer, Cyclops springs up, grabs two of Odysseus's companions, and 'slapped them, like killing puppies, against the ground, / and their brains ran out over the floor and soaked the ground' (289–90). We now see the daunting challenge facing Odysseus. How is he to respond? His initial, instinctive response is to go for his sword (300). If this sounds familiar to us, it should. When faced with his own challenging circumstances in the assembly of *Iliad* 1, Achilles also goes for his sword (190). By recalling that scene, the *Odyssey* suggests that the typical reaction of the epic hero to a crisis is a show of strength. But, whereas going for one's sword when faced by a cannibalistic monster might seem the right course of action (in contrast to Achilles' frustration with debate), it isn't. Indeed, Odysseus holds *himself* back – he needs no god to pull him back by the hair – calculating that, were he to kill Polyphemus, he and his men would be trapped inside the cave, unable to move the massive boulder (304–5). In this monstrous world, where one encounters terrible beasts that lie and eat you alive, there is really only one reasonable response – to lie back and think of Ithaca. Of course, this waiting game also means consigning more men to gruesome deaths.

The rules are established and the challenge is issued: Odysseus must bide his time while his men get picked off two-by-two. But he has a cunning plan. Here Odysseus's insistence on guest-gifts becomes pointed. He offers Polyphemus wine. Neat. Such was the strength of neat wine that (civilised) Greeks always took their wine mixed (normally three parts water for one part wine). By offering Cyclops neat wine, Odysseus's intention is to get Polyphemus drunk. As his wits become addled, Polyphemus asks Odysseus his name, in return for which he promises a guest-gift of his own – to eat this man last! Thus, Odysseus (the narrator) uses the exchange of 'gifts' to draw the contrast between his offer of wine (in normal circumstances a token of civilisation, but here a weapon of sorts) and Cyclops's 'gift' of being eaten last (barbaric beyond all measure). But there is more to come. For, like his offer of wine, Odysseus provides a name designed to pull the wool over Cyclops's eye. He is 'Nobody' (366), or *Outis* in Greek (this will be important). *Both* sides in this exchange break the rules of hospitality, but, whereas Cyclops does it for his appetite, Odysseus lies in order to survive and save his men.

The wine has its intended effect, and Cyclops soon falls into a drunken stupor, at which point Odysseus and his men get to work. Homer breathes life into this scene (which appears frequently on vases) through his skilled use of language and, in particular, simile. Odysseus first compares their assault on Cyclops with building a ship: his companions 'took the stake of olivewood, sharp at the point, / and thrust it into his eye. Meanwhile I threw my weight upon it from above, / whirled it round, as when a man bores a ship's timber / with a drill, and those below keep it spinning with a leather strap, / holding on to it at either end, and the drill turns unceasingly' (382–6). Then to a blacksmith forging iron: Polyphemus's eye sizzles grotesquely as the stake, its point hardened in the embers of the fire, is driven in, 'as when a blacksmith dips a great axe or an adze / in cold water to temper it, and it hisses loudly' (391–4). The two similes point to acts of civilisation (ship building, forging iron) that contrast with the barbarity of the present scene (poking some monster's eye out). Even so, the payoff for Odysseus's cleverness still awaits us. As Polyphemus cries out in agony, the other Cyclopes rush to his cave to offer assistance. But, when they ask him whether he is OK or whether anyone is doing him harm, he replies: 'Friends, Nobody is killing me by trickery not by force' (408). At this non-answer, the other Cyclopes think that Polyphemus has lost his wits, tell him to pray to his father, and depart.

The game of punning here reveals the sophistication of the *Odyssey* and distinguishes the epic poem from other representations of the Cyclops story. Clearly, Odysseus's pseudonym works spectacularly well – the other Cyclopes take off when they hear from Polyphemus that 'Nobody' (*Outis*) is harming him. But there's more going on in the Greek. In response to Polyphemus's claim that '*Outis*' is harming him, the Cyclopes use a conditional ('if') clause that transforms the Greek '*ou tis*' form of 'Nobody' into '*mē tis*': 'well, if Nobody (*mē tis*) is harming you...' (410). Combined, '*mē tis*' forms *mētis*, the Greek word for 'cunning'. Odysseus spells out his pun in the very next sentence, as he comments on the success of his trick: 'my dear heart laughed / at how my name and my blameless cunning [*mētis*] had fooled him' (413–14). Here, Odysseus's pseudonym *Outis/Mētis* recalls the very 'cunning' for which the hero is known throughout the tradition. In fact, this pun is a performance of his trickiness and demonstrates just how Odysseus's verbal artistry is helping his fame reach the skies.

All this makes the end of the tale, which has such catastrophic consequences for Odysseus and his companions, all the odder. After Polyphemus is blinded, Odysseus engineers an escape from the cave by tying his men under sheep, while picking for himself the strongest ram (incidentally recalling Helen's description of Odysseus in *Iliad* 3: he stood out 'like a ram'). Once all are out, they make for their ships. But, as soon as they are some way offshore, Odysseus halts their flight and begins taunting Cyclops, who responds by hurling rocks out to sea. As the sound of his voice brings Polyphemus's boulders closer, Odysseus's men beg him to stop. They cannot understand why he wants to 'rile this wild man' (494). Odysseus ignores the group, as Agamemnon does at the beginning of the *Iliad*, and Achilles later, because of his 'great-hearted spirit' (500). (The same adjective, 'great-hearted', is used for Achilles three times in *Iliad* 9, at 255, 629, 675). Even though Odysseus has demonstrated great restraint before by resisting angry impulse (like unsheathing his sword), here he gives in to it. In a final boast, he flings his name at Cyclops, complete with his formal epithets 'sacker of cities' and 'son of Laertes'. With this triple declaration, Odysseus presents himself as a hero from the *Iliad*.

And that very nearly leads to his undoing. Polyphemus's immediate response is to throw an even larger boulder, which all but sinks Odysseus's ship. But, more importantly, now that he has a name, he can curse Odysseus to years of suffering, for Polyphemus's father turns out to be Poseidon, god of the sea. Hence, the Cyclops episode is made central to the *Odyssey* as the *cause* of Odysseus's wanderings – Poseidon has been resisting Odysseus's homecoming all this time because of what Odysseus did to his son. But why does Odysseus fling his name in Cyclops's face, when before he was so careful to protect it (as 'Nobody')? Once we start picking away at Odysseus's narrative, other loose ends appear. Why does Odysseus lead his men into Cyclops's cave and insist upon staying for a 'guest-gift'? Or, rather, since he is the one responsible for this account, why does he tell us? Why not simply blame this fault on the foolishness of his companions, as he does elsewhere? For one answer, we may point to his initial response to Polyphemus, when he proclaims them to be the men of Agamemnon, Achaeans recently departed from Troy. Odysseus walks into Cyclops's cave still a hero from the *Iliad*. The events that issue from that cave transform him into a different kind of hero, who can only survive in the brave new world of the *Odyssey* through endurance, trickery, and, above all, telling lies. Even after escaping the cave, Odysseus still struggles to free himself from being an Iliadic man – so he declares his patronymic and demands recognition for his accomplishments, as one did at Troy. He discloses his identity to Polyphemus because he knows no other way to secure his epic fame.

The irony is that his desire to validate his accomplishments risks depriving him of what he really wants – to get home. Odysseus must learn that he won't get glory by advertising himself, but – paradoxically – by keeping silent and disguising his true identity. What was anathema to Achilles, who hated like the gates of Hades the man who says one thing while keeping another in his heart, becomes the only way to survive the *Odyssey*. When Odysseus reveals his name to Polyphemus, it is the final act of the Iliadic hero, who must boast over the vanquished to start the process of epic fame.

In Odysseus's (or is it Homer's?) hands, the Cyclops episode is transformed from a collective action undertaken by Odysseus and his men into a demonstration of why being a hero from the *Iliad* is insufficient in this poem. Gone are the usual customs of hospitality, the conventional codes of martial conduct. The hero now must learn to live by his wits alone, to use his intelligence, to lie his way out of danger, to endure unbearable suffering until the time is right to strike. The encounter with the monster justifies Odysseus's behaviour once he has landed back in the all-too-familiar, but equally threatening, world of Ithaca.

Waking the dead

After his encounter with Polyphemus, Odysseus roams the seas for years on end, gradually losing more and more of his companions. His longest encounter is with the witch, Circe, who turns Odysseus's men into pigs – a nice literal transformation of men's piggy appetites (for food and sex). Odysseus himself, forewarned and forearmed by Hermes (with a stick of the herb moly), remains impervious to Circe's charms, until she gives up trying to turn him into a pig and takes him to bed instead (10.347). In other versions of their affair, such as the *Telegony*, Odysseus apparently has at least one child with Circe. While the *Odyssey* is silent on that issue, there is more than a suggestion that she has cast a spell over the hero. With little fanfare, we learn that a full year has passed, and Odysseus's men are as impatient with him for their return home as he was with them when they ate Lotus flowers.

Circe, though, is pivotal for Odysseus's return, since she instructs him how to overcome the dangers ahead. Featuring some of the most famous perils from Greek myth, these episodes serve to mark Odysseus out from his men as the privileged survivor. The first famous threat that Odysseus must negotiate are the Sirens, who probably featured in the epic of Jason and the Argonauts (though only Apollodorus's third-century BC version survives). The Sirens' song is so enchanting that all who listen to it wreck their ships in desperate longing to hear more. The answer? Odysseus is to block his men's ears full of wax, while instructing them to tie him to the mast of the ship to listen. Intriguingly, the theme of the Sirens' deadly song for Odysseus is 'everything that in wide Troy / the Argives [another of Homer's names for the Achaeans] and Trojans toiled by the will of the

Odysseus and the Sirens by the Siren painter, Attic red-figured stamnos (a type of pot for storing liquid), c. 480–470 BC, found in Vulci (an Etruscan city north of Rome), British Museum

Odysseus is depicted tied to the mast of his ship, his head thrown back in a sign of ecstasy, while his men (of course deaf to the Sirens' song with wax in their ears) row on regardless. Meanwhile, the painter represents the Sirens as birds with large women's heads, bird feathers, and scaly feet, rather similar to those other mythological scourges, the Harpies.

gods' (12.189–90). The promise of 'everything about Troy' suggests an epic even longer than *Iliad* – no wonder the Sirens present such a danger to the man trying to get home! Perhaps too it is a tale of martial exploits, such as those in the *Iliad*, that proves so perilously enchanting to the listener. Either way, we may again note the *Odyssey*'s intense interest in poetic composition, even (or especially?) the seductive dangers that such creations present for an audience.

During these adventures, Odysseus no longer even contemplates meeting such challenges with sword and strength; only cunning will do the trick. He counters Circe's magic with a magical antidote and counteracts the Sirens' spell with a ruse. As for the sea monsters Scylla and Charybdis – well, confides Circe, there's no getting past them without a cost. Six-headed Scylla may take six of your men at a time, but Charybdis will drown you all in her whirlpool. Prudent Odysseus opts for the former option, and, even more prudently, omits to inform his men that some are certain to die. Formerly, he failed to inform his men that the gift bag he had received from Aeolus, the god of winds, contained unfavourable weather. With predictable consequences, as soon as Odysseus is asleep, his curious men open the bag to see what treasure he has been hiding – and accidently let out all the winds, which drives them all the way back to where they started. (This is the opening episode of *Odyssey* 10.) Now Odysseus's limited disclosure is (represented as) a model of necessity. Equally importantly, he displays his own, perhaps manipulative, ability to 'perform' for his men. When they approach the monster, Odysseus stands to defend them in full armour. Some men die, but those who remain look to him for salvation, believing that they still have a chance to return home.

The most detailed episode of Odysseus's other encounters is his trip to wake the dead in *Odyssey* 11. Odysseus is keen to get information from the (dead) prophet Teiresias about what awaits him in Ithaca. Yet Odysseus also needs to have an underworld trip because that is what great heroes do in myth. Heracles, for example, gains entry into Hades by placating the hellhound Cerberus. Odysseus's underworld experience, however, is strikingly different. Once again, Circe is instrumental is helping Odysseus achieve his ends with strict instructions about how to summon the ghost of Teiresias (it involves a ritual of bloodletting). As a result, Odysseus doesn't so much descend into hell as Hades, with its shadowy cast of figures, comes to him.

As with other famous underworld trips (most notably Aeneas's in *Aeneid* 6), Odysseus's conversations with the dead position him in the unfolding story and the mythical tradition more generally. First, Teiresias provides Odysseus (and the audience) with a road-map for what will happen when he arrives on Ithaca – he will defeat the suitors through a combination of violence and cunning. In this way, the pronouncements of Circe and Teiresias stand in for the *Iliad*'s plans of Zeus. The fact that it is no longer Zeus that charts the future, but quasi-human figures (a witch and a prophet), further demonstrates the *Odyssey*'s progress in cosmic evolution. Like Zeus's plan, too, Teiresias's prophecy goes beyond the borders of this epic to foretell yet more wandering for Odysseus and an eventual death that comes, mysteriously, 'from the sea'.

After Teiresias's prophecy, Odysseus turns to his mother, Anticleia, who died of a broken heart, having waited so long for him to return. (It's not only Odysseus who has suffered.)

She provides a fleeting insight into events in Ithaca during his absence. But her appearance also ushers in a catalogue of women (recalling the fragmentary Hesiodic *Catalogue of Women*) and their male progeny – heroes like Amphion and Zethus, who built the walls of Thebes, and, of course, Heracles (to name but a few). By starting with his mother, Odysseus slyly inserts himself into the catalogue and invites comparison to these great figures of bygone days. And his name is first on the list...

That same impulse is most clearly evident in the final ghostly apparitions to appear – Odysseus's former Trojan War comrades. Through these conversations with the dead, the *Odyssey* directly addresses and explores its relationship to the *Iliad*. Already suffering as the unfortunate counter-model offered by the *Odyssey*, the shade of Agamemnon provides Odysseus with a lesson about women. Self-pitying and ever proud, Agamemnon's shade regales Odysseus with the story of his betrayal and murder at the hands of his wife, Clytemnestra. Odysseus dutifully offers his condolences, but then spies the spirit of swift-footed Achilles. Typically, the shade of Achilles doesn't wait to be asked to speak but addresses Odysseus directly: how on earth did this wily man break into Hades of all places?! In reply, Odysseus grants Achilles what he seemed most to crave in the *Iliad* – respect and honour. Achilles' life was so 'blessed', Odysseus comments, that he was honoured like a god when he was alive; now he reigns supreme over the dead (478–86). Odysseus's message is clear: Achilles is best because he lived gloriously and, by dying gloriously, his name lives on forever.

Interestingly, while this may have been music to the ears of the *Iliad*'s Achilles, it certainly is *not* for *this* Achilles. Instead, ironically mimicking his *Iliad* 9 persona, he objects: 'Don't try to talk me around about death, shining Odysseus. / I would rather be a serf in slave to another man, / someone with no land allotted him and not much to live on, / than be a king over all the perished dead' (488–91). Thus, Achilles' ghost categorically rejects Odysseus's invitation to glory in the memory of his martial prowess. Honour, respect, epic fame – the very things that the *Iliad*'s Achilles longs after – here he rejects in favour of *life*. In fact, so much is this Achilles desirous of life that he claims he would rather be a *slave* to another than lord of the dead. While this attitude undercuts the *Iliad*'s drive towards a glorious death (even if that other poem is in truth far more complex), the emphasis on survival suits the hero Achilles addresses – Odysseus, epic's great survivor.

Indeed, Achilles has something else on his mind than his epic fame: he wants to know about his *family*. He asks about his father, Peleus, whom we last saw Achilles imagining surrounded by enemies, alone, far from his son (in *Iliad* 24). That worry pre-occupies him still, and he wants to know: 'whether he still keeps his honour among the Myrmidons, / or whether he is dishonoured in Hellas and Phthia, / because old age constrains his hands and feet' (495–7). Here Achilles' wish to be alive translates into a wish to protect his father, to scare away the men who 'use force on him and keep him from honour' (503). More surprisingly, Achilles also asks about his *son*, Neoptolemus. Only once in the *Iliad* does Achilles even mention his son, and then only in passing. Here he asks whether Neoptolemus has tasted battle. He would not like to know the answer. Neoptolemus is famous, *infamous*, in myth for one act above all others – killing Priam at the altar of Athena. With such a sacrilegious action, Achilles' son is enshrined in the tradition for undoing arguably his father's greatest deed (as represented by the *Iliad*), which was to pity Priam. The point here is that the things that now concern the dead Achilles so much – his father's health, his son's reputation – are the very features that mark Odysseus out as the hero who trumps all comers. Odysseus is the hero who survives to make it home to be reunited with his son (not to mention his wife), and to rescue his father, Laertes, from the depths of despair. In this poem, the individual hero's fame extends to encompass his whole family.

Odysseus's conversations with the dead engage with other traditions as well. The *Odyssey* provides, through Odysseus's eyes, our earliest view of a punitive afterlife where Minos judges the dead and great sinners from myth are punished. We see Tantalus, denied food or drink for having fed the gods human flesh, and Sisyphus, a trickster figure who tried to evade death itself, condemned forever to roll a stone up a hill. Finally, Odysseus meets Heracles, *the* great hero whose labours are enshrined in myth – he offers his commiserations for the pains this new hero still endures. Thus, Odysseus's underworld portrait emphasises key traits of his story – enduring, surviving, suffering – and his own place in the race of heroes. He begins the tale with his mother, and ends it by being recognised by the (previously) greatest hero of them all.

A wine bowl depicting the suicide of Ajax, ca. 400–350 BC. Said to be from Vulci, British Museum

When Achilles dies (by an arrow from Paris), Odysseus retrieves his body, while Ajax holds the Trojans back. Afterwards, the two comrades both claim Achilles' armour. Ajax believes that he is entitled to inherit them, since he was most like Achilles in strength and might. Instead, Odysseus receives them. (The story was apparently told in the *Aethiopis*.) In the *Odyssey*, some captured Trojans apparently vote Odysseus to be most worthy of them (as representing the greatest danger to them), while in Sophocles's tragedy, *Ajax*, the judgement is made by the Achaean leaders. Either way, humiliated by this slight, Ajax commits suicide. He takes his anger with Odysseus to the grave: in *Odyssey* 11, Ajax refuses Odysseus's invitation to parley.

The last episode of Odysseus's adventures provides the clearest explanation for why he sits before the Phaeacians alone. As well as the dangers of Scylla and Charybdis, Circe also warns Odysseus about the cattle of the Sun, which, she insists, must not be eaten. In spite of his own insistent warnings, however, Odysseus's half-starved companions find this final command a step too far. While Odysseus dozes, again, they disobey his instructions, again: they kill the cattle and sacrifice to the sun god, Helios, hoping to placate him. But, even as they turn on the spits, the slaughtered cattle low as if still alive – the uncanny event marks the transgressive nature of the companions' actions. To the last, they 'perish because of their own recklessness'. In fact, Homer trails their killing of the Sun's cattle as the cause of their lost homecoming in the opening lines of the epic (1.8–9). Only the remarkable Odysseus 'of many turns' remains alive, with many more years yet before he finally makes it to Scheria.

We do not have to speculate about the effect of Odysseus's words on an audience. Homer provides us with one. The Phaeacians are so stunned that, like the embassy when Achilles rejected Agamemnon's offer in *Iliad* 9, 'all were in silence'. But that is where the comparison ends. Odysseus's audience 'were held *enchanted* through the shadowy halls' (11.333–4). Where Achilles provokes silence due to force of will, Odysseus engenders it through the power of the story he composes. And, like the Sirens' song, there is something slightly disquieting about the enchanting effect. This – Homer's description – occurs a little over two-thirds through Odysseus's story, when he breaks off suddenly from cataloguing the women he met in Hades – the night wasn't long enough to name them all. At this, Arete, the Phaeacian queen, whose importance Athena has previously stressed, praises Odysseus and promises him gifts. The catalogue of women has obviously appealed to her. Not to be outdone by his wife, Alcinous asks for an encore: 'But let our guest endure, much though he longs for his homecoming, / and wait until tomorrow, by which time / I will fulfil all of his gifts' (350–2). The theme of endurance returns, only this time with a twist. The task of singing epic poetry apparently also requires great endurance. This is the poet as hero, as Homer smuggles in a nod to his own art. Simultaneously, however, Alcinous's assessment reminds us that Odysseus is *playing* at being an epic poet. Indeed, in response, Odysseus expresses himself willing to sing for another year (!), if that means he can return to Ithaca with riches sufficient to earn the respect of his people. The fact that Odysseus so blatantly sings for an end complicates our judgement of him as an epic poet. More worryingly, it may also cause us to question Homer's own performance. Who is under the spell here?

Alcinous's request is for a 'whatever happened to...?' account of Odysseus's former comrades at Troy. Evidently, news of the Trojan War *has* reached the Phaeacians, which marks their culture as the epitome of civilisation, just as Cyclops's ignorance of Agamemnon marks him out as a barbaric monster. But, while the tales of Troy – should we imagine the particular version depicted by the *Iliad*? – are at the forefront of the audience's mind, Odysseus's story wins the day. He represents his former comrades from Troy as but shadows of their former selves, eager to hear news of their families, dismissive of their fame hard won on the battlefield, desperate to be alive. They all want to be like this man, Odysseus, in this epic, the *Odyssey*. Alcinous and his fellow Phaeacians, however, fail to see Odysseus's story as anything other than truthful: no wise can Odysseus be considered crafty or thievish, Alcinous remarks (11.364–6). The irony of this judgement is not lost on Homer. He has Athena make precisely the *opposite* judgement, when she and Odysseus meet on the Ithacan shoreline. *She* pronounces, 'he would be crafty or thievish whoever could get past you / in any kind of contriving, even if a god were against you' (13.291–2). For Athena, Odysseus is not only a liar but also her favourite *because* of his tricks. Yet, her assessment here does not just put Odysseus's lying activity into a favourable light, as something that he must do in order to survive; it also casts doubt on Odysseus's Phaeacian audience, who singularly fail either to grasp the trickiness of the tale or to understand their manipulation. What the lessons are for Homer's audience – whether we should imagine his tale as truthful and accurate or as enchanting and manipulative, and what difference either view makes for how we think about Odysseus's return home – are very much harder to decode.

After being AWOL for the first four books of his epic, within the space of the next four books Odysseus moves from the margins of human society (5–8) to take centre stage in book nine, where he assumes control of the narrative to initiate the last leg of his journey home. During three whole books of the poem, Odysseus – without the mediation of the epic poet – sings about his torturous route back from Troy, from a post-*Iliad* world, in which he and his men sack cities and distribute booty, to a world beyond any map and moral compass, where fantastical creatures care not a jot for tales of martial glory or even for the gods. Above all, his story functions to set the agenda for a successful homecoming. Odysseus demonstrates that he must shed his

Iliadic pretensions and learn to be a new kind of hero who uses tricks to escape impossible situations; who endures all manner of suffering to secure what he wants; who survives. In the equivalent book of the *Iliad*, when we are finally reintroduced to Achilles, we find him 'delighting his mind with a clear lyre...with which he delighted his spirit, and sang the glories of men' (9.186, 189). The *Odyssey* goes one step further. By presenting its hero singing about his *own* glory, it reproduces, if not *creates*, his fame for telling stories. And, by performing his identity through storytelling, Odysseus continues the process of reinventing himself as the new model man.

At the same time, precisely because his journey charts unknown and unknowable waters, Odysseus becomes a model for all Greeks (and, indeed, other peoples) in boldly going where no man has gone before. His travels take him through time and space, through a world full of gods and fabled monsters, to make it to Scheria – a world in-between where gods still commune with the inhabitants and crops grow bounteously without effort. That world is soon to be over. By the time the Phaeacians deposit Odysseus, asleep, back on Ithaca, Poseidon is already acting to make sure that they will suffer for their pains – he turns their ship into a rock and erects a mountain range to cut off their land forever more and after. The *Odyssey* dramatises the end of a golden age and the irrevocable separation of gods from men. The rest of the poem (13–24) explores how one man, Odysseus, makes it home.

For landing back on Ithaca is only half of the story. Odysseus must still gain entry to his palace, reunite with his wife, son, and father, and resume his place as lord of the island. And it won't be easy. Back at home, consuming his household, attempting to seduce his wife, and plotting to kill his son, are the suitors – far more monstrous than any one-eyed creature from fable, precisely because they are real. Men like these exist in any city. Like Odysseus's companions, their recklessness relates to their inability to control their appetite. They are living it up in Odysseus's palace in a never-ending bout of eating, drinking, and sex. Like Odysseus's companions, they too will die as a result of their recklessness, as they learn too late that they are part of an epic narrative and not some endless symposium. The *Odyssey* is about to take an Iliadic turn.

Ithaca, home

After ten long years of wandering, Odysseus is finally back on Ithaca. But he is not yet *home*. The second half of the *Odyssey* (13–24) charts the by-now familiar path Odysseus takes from the margins (in this case, the Ithacan shore) to take centre stage (in his house). And Odysseus achieves his goal through the also familiar strategy of disguise, trickery, endurance, and, above all, telling stories. More explicitly than ever, Odysseus uses storytelling as a weapon to test the mettle and loyalty (or otherwise) of his audience. This strategy in turn leads to a series of recognitions – those carefully managed (Telemachus, Eumaeus), spontaneous (Eurycleia), ambiguous (Penelope), flirtatious (Athena), and failed (the suitors) – which enables the one man (Odysseus) to defeat the many.

This theme of recognition is important. It provides what is essentially a rollercoaster ride of adventure, romance, and action with depth and complexity. But recognition – how to read the signs properly – is also an essential part of what it is to be an audience. The issue comes down to the close association between poet and hero, first noticed when Odysseus took up the telling of the tale. The fallout from the hero taking over the poem impacts on the rest of the *Odyssey*, as Odysseus continues to tell tales and Homer describes the suitors in terms that echo Odysseus's account of the Cyclops. Is it possible to avoid falling under the spell of the story's manipulative charm, as Alcinous's Phaeacians so patently failed?

The modern Greek poet Constantine Cavafy (1863–1933) captures this aspect of the *Odyssey* in his aptly named poem *Ithaka*. 'As you set out for Ithaka,' he begins, 'hope the voyage is a long one, / full of adventure, full of discovery.' Odysseus's Ithaca has become the reader's – the 'you' of Cavafy's poem – and brings out the idea that Ithaca itself represents a journey rather than an end goal. So, too, in the *Odyssey*, Odysseus rediscovers who he is, and discovers who he must be, as he makes his way home; and the audience learn with him, about what kind of man he is, and what kind of man he must be. Cavafy returns to the theme in his closing stanza:

> And if you find her poor, Ithaka won't have fooled you.
> Wise as you will have become, so full of experience,
> you will have understood by then what these Ithakas mean.

The striking device of making Ithaca plural ('Ithakas') underlines the point that Ithaca means different things to different people. And this is one startling effect of Homer's poem. By virtue of the close association of poet and hero, the *Odyssey* enlists the audience on the side of Odysseus, as if we were returning to our own Ithacas, and learning about ourselves in the process.

Yet at no point in the *Odyssey* does Homer allow us to forget or to overlook what is at stake in taking sides. Homer's skilled and nuanced presentation of Odysseus prevents the poem from being a straightforward celebration of revenge. Instead, when our man slaughters the suitors, however deserved their fate may be, Homer makes us reflect on where we stand with his hero. Long-suffering exile, brutal leader, loving husband, and cunning trickster – Odysseus is all of these things, and more.

The return of the king

Odysseus arrives on Ithaca asleep. Throughout his adventures, Odysseus's slumbers usher in points of crisis, as when his men open the bag of winds or barbecue the cattle of the Sun. Similarly, when he wakes here, he suspects that the Phaeacians have betrayed him and dumped him on some unknown land, prompting him to wonder again whether he will meet men who are 'savage and wild and without justice, / or friendly to strangers with a mind that is god-fearing' (13.201–2) – barbaric Cyclopes, for example, or civilised (so he thought) Phaeacians. In this moment of transition between worlds, Odysseus articulates one of three critical themes of the second half of the epic. If the Phaeacians have deceived him, Odysseus curses, 'may Zeus, the god of suppliants, punish them, for he oversees / all mankind and punishes anyone who transgresses' (213–14). The watchword of events on Ithaca is *revenge*.

Of course, the Phaeacians have dutifully left Odysseus on Ithaca and paid for this assistance at the hands of Poseidon with their perpetual isolation from the world of men. Rather, Odysseus fails to recognise his homeland, because Athena has cast a great mist about the island. This confusion brings us to a second major theme – *recognition*, which is tied up with revenge in significant ways. On the one hand, in order to carry out his vengeance, Odysseus must find out who's with him and who's against him. On the other hand, the audience of the *Odyssey* also need to recognise how to assess Odysseus's revenge properly – as an act of justified retribution or as a brutal suppression of his people.

Both points relate to a third crucial theme – *deception*. In the poetics of the *Iliad*, as famously articulated by Achilles, the man who says one thing but hides another in his heart is hateful. As we have already seen in the tale of Odysseus's adventures, that kind of straight-talking, straightforward hero has little chance of survival or success in this new world. We might, however, be tempted to limit the role of deception to the fantasy, where one-eyed creatures eat men raw and where the only way out of the cave is through trickery. Not so. And Odysseus's first encounter back on home soil shows us why not, as he rediscovers Ithaca under the tutelage of Athena.

The meeting between hero and goddess is complex and playful, but critical for understanding the second half of the poem. Athena's mist tests Odysseus and instructs the audience. Just as Odysseus learns to recognise Ithaca – not just its physical topography but what awaits him back home, what home *means* – so Homer's audience learn how to assess that homecoming. Disguised as a shepherd, Athena informs Odysseus that he is indeed on Ithaca. While secretly elated, Odysseus lies in turn, spinning the first of his many 'Cretan' tales (so called, because he adopts a Cretan persona each time). Here he is a Cretan on the run from murder, abandoned by his men after a storm. Far from reacting angrily to this fabrication, Athena smiles. She unveils her true self and 'outs' Odysseus as a 'wretch, so full of cunning and insatiable for trickery that you will not, / even when back on your own land, give up deception / and thievish tales' (293–4). Just as well, for she warns him that he must 'in silence / suffer many pains, and welcome men's violence' (309–10). So nearly home, Odysseus must still play the role of the hero who suffers. He must take more pain before he can deal it out.

Even now, however, Odysseus expresses doubt whether he is indeed back home – more than anything it is his capacity to question a goddess standing in front of him that sets him apart from other men. In the *Iliad*, the gods can deceive men in many ways but when they reveal themselves (such as when Athena appears to Achilles in *Iliad* 1) their epiphany is recognised instantly and men instantly obey. Odysseus, however, either as a result of his prolonged suffering or as part of his nature, doubts what is in front of his eyes. To prove that he is home, Athena draws his attention to the harbour and cave about them. This 'sign' of the land, the physical symbol that positively identifies Ithaca, anticipates symbols that will come to identify Odysseus – his scar, his bed, and his bow. As for his hesitation, Athena again praises him: 'Any other man who had returned from wandering would have happily / gone straight off home to see his children and wife; / but it is not dear to you to learn and inquire / until you have tested your wife' (333–6). Interesting here is not so much Athena's general warning – Odysseus has already shown that he wouldn't have blundered straight home like an Agamemnon – as the singling out of Penelope as the one person he must test. Just what Penelope thinks is an issue not only for Odysseus to ponder but for us too. Forewarned, Odysseus is now forearmed, as Athena transforms him into a beggar. While obviously serving a practical purpose, the disguise also introduces a hero foreign to the *Iliad* – a man of tricks, who passes through the company of men incognito. In turn, the motif of disguise resonates with a famous story in the tradition, in which Odysseus disguises himself as a beggar to infiltrate Troy and steal the Palladion, a sacred object that preserved the city while it remained in its walls. Here, however, the risks are higher, the gains more personal. Odysseus must play the role of the beggar to gain access to and reclaim his *own* home. This disguise and trickery is no game. For Odysseus to reclaim his rightful place, he must adopt the same strategy that served him so well in Cyclops's cave. He must, in effect, be 'no man', in order to slay the monster – the suitors eating him out of house and home.

This, the first of Odysseus's encounters back on Ithaca, establishes a pattern by which Odysseus (and the audience) may *recognise* who's with him and who's against him. The first human character whom Odysseus meets is the swineherd – the lowest of the low in the herding pecking order. Even if Eumaeus turns out to be of noble blood (he was kidnapped by pirates), the swineherd's presence shows the lengths to which the *Odyssey* questions what it means to be heroic or noble. With Eumaeus, we learn the importance of good hospitality but especially of storytelling, as Odysseus enacts his strategy of weaving Cretan yarns that mix fact with fiction – or, as Homer later puts it, make 'lies like the truth' (19.203) – in order to test the loyalty of his interlocutor. Meanwhile, the vultures are gathering. Athena spirits Telemachus home, who strategically bypasses Nestor on the return home for fear of being delayed any longer by the old man's war stories (15.198–201). There is a time and a place for storytelling, and for Telemachus this is not it – not, at any rate, if he wants to play a role in the current story unfolding. Instead, he hurries back to Eumaeus's hut – more proof of the swineherd's loyalty and importance – where he meets the beggar. As soon as Eumaeus is out of the way, Odysseus openly declares who he is, while Athena gives him a divine makeover – he is a returning Trojan War hero after all. When his son refuses to believe what is before his eyes (like father, like son), Odysseus bluntly states: 'No other Odysseus will ever come back to you here / than this one here' (16.204–5). The over-determination of Telemachus's recognition of his father – Odysseus announces who he is, Athena supports the claim, Odysseus repeats it – underscores the problem of Odysseus's identity. For what sign can be ultimate proof of a father you've never seen? How does a man separated from his family return to them after war?

However we interpret Telemachus's recognition of his father, one thing is for certain: by the end of *Odyssey* 16, the odysseys of father and son have finally come together. This is encapsulated by their readiness, if not impatience, to exact vengeance on the suitors. Odysseus plans to enter the house as a beggar and accept mistreatment at the hands of the suitors, relying on Zeus and Athena to bring them their day of reckoning. Telemachus is to keep all the weapons under lock and key, until they know which of the servants stand with them. It is at this point that Odysseus declares his son a man.

The scar and the bow

Odysseus's identity is reconstructed through the growing intensity of his reunions, in the memories of those he left behind, with the signs written on his body, and above all by the stories he tells. If Odysseus's meeting with his son seems complex, it pales in comparison to the reunion between man and wife in *Odyssey* 19. When Penelope witnesses even a slave, the wicked Melantho, abusing Odysseus-the-beggar in her house, it prompts her to intercede and find out more about this man. Their meeting takes place in the shadowy half-light of the hearth-fire. Here, at the symbolic centre of Odysseus's hall, husband and wife flirt with each other, revelation, and the truth. (It is in this context that Homer tells us that Odysseus made 'lies that sound like the truth'.) The beggar immediately praises Penelope: 'your fame (*kleos*) reaches the broad heaven' (19.108) – a phrase that recalls Odysseus's declaration to the Phaeacians in book nine and that casts both man and wife in epic glory. In turn, Penelope picks up on their shared suffering. The beggar's self-identification as the 'man of many sorrows' prompts her account of her own struggles to keep the suitors at bay with her trick of weaving and unweaving Laertes's death shroud, and the pain of having to complete it now that her ruse has been discovered (as the suitor Antinous reveals in *Odyssey* 2). At this point, the beggar reveals himself to be a certain Aethon (brother of Idomeneus, the Cretan hero of the *Iliad*), who entertained 'Odysseus' on his way to Troy. Penelope asks for details of the clothing Odysseus had worn – and, in the beggar's answer, she recognises her husband and mourns his passing. The beggar counters, prophesying Odysseus's return with details from the *Odyssey* itself to support his assertion, such as the 'fact' that Odysseus's companions perished for slaughtering the cattle of the Sun.

At this critical juncture, Homer breaks off and has Penelope arrange for the beggar to be bathed. As she retreats further into the shadows to give the beggar privacy, Odysseus's old nurse, Eurycleia (whose name means 'wide fame'), steps into the light to bathe him. And immediately she notices his scar (19.392–3). The discovery threatens to unpick Odysseus's carefully woven plans.

Upon Eurycleia recognising the scar, Homer takes us on a trip down memory lane, to the point when Odysseus received the wound. It happened, or rather was won, on a hunting expedition, the classic rite of passage for a male youth; it testifies to Odysseus's heroic pedigree as well as, of course, to his identity. What is more, we learn that Odysseus owes his name, unusually, not to his father but to his maternal grandfather, Autolycus, a notorious trickster and thus an appropriate figure to name this tricky hero. Odysseus carries all of these details on the story of his body. The actual moment of recognition, however, passes in an instant. Eurycleia recognises the scar, opens her mouth to acclaim the return of the king – only for Odysseus to leap up and clasp his hand over her mouth. Odysseus is not only a master storyteller; he also shows himself to be in control of the story. Just when his deception threatens to be prematurely exposed, when his scar – hidden throughout the epic and a tangible sign of his adolescent rite of passage – opens up a tear in his closely woven story that risks endangering his life, he quickly reasserts his authority and stitches up the tale. This won't be the last time that Odysseus silences word of his 'wide fame'. The *Odyssey* delights in the paradox of Odysseus gaining glory by suppressing it.

Immediately after this scene of interrupted recognition, Odysseus returns closer to the fire, where Penelope asks the stranger to interpret a strange dream she has been having, in which an eagle kills some geese. Curiously, 'Odysseus' appears in her dream to interpret it for her – he is the eagle; the suitors, the geese. The beggar Odysseus draws the obvious conclusion: 'Woman [the Greek can also be translated as 'wife'], it is not possible to interpret this dream / in any other way, since Odysseus himself has declared how he will bring it to pass: the suitor's destruction / is plain for all to see' (555–8). Curiouser still, however, Penelope admits to *enjoying* watching the geese and was angry when the eagle killed them. How are we to understand this ambivalence in Penelope's attitude towards her husband? Is she testing this beggar? Are there hints here of the alternative Penelope known to the tradition – the one who sleeps with all the suitors? Or is Homer testing our abilities of analysis? Before we have much time to ponder, Penelope dismisses all interpretations of the dream and suddenly announces a contest of the bow for her hand in marriage. Why here? Why now?

In *Odyssey* 24, as the dead suitors descend into the underworld, Amphimedon, the one suitor with a moral compass (his actions spare Telemachus's life at one point), assumes that Odysseus and Penelope plot the contest of the bow together (24.167–9). Is that what has happened here? Has Penelope recognised Odysseus and decided to bring events to a head now that he has returned? Yet, right before Penelope sets the contest, she cries privately as if she were a woman consigned to a miserable fate (21.57–60). The audience have a judgement to make here. Are we satisfied that it is merely coincidence that she announces the test? Or do we prefer to surmise that Penelope has secretly recognised her husband? The *Odyssey* is playing a complex game, testing whether we are picking out the (right) signs and putting them together (correctly) – the essence of recognition or *reading*. But we should be careful. If we feel sure that Penelope and Odysseus have recognised each other in the shadowy firelight, we find ourselves reading the events like the suitors. And the poem shows them to be particularly inept at interpreting the signs...

More equivocation is to follow. Stepping before the suitors with the bow, Penelope declares that 'here is the contest set before you' (21.73). We can readily understand the contest to be about stringing the bow, but we can also understand it as the battle for her hand. To the end Penelope flirts and chastises in equal measure, just as the poem itself flirts between her devotion to her husband and her potential disloyalty (by putting on the contest to decide which suitor will be her man). Even the choice of weapon is significant. The bow is *the* ambiguous weapon in

Homeric epic. Great heroes, like Heracles, can wield it, but it attracts little praise and more often than not outright censure. (The archer uses his weapon safely from afar unlike the hand-to-hand combatant.) Paris, for example, uses the bow, and he's hardly the *Iliad*'s model of a courageous and honourable fighter. Its duality makes the bow perfect for the *Odyssey*. Moreover, this bow, like the scar before it, has a backstory. It was a gift from a man in Sparta named Iphitus who received the bow from his father, Eurytus, a man, according to Odysseus (8.223–9), good enough an archer to rival the gods. The later Athenian tragedian Sophocles preserves a version of this story (in the *Trachiniae*) in which Eurytus dared to compare himself to Heracles in archery, which prompts Heracles, bow in hand, to sack his city. It is suggestive to think that Homer knows this story, since Odysseus will soon play the role of Heracles, taking revenge on a rival (group) for daring to challenge his authority.

The bow contest presents a suitably epic challenge. It is not just a question of stringing the bow – a deed that requires strength far greater than any that the suitors can muster. The archer must also use that tool with the necessary skill to shoot an arrow through twelve axe heads. It is a task that brings the startling admission from the wicked Antinous that 'there is no man among the lot of us who is such a one / as Odysseus used to be. I myself have seen him, / and I remember well, though I was still young and childish' (21.93–5). Not only is this declaration a case of a suitor condemning himself out of his own mouth, but the irony is also heavy. Odysseus is there, but he is not as he was. No wonder, then, that Antinous does not recognise him. At this moment, Telemachus steps up to the plate and *he*, Homer narrates, *could have* strung the bow. A crisis point is reached. Not only would Telemachus imperil the carefully laid plans of his father and Athena by stringing the bow. He would also be prematurely usurping his father's place – a would-be Oedipus (who killed his father) rather than an Orestes (who avenged him). But a glance from Odysseus is enough to keep Telemachus to his role and this story on track. Indeed, as Telemachus backs down, he delivers a speech right out of his father's manual, deprecating his strength and hiding his true intent. Thus, he proves himself to be his father's son ironically at the moment when he 'fails' to string the bow. For it is the skill of deception and not the ability to perform the traditional rite of passage that is proof of coming-of-age in the *Odyssey*. It is also characteristic of Odysseus to leave aside his weapon and endure, as he does when faced by Cyclops or all the time he has mixed with the suitors. The real weapon is disguise and deception. So too his son delays gratification – if only for a moment. Telemachus is so much like his father now. It is just left for the suitors to fail (inevitably), while Odysseus takes Eumaeus and the cowherd Philoetius to one side, shows them his scar, and enlists their support. The time is ready. The scene of feasting is about to become a bloody Iliadic battlefield.

Not that the suitors have any inkling of what fate awaits them. So far removed from the narrative thrust of the poem is Antinous that, when he sees his closest rival Eurymachus fail to string the bow, he declares the contest over – Apollo must be on a holiday, he announces! Antinous doesn't even *try* to string the bow. Then the irksome beggar has the audacity to ask for a go, which prompts more bluster from Antinous and his cohorts (it risks ruining their feast!). Penelope has just enough time to offer the beggar the reward of a cloak along with safe passage to 'wherever his heart and spirit command' (342) should he suc-ceed, before Telemachus intervenes to send her to her quarters. While he ensures that the bow ends up in his father's hands, Eumaeus locks the doors and Philoetius bars the courtyard. The stage is set.

As he handles the bow – skilfully – Odysseus endures yet more filth and fury from the suitors. Homer sees things differently and, in a sublime moment, shares his vision with the audience. He compares Odysseus handling the bow to *a bard getting to know his lyre*, stretching the string out, and then testing its resolution (405–9). Indeed, the metaphor spills over into the description of the bow. When Odysseus strings the bow and plucks it, it sings beautifully like a swallow (410–11). At this moment, the identity of the martial hero and epic poet merge. The bow becomes a symbol for both Odysseus's power over words and his potential to deal out pain, his ability to communicate his suffering and his promise to deal it out. Like Apollo, who bookends *Iliad* 1 by using his bow to spread plague and strife among the Achaeans and then his lyre to bring music and harmony to Olympus, Odysseus reigns as a master of song and a looser of arrows. Odysseus, too, is in on the joke. After he easily shoots the arrow through the axe-heads, he quips that now is the time to delight in 'the dance and the lyre; for these things come at the end of the feasting' (430). And, with that, he turns his bow on the suitors.

What the suitors think about the success of Odysseus the beggar is a moot point. Instead, Homer describes Antinous supping his wine, oblivious to the carnage that is about to unfold, 'For,' as he narrates, 'who would think that among the men feasting / one among many, even if he were really mighty, / would inflict evil death upon him and dark doom?' (22.12–14). Then an arrow flies through Antinous's neck (as he drinks) and he falls dead. At this point, Odysseus finally throws off his disguise and addresses the suitors, man to men. Consternation, *not* fear, grips them. Eurymachus chastises 'the stranger' (27) as if Antinous's death were a mistake! Even now, as Odysseus stands revealed before them, the suitors do not recognise the danger they are in. They have been so far marginalised from the poem's drive towards (Odysseus's) homecoming that they don't realise they are in an epic, where contest is deadly, and where the games of the symposium – the feasting, drinking, and sex – give way to death and slaughter. Epic fail. Eurymachus is next to fall, shot, appropriately for his appetite, in the stomach.

The banquet of death that follows in *Odyssey* 22 resonates powerfully with many of the battle scenes in Homer's other epic. The halls of the returning king echo (literally) with the sounds of the *Iliad*'s battlefield. Yet the killings, cast in the language of a heroic battle, do not revisit the Trojan plain perfectly. Odysseus fights against overwhelming odds, with only the help of Athena, the two servants, and his son, to exact his vengeance. Never have so few defeated so many – but then the many, for the most part, are unarmed. (The *Odyssey* affects hesitation at killing even condemned men in this manner: some of the suitors are armed by the traitorous Melanthius.) Like Achilles, Odysseus refuses the supplication of many of the suitors, including the relatively obscure Leiodes, whose head is memorably cut off even as his tongue wags in entreaty. After so much endurance, Odysseus now demonstrates a striking swiftness to action. In the end, however, and unlike Achilles, he heeds the battlefield supplication of two figures (at Telemachus's say-so). One is Medon, Ithaca's herald, the other Phemius, the bard. Both are spared – we might conjecture – for their respective roles in promoting the latest homecoming tale about a Trojan War veteran, that of the wily Odysseus, this poem in progress, the *Odyssey*.

The resolution is as shocking as it is sudden and leaves open the question what to make of the slaughter. The second-century BC mythographer Apollodorus describes Odysseus being judged and exiled by Achilles' son Neoptolemus for killing the suitors. The *Odyssey* itself offers rival alternatives. For 'Ms Wide Fame' Eurycleia, it is an occasion to celebrate. Though Odysseus stops her victory song, he is powerless to prevent her from running off to inform Penelope, deliriously happy. Penelope thinks the woman has lost her mind – the slaughter of so many suitors must be due to the gods. Besides, how is it possible for her husband to have returned now? As she goes to see Odysseus, she is unsure whether she should test him or embrace him, perhaps reflecting an ambivalence that the audience should feel. Fresh and exultant from his first taste of battle, Telemachus cannot believe how cruel his mother can be. Odysseus is more cautious. He knows the severity of the situation: 'when one has killed only one man in a community... / even that man flees into exile, leaving kinsmen and fatherland behind. / But we have killed the support of the city, who were the best / of youths in Ithaca' (23.118–22). He may have had mixed success in silencing Eurycleia's jubilation, but now he takes control. He issues instructions to strike up wedding celebrations to cover the noise of the slaughter (130–40), as if husband and wife were renewing their vows, which, in an odd kind of way, they are. Far from shouting out his success from the rooftops, which is the essence of fame (*kleos*), Odysseus tries to keep it hidden. But that, of course, is the very way in which he claims his fame.

The ends of the *Odyssey*

One of Homer's first editors, the Alexandrian scholar Aristophanes of Byzantium (c. 257–180 BC), argued that the *Odyssey*'s proper end comes at 23.296 when Odysseus and Penelope 'gladly come to the holy site of their ancient bed', a theory which, revived by Romantic-influenced Victorian critics, lingers on in scholarship to this day. It is certainly true that the twenty-fourth and final book of the *Odyssey is* difficult to make sense of. There is another visit to the heroes of the *Iliad* in their shadowy underworld existence. Odysseus's father Laertes makes a belated appearance. Athena and Zeus intervene again to bring the poem to a shuddering halt. And some episodes *are* difficult to stomach – such as Odysseus putting his father to the test or the spillover of the conflict to the rest of the Ithacan population. Yet the poem explicitly sets up its ending as a problem. At almost exactly the halfway point, in *Odyssey* 11, Teiresias prophesies that Odysseus's journey will continue even once he has arrived back on Ithaca.

As the closing credits roll, the story of Odysseus's homecoming is *not* at an end after all, and he must leave on another odyssey at some undetermined point in the future. (According to the summary of the lost epic *Telegony*, Odysseus eventually meets his end at the hands of a son he has with Circe, Telegonus, he who is 'born from afar'.) Through a series of moves, the *Odyssey* draws attention to the artificiality of its closure and asks the audience to reflect on where this epic ends, and why that matters.

The first of these closing gestures is Odysseus's reunion with his wife. After flirting with the possibility of their recognition in *Odyssey* 19, Homer finally brings man and wife together in *Odyssey* 23, but with a twist. When Telemachus chastises his mother for refusing to accept Eurycleia's account of the suitors' demise, she replies: 'if it really / is Odysseus and he has come home, then the two of us / shall find other ways, and better, to recognise each other, for we have / signs [*sēmata*, singular *sēma*], which the two of us know that are hidden from others' (107–10). The promise of shared secrets makes Odysseus smile, but soon he too turns angry when he hears Penelope ask for their bed to be brought out. 'What bitter word is this?' (183), he exclaims – and proceeds to relate the story of their bed, which he himself built around an olive tree. The symbolism is heavy: their bed, made from Athena's tree, stands rooted at the centre of the household. The union of husband and wife *is* the house. And it is on the basis of Odysseus's furious reaction that Penelope now acknowledges that her man is home – she has tricked him to find out the truth (only her man knows her bed). The typical Odyssean irony is that she recognises her husband at the one moment when he is not the man he has been in our epic, when he is the one deceived and angrily lets his guard slip.

Homer expresses Penelope's joy at recognising her husband through a simile that brings husband and wife together. Odysseus is as welcome to her as land is to a shipwrecked sailor (232–40) – here Penelope plays Odysseus's role as the sailor, Odysseus the home to which he returns. With Athena holding back the coming dawn, Odysseus relates the bad news of Teiresias's prophecy – that he must wander and suffer more, until eventually he comes across a 'sign' (*sēma*), when another wayfarer will confuse his oar for a winnowing fan. (More on this in due course.) Only then do husband and wife finally come together for lovemaking, and, for some, bring the *Odyssey* to an end.

But climaxing in bed with Odysseus and Penelope says as much about readers' assumptions as it does about the tone or content of the remainder of the poem. Immediately after their lovemaking, Odysseus relates to Penelope his adventures in a highly abridged version of his song to the Phaeacians, which continues the *Odyssey*'s performance of, and investigation into, storytelling. (Particularly noticeable, for example, is the fact that Odysseus leaves out his affairs with other women.) Indeed, the *Odyssey* seems self-consciously aware of the problem of ending at this point in at least two ways. First, Odysseus's mention of Teiresias's prophecy reminds the audience that the story has no *natural* end and that Odysseus's journey will (have to) continue even after *this* song has finished. Second, Homer explicitly poses the question of how to read (the signs). The Greek word for 'sign', *sēma*, relates to the reading of tokens correctly, to interpretation. We might recall that the *Iliad* ends its retelling of the Trojan War with a sign (*sēma*) – the burial mound of Hector – as if it were burying the Trojan War story. Now, as its own story draws to a close, the *Odyssey* reflects on not only the status of *this version* of Odysseus's homecoming in comparison to others (which Teiresias's prophecy recalls), or the performance of Odysseus's storytelling (in his version to his wife), but also the nature of interpretation itself – how we read the signs (*sēmata*). Wherever (we think) this tale ends fundamentally changes the way we read it.

The challenge starts at the very beginning of the last book, as we follow Hermes guiding the shades of the suitors to their final resting place. (On this occasion, we really do enter the underworld, where *Odyssey* 11 only approaches the border.) The role of Hermes as the 'leader of souls' brings to mind *Iliad* 24, when he leads Priam to Achilles' tent. There the underworld imagery of the journey signifies the grave threat to Priam's life in undertaking such an expedition. Where the *Iliad*'s Hermes only figuratively leads Priam to the underworld, however, the *Odyssey*'s Hermes literally guides the souls of the suitors to Hades. Nevertheless, if Hermes' role reminds us of the *Iliad*, then it should come as no surprise that the figures to whom Homer next turns are Achilles and Agamemnon. Yet these two shades are far removed from the warring heroes of the *Iliad*. This Achilles and this Agamemnon sing each other's praises (35–98)! This mutual backslapping saps both men of their vital energy and neither seems worthy to be called the best of the Achaeans. That title now surely belongs to Odysseus.

The suitors' shades admit as much. As the Trojan War veterans watch in bewilderment, the youth of Ithaca arrive en masse, one of them, the not-so-bad Amphimedon explains that they have all been laid low by the singular man, Odysseus, who has returned to punish them (121–90). Agamemnon blesses Odysseus for having such a virtuous wife (192–8) – before ranting (again) about his death at the hands of his own treacherous woman. And there we leave the great heroes from Troy, sore at their own demise, in awe of Odysseus's survival. The *Iliad* inters the Trojan War tradition by burying Hector, Troy's great warrior and last defence. With Hector dead, Troy is doomed to fall, the story is over – there is no need for any other Trojan War poem after the *Iliad*. The *Odyssey* appropriates this strategy by burying Achilles – something that the *Iliad*, of course, foreshadows but resists. And, by burying Achilles, the *Odyssey* buries the *Iliad* with him as an epic that is as out of date as its hero, all brawn and no brains, hardly a match for this poem and its epic survivor.

An audience alert to the *Odyssey*'s interplay with the *Iliad* might wonder whether the poem should end here, particularly given the forceful closural device of burial. But they would be reading as much into the events as Amphimedon, who imagines an understanding between Odysseus and Penelope where the poem equivocates. Instead, the epic twists again. Back on Ithaca, son meets father.

Turning to Laertes may come as a bit of a shock: but, although Laertes himself has remained on the very margins of Ithaca and the poem, his presence, like that of Peleus in the *Iliad*, is felt throughout. His name has shadowed the hero throughout his trials in the form of Odysseus's patronym *Laertides*, 'son of Laertes'. Penelope's famous trick of weaving a death shroud that she unpicks each night aptly symbolises Laertes's precarious existence between life and death. Like the *Iliad*'s Peleus, he is on the 'threshold of old age' (15.348; the very words with which Priam imagines Peleus, 24.487). Whereas the *Iliad* ends with this poignant moment between *a* father (Priam) and *a* son (Achilles), the pair of them doomed never to see their loved ones again (Hector, Peleus), the *Odyssey* ends with *the* father (Laertes) and *the* son (Odysseus). *This* hero gets home to his father.

However, Odysseus's reunion with his father is disturbing. Odysseus finds Laertes in the 'well-built orchard' (226), digging about a plant, clothed in shoddy rags. When he spies him, 'worn down by old age, with great suffering in his chest' (233), Odysseus's resolve falters, and he debates in his mind and spirit 'whether to kiss and embrace his father, and to tell him / everything, how he has come and made it back again to his dear fatherland, / or whether to question him first and test him on each thing' (236–8). By this point in the narrative, the threat of discovery has passed. There is no obvious reason for Odysseus to lie. But, proving himself unwilling, or unable, to put away his disguises, Odysseus hails Laertes and spins another Cretan yarn. The problem of this final recognition scene is indicated by Odysseus's vacillation. But the effect is even more unsettling, as, upon news of his son's still further (allegedly) wanderings, Laertes collapses to the floor.

After nearly giving his aged father a heart attack, Odysseus is panicked into finally revealing himself. Where the recognition between husband and wife takes place by virtue of the trickster being tricked, here the recognition between father and son takes place when the son almost kills his father (that Oedipus complex again). Now he has been forced to drop all pretence, Odysseus labours to prove his identity to his father. First he shows his scar, but that is not enough. We may remember that Odysseus won his scar – and his name – on a hunting expedition with his maternal grandfather. Laertes was not part of that story. Instead, he takes his father around their orchard, recounting their inheritance and the many memories they shared there. This works. After all, Laertes has been lovingly tending this orchard all these years (and all through the *Odyssey*). But what shared memories they have, Homer gives us no indication. This last example of recognition probes the efficacy of Odysseus's testing strategy and conceals rather than reveals the tokens by which father and son recognise each other. Here, we find that there are limits to how much an audience can glean from the stories being told.

There is, Odysseus acknowledges to his father, trouble ahead, and this trouble – the fall-out from Odysseus's slaughter of the suitors – provides one last problem encounter to consider. Odysseus has already anticipated, in a brief aside to his son, that killing so many young men will have consequences. Such is the logic of revenge that he expects payback from the families of their victims. The challenge comes in the shape of Antinous's father, Eupeithes, whose name itself, 'very persuasive', demonstrates the extent of this last crisis that Odysseus faces. 'Mr Persuasion' calls an assembly of the Ithacan people, in which he presents an alternative version of the events presented in the *Odyssey*. Drawing upon the language used by the *Iliad* to denote

Agamemnon's failure as a leader, Eupeithes roundly denounces Odysseus. 'He has lost his hollow ships and he has destroyed his people' (428), he bluntly states. By this, he means not only the companions who accompanied their leader to Troy and who failed to make it back, but also the men at home, the suitors, the flower of Ithacan youth. Eupeithes even robs Odysseus of his name and, thereby, of his heroic identity. Labelling him simply 'this *man* here' (426), Eupeithes recalls the anonymity of the poem's first word, 'man' (*andra*).

This speech, unique in its frank criticism of Odysseus's authority, threatens to unravel his carefully constructed persona and to undo the *Odyssey*'s equally carefully wrought narrative. For Eupeithes *is* persuasive. Homer tells us that the crowd 'sprang up with a great hue and cry, / more than half of them' (463–4), which comes as some surprise, given the fact that Medon, the recently spared herald, and Halitherses, the bird interpreter from book two, both bluntly warn the people that 'god' is on Odysseus's side and that their sons died by their own recklessness. If the suitors' relations fail to get the message, Homer makes sure that the audience don't. 'Eupeithes', he narrates, 'led the fools: / he said he was going to avenge his son's murder. But he wasn't going / to come back' (469–71). 'To come back' is the privilege that only Odysseus and son have in this narrative. Even as we may feel troubled by the issues raised by Eupeithes's speech, or flinch at his impending doom, that does not – *cannot* – mean taking sides against Odysseus.

Like any good Hollywood blockbuster, the *Odyssey* ends with a full-on battle. Lined up against the revolting Ithacans are Odysseus, with son *and* father, his loyal servants, and also some newly acquired and aptly named allies – Dolios ('Mr Tricky') and sons. To the last, this is a tricky tale. As they ready themselves for war, Laertes's heart leaps in delight seeing 'my son and my son's son contesting over being excellent' (515). So inspired is he that he even flings the first spear – killing, you've guessed it, Eupeithes, that enemy of the tale (523–5). Soon thereafter, Athena intervenes to declare peace. We might wonder how else the killing could be stopped, when the cycle of vengeance dominates men's minds.

Yet, a few hundred lines before this, Zeus and Athena appear to have wrapped things up:

> Since Odysseus has taken his revenge on the suitors,
> Let them take trusty oaths and let him be king forever,
> And let us put a forgetting on the murder of
> Their sons and brothers: in fact let them love each other
> As before, and let wealth and peace flourish.
>
> (24.482–6)

As resolutions go, this one is pretty definitive and conclusive. It demonstrates, again, the gods' care for men, as we have seen in the *Iliad*. But the tone is somewhat different here, as captured by Zeus's odd pronouncement that he will 'put a forgetting' on both sides. Besides, these prudent sentiments do *not* stop conflict from breaking out. Even when Athena then formally intervenes, 'and pale fear seized' the Ithacans (533), one man fights on still, mowing down all in his path – Odysseus. It takes Athena appearing in person (along with a thunderbolt from Zeus) to prevent him from wreaking any more destruction (542–5). It is not so easy, it seems, to dismiss from our minds the slaughter as Zeus instructs. Odysseus earns epic fame because he gets home, because he survives, and because he does this through the power of his intellect. His slaughter of the suitors and their relations is more difficult to swallow; it is the behaviour of a Heracles or an Achilles. The fact that Odysseus goes on killing, even after the gods intervene, and that he must be held back by Athena at the end, forces us to confront the uncomfortable truth that epic glory is but a short step away from indiscriminate violence. Still more uncomfortable is the role that the audience plays in its legitimisation.

So, the last twist in this 'much turning', tricky poem is, ironically, its unflinching honesty. Even as it suppresses alternatives as brutally as Odysseus kills challengers to his authority, simultaneously the *Odyssey* draws attention to the very mechanics by which an audience is persuaded (through the voice of the narrator, characterisation, the gods, etc.). This final sting in the tale forces us to question the extent to which we are implicated in cheering Odysseus on.

The end of epic

We have followed Odysseus from the margins of his society, on the shoreline where he was left by the Phaeacians, via the swineherd's hut and his banqueting hall, to the centre of his home, the olive-tree bed, to which he and his wife retire after the slaughtering of the suitors and a twenty-year separation. But Odysseus's homecoming is not only a physical return. Homecoming also entails an investigation into what one means to others. In part, the *Odyssey* provides the first post-traumatic stress account of a warrior returning from war, trying not only to regain his place in society and re-establish his bonds with his family, but also to recover his identity. In part too, it helps to explain the durability and flexibility of Odysseus (or his Latin alter ego, Ulysses) in popular culture throughout the ages and all over the world. Philosopher, poet, politician, warrior, trickster, beggar, king, sufferer, executor, thief – Odysseus of the *Odyssey* is none and all of the above. A man for all seasons, the man from Troy, husband of Penelope – Odysseus as '*andra*' (man/husband) dominates the poem.

However, the *Odyssey* is far more than Odysseus. During its narrative 'of many turns', the poem constantly draws attention to its own construction. Think of the songs of bards, such as Phemius entertaining the suitors with the tales of the failed homecomings of the Trojan War veterans (prompting Penelope's heartfelt plea to change the tune), or Demodocus singing about Odysseus's Trojan horse trick. Or of Odysseus himself, who takes over the telling of the tale for three whole books. Or of Athena and Zeus stage-managing Odysseus's return and setting the story on its way, and then bringing about its sudden end *dea ex machina*. Or of the poem's first speaker, Zeus, complaining about how men don't heed warnings. Or of Penelope's challenge to her husband (and us) to read the signs properly. The *Odyssey* is one of the richest, most elusive, and most self-conscious texts in literary history.

At its centre in *Odyssey* 11 stands Teiresias's prophecy. We have already mentioned how it foretells that Odysseus's journey doesn't end with the *Odyssey* – hence, the 'false' endings, as the poem veers this way and that in search of some kind of closure. But it has more to offer, particularly with what it has to say about epic as a genre. Delivering his prophecy on the 'borders' (13) of the world next to the great sea 'Oceanus', Teiresias anticipates Odysseus's return to Ithaca (he will slaughter the suitors by force and by guile) *and* his post-*Odyssey* wandering. For, at some unspecified point in the future, Odysseus must take up his 'well-shaped oar' and walk until he meets 'men who know nothing about the sea' (122–3). Then, when a passing wayfarer confuses his oar for a winnowing fan, Odysseus should plant the oar in the ground and sacrifice to Poseidon. Only then will a peaceful death come to Odysseus 'from the sea' (134), and his people will be happy.

While the instructions are clear – Teiresias asserts that 'I will give you a very clear sign [*sēma*] and you won't miss it' – interpretation, typically of divine communications, is not. Indeed, misrecognition is embedded within the story, as the wayfarer whom Odysseus is prophesied to meet will *mistake* his oar for a winnowing shovel (a kind of agricultural instrument). When Odysseus relates Teiresias's instructions to his wife in *Odyssey* 23, he talks about them not yet having reached the 'borders' (23.248) of their trials, explicitly acknowledging that the prophecy goes beyond the borders of this poem into a post-*Odyssey* terrain. But what kind of terrain should we be imagining? Significantly

Odysseus glosses his future journey as 'unmeasured' (*ametrētos*, 23.249) toil. By this, Odysseus means that his wandering and suffering will continue without end (or 'measure'). But the Greek for measure, *metra*, also signifies poetic *metre*. So, Odysseus is also saying that the future outside this poem will be without *metre* – or, to put that differently, that this poem heralds the end of this kind of verse, the hexameter metre of heroic epic.

Within two or three generations of the *Odyssey* being written down, other authors begin to associate Homeric epic with the great sea (Oceanus) surrounding the Earth – until we get that image of all literature springing from and flowing back into Homer. It is interesting then that Teiresias's prophecy describes Odysseus wandering *far from the sea*, as if the *Odyssey* were already anticipating the end of this kind of poetry. Indeed, there may even be a hint of this awareness in the description of Odysseus's oar. If Homeric poetry can be understood as the sea, then the oar can be thought of as the means by which one moves through it. Teiresias himself uses epic language to refer to the oar as 'the wings of a ship'. But the oar gets mistaken by someone far from the sea – someone far from the world of Homeric epic, that is – as a land-based tool for agriculture, mistranslating a poetic figure ('the wings of a ship') as a prosaic object ('a winnowing fan'). Taken together, Teiresias's prophecy and Odysseus's translation of it point to a literary terrain far removed from the *Odyssey*, far even from the kind of heroic epic that Homer's poem represents. From its elusive beginnings to its abrupt end, the *Odyssey* presents itself as the epic to end all epics.

Odysseus's final odyssey will take him far from the great sea, far beyond the boundaries, that is, of Homeric geography and poetics, into a world where Homeric verse is unfamiliar, which doesn't understand the metaphorical way Homeric language works (the 'wings of a ship'?), and whose residents may not know the stories of the Trojan War and of Odysseus. In the final reckoning Homer's *Odyssey* anticipates a world beyond the borders not only of this poem but even of heroic epic itself, where death comes naturally to (the) man and the people who live round about are finally blessed and not dependent on a leader for salvation. The never-ending story of Odysseus's wandering is a journey into other literary forms.

Epilogue
Homer: the much-resounding sea

The world of Homer, with its tales of gods, heroes, and fantastical creatures, can seem far removed from our own. Nevertheless, the themes the epics present and the questions they raise still speak to us. Indeed, there is something about the very distance of epic that allows its audiences to confront deeply problematic issues, experience tensions that threaten to rip apart the very fabric of human society, and reflect on who they are and where they come from.

This epilogue, like the Homeric epics themselves, both looks back to how they relate to the oral tradition from out of which they arose, *and* traces the story of how they stimulated and continue to stimulate responses in the centuries that follow. We draw upon a range of ancient testimony to explore what became of Homer's heroes, to replay how the poems' heroic themes and values were played out in different environments (e.g. the symposium and the theatre) or in different cities (Athens, Alexandria, Rome), and to reflect on what their successors made of the competing narrative forms that these poems bequeathed. For it is in the difference between the *Iliad*'s intense reflection on mortality and the *Odyssey*'s adventurous exploration of survival and identity that the Homeric legacy is most keenly felt in antiquity, whether we are talking about the rivalry between tragedy and comedy in Athens, or between authors of the same genre, such as the Odyssean and Iliadic histories by Herodotus and

Thucydides, respectively. All ancient Greek and Roman literary productions that follow epic look for their inspiration (or authority) from Homer, while also seeking to challenge and contest that hegemony. Even from the vantage of our own contemporary culture, the rushing force of epic can still be felt in rapidly developing digital media and the forging of yet more new artistic productions such as film, pop music, and fantasy fiction.

Of arms and the man

The primary question of Homer's influence is our near-complete ignorance about the origin of the poems ascribed to him and the nature of their authorship. As we have discussed, we simply do not know who Homer was (if he was an individual), where he was from, when (or if) he composed the *Iliad* and/or the *Odyssey*, and how these poems became fixed in the form we possess. Nonetheless, something of their story can be traced from how other works refer to, engage with, and rework them. This – the story of Homer's reception in antiquity – can be a useful frame for thinking about the nature of the poems themselves.

Take the story of Homer's battle with Hesiod, the *Certamen* (or, simply, the 'Contest'), for example. Modern critics have tended to dismiss this anonymous late fourth-century BC reimagination of a 'contest' between the two epic superpowers, because it disappoints as a biographical portrait of real people. To answer who Homer was, where he was from, and how his poems enjoyed such cultural authority, the *Certamen* constructs an image of Homer based on his poems. But this is what makes it invaluable as a source for thinking about his poetry. Its representation of the number of places that call Homer their own or through which he is portrayed as travelling show not so much the *Certamen* hedging its bets about Homer's life story as his wide reception throughout the Greek world. Moreover, the imagined contest with Hesiod encapsulates an essential competitive feature of Greek poetic performance, often in such a formal environment as the one imagined here, and reflects an understanding of the world of archaic Greek hexameter poetry, which Homer and Hesiod dominate together. But it does more than that. It offers a critical insight into their difference at the moment when it comes to deciding who is best:

> Being in wonder also at this, the Greeks praised Homer, so far did his verses exceed the standard, and they ordered that he be given the victory. But the king crowned Hesiod.
>
> (*Certamen* 205–10)

What is striking about this scene is not only how it mimics Homer's own scene of judgement at the beginning of the *Iliad*, where the people acclaim the priest Chryses but Agamemnon dismisses him. It is also notable that the king votes for Hesiod – who, after all, at the beginning of his *Works and Days* warns kings against making crooked judgements – while the people vote for Homer. This story displays an intimate awareness of the *Iliad's* agonistic dynamic and perhaps explains just why Homer's poems were performed in Athens at the Great Panatheneia for some two centuries. Homer's poems were better able than other (lost) epics to respond to, and perhaps even help shape, the growing group political consciousness in Greek communities all around the Mediterranean.

Arguably, this stimulation and shaping of political consciousness is nowhere better illustrated than in Athens, where the Homeric poems probably achieved their final form (however we imagine these oral poems becoming fixed in writing). It is somewhat ironic that they become institutionalised under a dictatorship (Peisistratus and sons). But tyrannical regimes frequently represent early stirrings of disaffection with a traditional elite. (This is certainly the case in ancient Greek cities such as Athens,

Corinth, Syracuse, and the like – only Sparta was said to have avoided tyranny, and, yet, with its communal messes, state education from the age of three, and being on a perpetual war footing, Sparta was a very *odd* place.) What is more, tyrannies often prove to be adept at enlisting popular support through the sponsoring of public art (which is still the case to this day). Even so, the politics of performance was no less powerful once the Athenians established democracy, for now the Athenian Homer underpinned the city's claims of supremacy in the Greek world. Pericles, the prominent Athenian statesman at the height of the city's power, may claim that Athens needs no Homer to sing its praises (Thucydides 1.21.2). But it is significant that he must still cite Homer as the authority supposedly surplus to requirements.

Later, as Alexandria becomes the new cultural hub of the Mediterranean in the third century BC, Homer again is *the* cultural marker. The first efforts at editing Homer's poems are part of Alexandria's claims to being Greek and the (natural) inheritor of the Greek legacy. (Hence, the label for this period, the *Hellen*istic world – from the word *Hellenes*, or Greeks.) In this scenario, even the work of scholars such as Aristarchus, Zenodotus, and Aristophanes of Byzantium performs the role of asserting cultural legitimacy and power. Alexandria's poets rework Homeric subjects even as they dismiss epic itself as a viable genre. Thus, Apollonius's *Argonautica* (the story of Jason and the Argonauts) masquerades as a prequel to the *Odyssey* that is intimately connected to, and heavily derivative of, Homer's poem. Here we have a kind of post-Odyssean pre-*Odyssey*, if you will, in much the same way as Christopher Nolan's *Batman Begins*, or *Casino Royale* (starring Daniel Craig as James Bond), reboot their franchises with a knowing understanding of their inheritance, even as they radically depart from it. (In *Casino Royale*, for example, we learn where Bond's ice-cool womanising persona comes from – the woman he loves dies, and he *hurts* – even as *this* Bond professes not to care whether his Martini is shaken or stirred.)

Another poet, the Sicilian Theocritus, invents a new genre of poetry called Bucolic (literally 'country' poems) rooted in Homer's *Odyssey*, which are anything but as rustic and unsophisticated as they claim to be. For instance, Theocritus reimagines Homer's one-eyed monster, Polyphemus, as a poet-goatherd, tending his flocks and looking longingly (out of his one still good eye) to his beloved nymph in those halcyon days before the wretched man came and took away his sight. Similarly, Callimachus, champion of the new 'small is beautiful' aesthetic, borrows a famous image from Homer for the metaphor that articulates this radical literary programme of writing short, but densely sophisticated, works. New poets should steer clear of the great sea of epic for fear of muddying its waters.

The story continues as Homer's epics spread throughout the Mediterranean World through a process of translation, imitation, and opposition. Even when the Romans assume control of the Mediterranean, Homer looms large, first via translation (in the form of Livius Andronicus's Latin *Odyssey*, c. 280–200 BC), then by imitation. Rome's first epic, the *Annales*, picked up the story of Rome from Troy's destruction; its poet, Ennius (c. 239–169 BC), claimed to be Homer reincarnated. Virgil's *Aeneid*, published posthumously after his death in 19 BC and arguably the most taught and read narrative in Europe after the *Bible*, draws heavily on Homer, as well as on interpretations of Homer by Latin authors like Livius and Ennius. Virgil advertises his debt in the very first words of his poem: 'Arms *and* the man I sing' (*Arma virumque cano*). His epic will be a synthesis of an *Iliad* and *Odyssey* in half as many books as either (twelve). In content, the *Aeneid* looks back to the *Iliad*, by tracing what happens immediately after the fall of Troy to the city's refugees (Aeneas; his aged father, Anchises; and his son, Ascanius, chief among them). But it retraces the *Odyssey*'s steps, as these Trojans wander the Mediterranean in search of home, though, in this case, 'home' is an unknown, and as yet unfounded, Rome.

Indeed, to understand Homer better, one could do worse than read the *Aeneid*, since Virgil is one of Homer's most astute readers. For example, like Homer before him, Virgil has the gods make arms for his hero, and, like Homer, singles out the shield for special mention (*Aeneid* 8.617–731; *Iliad* 18.478–608). In the *Aeneid*, the scenes emblazoned on the shield explicitly depict later history, primarily scenes from the Battle of Actium (31 BC), where Octavian (as Augustus was known then) defeated the combined forces of Antony and Cleopatra. In effect, when Aeneas re-enters the fray, he carries on his back Augustus's New World Order. Homer is far less gung-ho, but a similar idea may be implied by Achilles' shield. Its most detailed scene presents a trial taking place in the public assembly and involving the whole community (plaintiffs, the people, a moderator, a panel of judges). With Virgil's representation in mind, we can imagine Homer similarly anticipating a future beyond his epic, where such scenes of civic participation are commonplace. In fact, we might even suppose that such scenes owe a debt to Achilles (whose shield this is), for setting in motion the move towards participatory politics, when he stood up to Agamemnon in *Iliad* 1. As Achilles re-enters the fray, plunging this peaceful scene of a community forever frozen in the process of coming to judgement back into the ferocity of war, he carries on his shoulders a world known better to the audience than to himself, a world worth fighting for, a world which the *Iliad* can claim as its legacy.

Virgil's model did not silence successors, but it did change the rules. Now Homeric epic becomes filtered through the *Aeneid's* exploration of destiny and power. Virgil's near-contemporary Ovid pushes epic to the limits. His *Metamorphoses* goes back to the beginning of time – so, back to Hesiod's *Theogony* and a big-bang theory of chaos and atoms – and brings the action right up to the present-day apotheosis of Julius Caesar (42 BC). A generation or two later, Lucan refashions epic as recent history in a highly calculated, and powerful, gambit. For, in his *Pharsalia*, the poet, perhaps more than any figure within the narrative, is the hero of the day. At every turn, Lucan struggles (but fails, of course) to stop telling the story. For his story has a tragedy to tell – the inexorable march towards the triumph of Julius Caesar and the establishment of the rule of one man. (Lucan was soon forced to commit suicide by *his* Caesar, Nero.) Epic is *always* about the present, even as it is set in the past.

Arguably some of the most remarkable artistic productions to survive from this period (roughly first century AD) are a collection of twenty-two miniature marble reliefs depicting Homer's *Iliad* in relation to other stories about the fall of Troy. (Hence their name: the *Tabulae Iliacae*, or the 'Iliac tablets'.) The most complete fragment, held in the Capitoline Museums in Rome, measures just 25 x 30 cm. (Its original length would probably have been somewhat over 40 cm.) Despite these tiny proportions, there are over 250 surviving figurines, with accompanying Greek text summarising each book of the *Iliad*, which offer a panoramic overview of the Greek Troy story cycle – the *Iliopersis* (or *Sack of Troy*) in the middle, the *Aethiopis* and *Little Iliad* below, and the twenty-four books of the *Iliad* to the side. In spite of the fact that only scenes from book one (at the top) and books thirteen to twenty-four (to the right) survive, it is possible to make out how the complex compositional arrangement demonstrates great intimacy with the *Iliad* and encourages the viewer – handling it as one might now handle a tablet computer – to make connections across the various panels and reread the *Iliad* in the light of its careful iconography. One example demonstrates how this might work. For at the centre of the composition stands Aeneas, at the moment of his departure from Troy, rescuing his father and son. Homer's *Iliad* is quite literally being read in the light of the greater story that will unfold (alluded to in the bottom right-hand corner of the central frieze): Aeneas's escape from Troy and his founding of the Roman people.

Tabula Iliaca Capitolina, c. first century AD, Capitoline Museums, Rome

The *Tabulae Iliacae* are a collection of twenty-two miniature marble reliefs depicting Homer's *Iliad* in relation to other stories about the fall of Troy. This, the most complete fragment, measuring just 25 x 30 cm, depicts over 250 surviving figurines, with accompanying Greek text summarising each book of the *Iliad*. As well as offering a panoramic overview of the Greek Troy story cycle, by including images from the *Sack of Troy*, the *Aethiopis* and *Little Iliad*, the tablet invites the viewer to explore interconnections across the Iliad's twenty-four books. So, for example, the panel at the top, representing *Iliad* 1, ends with Thetis's supplication of Zeus (*Iliad* 1.493–530). As Thetis kneels before the god, Zeus turns away – and looks to the next panel, representing *Iliad* 24, which quite literally points viewers to the consequences of Thetis's act. It is worth observing too how the depiction of Achilles, beseeched by Priam, itself mirrors that of Zeus supplicated by Thetis, thereby encouraging the viewer to think of the similarities (and differences) between the two acts.

In a manner that is typical of Greece (and Rome), Homer's cultural predominance meant that other authors both looked to him for authority *and* contested that authority to make their own mark. Given the surviving record, Homer's influence is seen most clearly, and most keenly felt, in Athens. In the *Poetics* (the first formal work of literary criticism that comes down to us), Aristotle uses Homeric epic as a way into thinking about the qualities of tragedy. This is a calculated move: for Athenian tragedy feeds heavily from Homer's table. Of course, many tragedies rework material other than what is found in Homer. Thebes in particular provides the Athenian tragedians with especially rich pickings, acting as both an alter-Athens and as a city that is always being besieged (by armies, plague, or other horrors closer to home). Still, there remains an impressive roll call of Trojan War plays (many based on Homeric material) in the extant tragic corpus – Aeschylus's *Oresteia* trilogy (*Agamemnon*, *Libation Bearers*, *Eumenides*); Sophocles's *Ajax*, *Philoctetes*, and *Electra*; Euripides's *Trojan Women*, *Hecuba*, *Andromache*, *Helen*, *Electra*, *Orestes*, and *Cyclops* (a satyr-play, performed after tragic trilogies to lighten the mood, which retells Odysseus's encounter with Polyphemus with emphasis on the pair's mutual drunkenness, gluttony, and buffoonery) – not to mention those plays lost to us (such as Aeschylus's *Myrmidons*) or those of doubtful authorship (such as the *Rhesus*, which drama-tises the events covered in *Iliad* 10).

And the engagement with Homer goes deeper than subject matter alone. Characters step on the tragic stage carrying with them their Homeric baggage. Aeschylus's Agamemnon returns in great pomp and circumstance only to be stabbed in the back by his wife: the subject is anticipated in the *Odyssey*, where he com-plains about his wife's treachery, but it is his arrogance, as explored in the *Iliad*, which provides Aeschylus with the character of the king. In Sophocles's *Philoctetes*, Achilles' son Neoptolemus wres-tles with questions of loyalty in ways similar to his father in the *Iliad*, even as Odysseus tries to educate him in the dark arts of deceit (as if he were a Telemachus learning the ropes in the *Odyssey*). Odysseus himself is recast as a consummate politician who says one thing but keeps another in his heart (as too in Euripides's *Trojan Women* and *Hecuba*; his role in Sophocles's *Ajax* is a notable exception). In democratic Athens, Homer's Odysseus becomes the ideal figure through which to investigate and re-enact the audience's anxieties about the impact of spin on political discourse and debate.

All the same, however, tragedy marks a critical difference from Homer's epics. The dramas offer the view of those from below – women, slaves, and especially the group at large, the Chorus. All have their antecedents in Homer – Aristotle calls the Chorus tragedy's version of the epic 'people' (*laos*, or 'laity'). But something has changed. Euripides in particular interrogates Trojan War material by exploring *responses* to the hero through the views of marginalised groups, especially women. In his *Trojan Women*, for example, Euripides recalls scenes in the *Iliad* when Troy's women mourn Hector in order to dramatise a city in ruin. (Troy is always the city being sacked.) Simultaneously, he uses the plight of these women to prompt the Athenians to think about their own actions in war: earlier in the same year it was performed (415 BC), Athens seized the neutral island of Melos, put to death the entire male population, and enslaved all women and children (an act unforgettably dramatised by Thucydides in his 'Melian Dialogue'). What is remarkable here is the fact that Homer's legacy leads not to a celebration of epic glory but to an agonised reflection on the problems engendered by the power and the glory of heroes, rendering tragedy one long extended footnote on the suffering and troubled heroism of Homer's epics.

Homer's poems bequeath to the tradition a pair of highly contrasting, yet complementary narrative patterns, whose influence leads to the development of many different poetic and prose-based genres. The early period of Greek literature (seventh to sixth centuries BC) is dominated by poetic genres (epic, lyric, elegiac, etc.), presumably because its metrical units are so closely tied to oral composition, memory, and performance. But, in the fifth century BC, we see the emergence of prose, which developed hand-in-hand with the invention of writing. Take the genre of history, for example, invented, as we know it, by Herodotus of Halicarnassus (modern-day Bodrum). In his opening gambit, he states that he has carried out investigations – the essential business of history – both to record the great deeds of men and to question why his people, the Greeks, came into conflict with the barbarians (the Persians). Both points reflect Homer's influence. He records great deeds 'so that they won't lose their glory' (*aklea*) – the negative of the Homeric *kleos* indicates that events now depend for their longevity on being *written* down. His question (why did the Greeks and barbarians go to war with each other?) not only mimics the structural device that opened the *Iliad* (a question of cause) but even recalls the context – two parties at war. But Herodotus's answer depends on his own investigations not the Muse – his eyewitness accounts, his ability to sift through competing versions of events. His enquiry (in Greek *historia* – from which we get the word *history*) is both Homeric and distinctly unHomeric. Yet, even as Herodotus subsequently distinguishes between his work from epic mythology, whose veracity cannot be vouched for, he recalls Homer. Like Odysseus, he comes to know 'cities of men both small and great alike' (1.5.3; compare *Odyssey* 1.3: 'Many were they whose cities he saw, whose minds he learned of'). And, his subsequent narrative, which combines ethnographic description with historical investigation, is greatly indebted to the precedent in Homer's *Odyssey* of a man gaining knowledge through travel and getting to know men's minds.

Perhaps it is not altogether surprising that Herodotus should turn to Homer, for epic was the primary model for a lengthy account of past events. Herodotus also draws on Homer's technique of combining narrative with the direct speech of historical agents – not, we might think, a natural feature of history writing. Herodotus's immediate successor, Thucydides, goes one step further by formalising speech in his history as debate, with one speech set in opposition to another. In turn, this reflects the focus of *his* history on Greek internal affairs and civil conflict, for which Thucydides looks to Homer's *Iliad* for precedent. Even if his narrative appears more objective – Thucydides is still read for his 'real politik' account of war – frequent Iliadic resonances destabilise dispassionate interpretations. In book six, for example, the Athenian general Nicias attempts to dissuade the Athenian assembly from its disastrous plans to invade Sicily by adopting a strategy of 'bigging up' the effort required. But, as Agamemnon found before him, playing the crowd is a dangerous game and the ruse backfires, as the Athenians become all the more eager for war. Where the gods in Homer prevent the Achaeans from rushing to the ships, in Thucydides's world of harsh realities no gods intervene and nothing holds the Athenians back from rushing to the ships. (Thucydides as the author dissents from the mass hysteria, as he sees it: but he can't stop his countrymen from pursuing their catastrophic course.) At the end of book seven, and bringing his account of the Sicilian expedition to a terrible climax, Thucydides describes the mass slaughter of Athenians in a river just outside Syracuse. The bloodbath recalls the Trojans choking up Scamander's waters as Achilles raged – only this time, there is, again, no god to step in to put a stop to the carnage. And so, with the words 'few out of the many returned', Thucydides anticipates a far more dangerous stage of the war, as Athens, the city renowned for cleverness (like Odysseus), will undergo an odyssey of sorts, besieged on all flanks by menacing suitors for her power.

Homer's influence can be traced elsewhere in prose – most obviously with the invention of the novel (or romance), whose stories of couples tragically separated but ultimately reunited after many travels and travails along the way recalls so clearly the

Odyssey (and Odysseus's Cretan tales). But it is there too even in a writer like Plato. This may at first surprise us, given the fact that Plato has Socrates recommend the banishment of Homer from the ideal philosophical republic. Yet Plato's dialogues are full of Homeric resonances – including over some two hundred quotations, by far the most of any ancient author. This evidence belies a deep engagement with Homer and probably points to Plato's efforts to cast Socrates as the new kind of hero for the challenges of this new world, in which one must turn away from politics and war and practise philosophy instead.

So much is relatively clear. Written texts of the *Iliad* and *Odyssey* can be located in a specific place (Athens) at a specific time (late sixth to early fourth century BC). Homer's influence during an earlier period is more difficult to ascertain, but some traces of the Greek oral traditions remain. Often, silence is telling. Hesiod's avoidance of Homeric material in his *Theogony* and *Works and Days* suggests that epics about the Trojan War, if not our *Iliad* and *Odyssey*, had already carved out a niche in the market. Other fragmentary witnesses, preserved as quotations in later authors, point once again to the authority of Homeric epic and the continual challenging of its hegemony. Presumably basing his lyric account on the 'happy' couple in the *Odyssey*, Sicilian poet Steisichorus (c. 640–555 BC) claims that the real Helen was in Egypt all the time (a phantom Helen went with Paris to Troy). Athenian lawgiver-cum-poet Solon (638–558 BC) turns to the *Odyssey* in trying to steer his city a course between the appetitive excesses of the rich and the emotional excesses of the common people: like the suitors or Odysseus's companions, the Athenians en masse are to blame 'by their own recklessness' for the fact that the city teeters on the brink of civil conflict and will, like Odysseus, 'suffer many pains' if they don't take note (Solon fragment 4). Sappho (c. 630–570 BC), one of our few surviving female voices from antiquity, positions her erotic poetry in direct opposition to Homeric martial poetry (fragment 16).

For her, the gleam of men in armour is nothing compared to her lover's glance, such is the power of love. The obvious example is, of course, Helen. But this is Helen not as an object (of male desire), but as a subject – what *she* loved. In turn, where logic would seem to insist on what Helen followed in pursuit of desire, Sappho instead reflects on what she left behind, which in turn brings to mind her own situation, her love for Anactoria, who has left Sappho behind. These shifting perspectives demonstrate Sappho's difference from Homer, as the narrator, once impartial and objective, becomes implicated in her own verse.

If Homer's direct influence on these poets is clear, the same cannot be said for Archilochus (c. 680–645 BC). Famous for throwing away his shield in flight, just as Odysseus relates he did during his 'Cretan' adventures, Archilochus may be reworking the *Odyssey*. Yet the early Greek philosopher Heraclitus ranks Archilochus alongside Hesiod and Homer as poets whom he would like to see thrown out of poetic contests. Perhaps it is better to think of Archilochus as a rival poet to Homer, working with the same materials (story patterns, themes, characters) but in the lyric and elegiac verse of the symposium (where the emphasis was on intimate and playful one-upmanship) rather than epic's foundational narratives.

If true, the *Odyssey*'s many scenes of banqueting would have a particular punch. Odysseus's men get ambushed on the beach while they have lunch; Cyclops makes his supper *out of* Odysseus's companions; the surviving companions perish when they barbecue the cattle of the Sun – all these tales of inappropriate feasting come to fruition back in the real world of Ithaca. In their endless partying, the suitors behave like the symposiasts for whom Archilochus would have performed. But, when Odysseus turns their banqueting hall into a bloody battlefield, Homer demonstrates the difference between epic and sympotic poetry: where drink and food and sex are the norms in the symposium, in epic poetry such indulgences are hardly worthy of praise and are just as likely to get you killed. In this framework, Homeric epic functions like a 'super genre' that consumes everything – not just other epic tales and traditions but even other genres such as lyric and elegy. In shooting Antinous through the neck as he sups his wine, and Eurymachus in the belly, Homer's Odysseus stakes a claim for epic's supremacy.

At all levels of their composition, from the surprising turn of formulaic phrase to the reversioning of story patterns, the Homeric epics render all prior heroic poems essentially obsolete. Far from representing the primitive beginnings of a Western tradition, they are better understood as sophisticated poems coming at the end of an oral tradition forever lost to us. In fact, they may well have played a part in its demise, but we will never be able to tell how or why other epic poems fell into silence. But what happens to the fragmentary opening of the *Cypria* may be telling. Whatever form the (or a) *Cypria* originally had, by the time that its story gets recorded (roughly the second century AD), it is as the prose synopsis *Chrestomathy* (literally the 'learning of useful things'). In a living oral context, not all the story has to be told because the audience would be familiar with the essentials. This later *summary* functions for readers cut off from the oral world of myth who need to know the background (such as how the Trojan War started, who Helen was, etc.). What is more, fragment 1 of the *Cypria* survives *only* because it exists in the margins of the tenth-century AD Venetus A manuscript of the *Iliad*. Its own particular, unique focus is lost forever; its only value now is to explain Homer. By some means or other, Homer's epics bring to an end the heroic oral tradition. Yet simultaneously they give rise to cultural and political musings far beyond those imagined within the scope of either poem.

In a galaxy far, far away

While we owe our texts of Homer to their being inscribed in animal hide (mediaeval manuscripts were made out of vellum) by monks holed up in European monasteries, the poems them-selves continue to survive and thrive by shifting form in various ways. This phenomenon is perhaps most keenly felt in the realm of translation, by which means successive generations of readers come to Homer afresh through the prism of their own cultures. The first complete English translation of Homer appeared in 1616 by George Chapman, and remained the most popular way most English speakers encountered these poems until Alexander Pope's *Iliad* (1715–20) and *Odyssey* (1726). Both writers' transla-tions were considered works of art in their own right. (The Romantic poet John Keats describes the thrill *On First Looking into Chapman's Homer* in terms of discovering a new continent or planet, while Samuel Johnson praised Pope's *Iliad* as 'a perfor-mance which no age or nation could hope to equal' – though it didn't impress classicist Richard Bentley: 'It is a pretty poem, Mr. Pope, but you must not call it Homer.') After the invention of the printing press, Homer in translation gained massive popu-lar appeal, remaining a phenomenon to this day: E.V. Rieu's 1946 prose translation of the *Odyssey* opened the *Penguin Classics* series and has sold millions of copies, while 2011 saw no fewer than four new English translations of Homer's *Iliad* alone. As the scientific advances of our day spawn the new digital age, we again find Homer at the vanguard of change. The Homer Multitext project, run by the Center for Hellenic Studies at Harvard University, is pioneering the use of online resources to capture textual variants to the Homeric poems, with the hope of shed-ding new light on the mechanics of oral composition and textu-alisation. The mediaeval manuscripts, to which we owe our texts of Homer, may struggle to contain his poems in the future.

Perhaps because they belong to a different medium, the visual arts have always shown a tangible sign of Homer's influence. Artists from different periods and different schools have continu-ally looked to Homer for inspiration. Ingres captures the moment when Thetis appeals to Zeus to honour her son in his 1811 *Jupiter and Thetis*. Henri Matisse's *Odysseus Blinding Polyphemus* (1935) singles out Odysseus vanquishing the monster, capturing the spirit, if not the letter, of Homer's representation. And frequently it is the spirit that seems most important, not the content. So, for example, in his *Ulysses and the Sirens* (1909), Herbert James Draper depicts the fearsome creatures very differently from the grotesque composite figures that graced ancient Greek vases, by reimagining them as beautiful mermaid-like seductresses crowding in on Ulysses (aka Odysseus). This alluring image owes something to Homer's description of their sweet words – the painter transfers the seductive power of the Sirens' song to their very bodies, thereby capturing their attraction and threat in his (visual) art. In his *Helen of Troy at the Scaean Gate* (1880), Gustave Moreau

Ulysses and the Sirens, Herbert James Draper, 1909, Hull

Far from being grotesque figures (as the Sirens are depicted on ancient Greek vases), Draper pictures them as beautiful mermaid-like seductresses crowding in on Ulysses (aka Odysseus). This alluring image owes something to Homer's description of their sweet words – the artist has transferred the seductive power of the Sirens' song to their very bodies, thereby capturing their attraction and threat in this visual art form. Compare, for example, John William Waterhouse's *Ulysses and the Sirens* 1891, in which the artist retains the harpy-like forms of the Sirens but pictures them with beautiful faces (as Homer relates).

depicts Helen richly and gorgeously attired, but her face stares out to us blankly. This visualisation allows us, the viewer, to fill in the canvas (sketched like a marble statue in outline), in much the same way as Homer invites us to ponder her *character* in his own ambiguous representation of the woman whose face launched a thousand ships.

Helen of Troy at the Scaean Gate, Gustave Moreau, 1880

> *Helen of Troy at the Scaean Gate* is one of a series of portraits of Helen that Moreau attempted in obsessively re-presenting her infamous, and disastrous, beauty. Here Moreau depicts Helen alone amidst the smouldering ruins of Troy, her face turned away from the city in outline like a marble statue. Just how do you read her blank face?

Frequently, modern reworkings of Homer announce themselves in their title and explicitly invite the audience to contemplate the interplay with Homer. Authors like James Joyce (*Ulysses*), Derek Walcott (*Omeros*), and Nikos Kazantzakis (*The Odyssey: A Modern Sequel*) use Homer's epic narratives, heroic characters, and poetic techniques to explore contemporary worlds (Ithaca relocated respectively to Ireland, the Caribbean, and modern Greece). Others present their creations as retellings of Homer. In her *Penelopiad*, Margaret Atwood allows Penelope to give her own account of her husband's prolonged absence. Madeline Miller's 2012 Orange prize-winning *The Song of Achilles* takes up the story of Achilles' relationship with Patroclus, recasting that intimacy in the light of modern sexuality and from Patroclus's viewpoint. Pop music is not immune to Homeric influence either. Led Zeppelin's 1976 'Achilles Last Stand', coming in at an epic ten minutes, was so named (perhaps apocryphally) because Robert Plant had severely broken his ankle. Metal group Symphony X journey even further into epic territory with their twenty-four-minute 'The Odyssey'. Homer has also inspired Cream's 'Tales of Brave Ulysses' and Suzanne Vega's 'Calypso', in which the singer muses on Odysseus's divine lover.

The continued (and increasing) attraction to Homer probably points to each epic's in-depth, multifaceted, and, ultimately, inexhaustible analysis of human behaviour in two paradigmatic contexts, the war and the return home. As Jonathan Shay notes in his own highly resonant book, *Achilles in Vietnam: Combat Trauma and the Undoing of Character*, the *Iliad* communicates and invites reflection on general reactions to war, such as grief at the death of a comrade or the loss of self in the rage of violence. In particular, it evokes for any contemporary society immersed in conflict the basic confusion of war – the way, for example, social, moral, or political order can be subverted, as happens in *Iliad* 1. The traumatic world wars of the past century have prompted many returns to Homer's ancient war epic, notably W.H. Auden's poetic explorations of violence and heroism in *The Shield of Achilles*, and Simone Weil's deliberation on the dehumanising nature of violence in *The* Iliad, *or the Poem of Force*. With each generation's experience of war and violence come new readings and appreciation of the *Iliad*. In turn, the poem is born again to engage different voices in the debate about the nature of war, heroism, friendship, and coming to terms with death.

If anything the *Odyssey* proves to be even more versatile – as befits this poem's 'much-turning' 'many-wayed' narrative. The *Odyssey*'s fundamental questions of identity lost and redefined through storytelling are present in the book/movie *Fight Club*, while David Foster Wallace's *Infinite Jest* contemplates the ways in which entertainment erases men's selves just as the Sirens wreck passing ships and others lose themselves in the land of the Lotus-Eaters through various forms of substance abuse. The critically acclaimed *Mad Men* addresses the *Odyssey*'s central theme of identity by similarly exploring the life and loves of its returning war 'hero' – the season four opener directly poses the question that has been rumbling through the first three series, just *who is Don Draper?* – even as it lifts the veil on the advertising industry, the modern art of storytelling. (Were Odysseus to be around now, or at least in the sixties, he would be in 'creative', like Don.) In Bryan Singer's 1995 film *The Usual Suspects*, the central character Verbal Kint, played by Kevin Spacey, weaves an Odyssean web of lies and deception to construct an arch-criminal figure (Keyser Söze), by which means he manufactures his release from police custody.

As Kint departs from the police station and his limp slowly transforms into an ever more purposeful, brisker step, the camera cuts to the duped police officer who notices, with increasing horror, details on the board behind him out of which Kint has woven his 'lies that sound like the truth'. (Thus, Kint even represents a good example of a bard, composing a story spontaneously from a store of clippings of previous tales gathered here and there.) Mike Leigh's 1993 film *Naked* follows Johnny (who remains the unnamed 'man' throughout) in an odyssey of our time through the streets of 1980s London, antagonising and aggressively interrogating everyone he meets. At one point, the film even blatantly advertises its debt to Homer as Johnny puns on Homer's name: 'I don't mean that to sound Homer-phobic. I mean I like the *Iliad*. And the *Odyssey. [Laughs]* Did you get that?' This nod to Homer is then followed up with a visual cue – Jonny takes a copy of Homer's *Odyssey* from a bookshelf, holds it to the camera, and asks: 'Do you get it now?' Homer would have heartily approved of such knowing playfulness with his creation.

In many ways, the *Odyssey* has been a touchstone of modernity – the challenge to identity, the struggle to find a place one can call home, the idea of the 'journey' (so beloved as a metaphor for business leaders or movie executives). All of these concerns feature in what is perhaps the seminal American novel, Mark Twain's *The Adventures of Huckleberry Finn*, where the Mississippi river represents Homer's wine-dark sea and different townspeople supply a new kind of ethnography. The motif of the journey in search for identity and a place to call home is also a feature of films like *O Brother, Where Art Thou?* and *2001: A Space Odyssey*. In the former, the homecoming of an ex-con during the Great Depression is playfully framed with scenes modelled on Homer and stars a Ulysses – played by George Clooney – obsessive about his appearance. In the latter, the journey is deadly serious as it is *mankind* whose identity is up for grabs on the journey from Earth to beyond.

A 'Space Odyssey' is a good place to end this Beginner's Guide to Homer. Several times through the course of this book we have referred to the ways in which Homer's epics both explore themes and issues that challenge cultural, ethical, and political norms, and invite their audience to contemplate the very fabric of their societies. Homer achieves these effects by locating his story in a distant heroic time and place, a world 'far, far away'. In the modern world, where documented histories go back centuries, science has made huge advances in knowledge, and religions are dogmatised through texts, there is not the same opportunity to use a heroic past. Instead, the period from the end of the nineteenth century to the present day has witnessed the development and flourishing of works of fantasy of various kinds in genres such as comics, horror, and science fiction.

Drawing on folklore traditions around Europe and in reaction to the rationalism of the Enlightenment, creative storytelling and cultural self-examination took seed in the early works of fantasy and horror by Mary Shelley (*Frankenstein*) and Edgar Allen Poe. Journeys, ethnography, and questions of civilisation found new expressions in science fiction writers such as Jules Verne and H.G. Wells. To this day, some of the bestselling books and highest-grossing movies hail from the fantastic genre – the new 'mythical' and epic realms. Superheroes, monsters, and aliens have replaced the extra-mortal characteristics of Homer's gods and heroes, while special technology or magic serves to reproduce the awe-inspiring and supernatural devices of the heroic realm. Like Homer's heroes, these are figures not only to be held in awe but also to fear and question. After reinventing how Batman begins his fight against crime, Christopher Nolan's *The Dark Knight* plays on the idea that its hero is as much an outsider – or 'freak', in the language of the Joker – as those whom he fights. Superheroes like *Superman* or *Spiderman* adopt disguises for the very reason that they cannot reveal their true identity and be themselves with the special powers they possess. Arguably, the classic example is *X-Men*, who, in their various manifestations in cartoon and film, explore the essential problem of outsiders in society, whether that outsider element is conceived of in terms of race, politics, or physical characteristics – the *X-Men* themselves are essentially 'mutants' who don't fit in.

The essential point about these 'modern' genres of fantasy, horror, and science fiction is that their distance from our every-day lives allows them, paradoxically, to scrutinise and engage in complex and troubling issues that affect us all. H.G. Wells's *The Time Machine* channels the *Odyssey* in its journey through future races of men, while addressing Victorian concerns about industrialism and the burgeoning ideological conflict between Marxism and Capitalism. The many versions of the *Star Trek* series send man on a voyage into the unknown that both refines and expands views on human identity (and significance), while also exploring the cultural values of its audience – we should not forget that it was this series that gave sixties America a multiracial cast and its first television interracial kiss. *Star Wars* (1977), the film that successfully made the crossover from sci-fi to mass pop-ular appeal, advertised in its opening credits its setting in a 'galaxy far, far away'.

Keeping one's distance is crucial. Debuting on US TV just two years after 11 September 2001, the rebooted *Battlestar Galactica* quickly establishes its other-worldliness, using – among other strategies – echoes of ancient Greek culture in a pantheon of twelve gods, call signs for pilots (such as 'Apollo' and 'Athena'), and musical cues for certain Cylons, which act like Homeric epithets in bringing to mind the character's past actions and feelings. And this distance is needed. For in its pilot episode this drama confronts the audience with the trauma of a surprise attack on a capital city, nuclear holocaust, and the near destruc-tion of the entire human race. At the end of that pilot, and setting the scene for the series to come, Commander Adama addresses the enormous personal loss that everyone has suffered, touches upon the guilt that each survivor feels, and offers hope. That hope is of finding a way to Earth, the 'home' planet of the original twelve tribes – 'in search of home' is the tagline used in the opening credits of each subsequent episode. *Battlestar Galactica* is essentially a homecoming narrative like the *Odyssey*. Above all, the humans are forced to contemplate why they *should* live, and *who* they are, now that their mechanical creations, Cylons, walk, talk, look, and sometimes even think and feel like real people. Using the narrative frame of a surviving group, *Battlestar Galactica* also confronts difficult social questions – such as whether being on a war footing justifies the suspension of a civilian government or the suppression of a free press, or whether in the context of mankind's possible extinction the government should outlaw abortion. Memorably, the season three opener depicts an insurgency resisting occupation, contemplating and, ultimately, carrying out suicide bombings – only in this case the insurgents are the sympathetic humans; the occupying power, the brutal Cylons. The fact that this played on prime-time TV in the US, even as US military forces and her coalition of the willing were engaged in increasingly fraught occupations of Iraq and Afghanistan, was in all likelihood possible only because of the distance afforded by this epic genre for the modern world.

As the result of millennia of storytelling and going on three thousand years of reception, Homer's epics give us a unique insight into the breadth and depth of responses to two human conditions, one related to war, conflict, and mortality, the other to the journey, search for home, and (re)discovery of identity. Over the centuries, the epics have sparked contemplation and reconsideration of the basic nature of what it means to be human. They have provided each new audience with new ways for understanding the worlds that came before and, simultaneously, new ways of thinking about the possible routes that still may be taken. Beginning with Homer is the beginning of a lifetime of enjoyment being caught up by stories of the past that always speak to the present.

As he holds up a copy of the *Odyssey* to the camera, the anti-hero of Mike Leigh's *Naked* asks:

> Johnny: Do you know this? I bet you do. You've most likely done it at school. You just can't remember. You know, like, uh, Achilles' heel, the wooden horse, Helen of Troy. You know them?
> Girl: Yeah.
> Johnny: Yeah. Well, that's all it is. Good stuff. Cyclops.

Further reading

Introduction

Barbara Graziosi, *Inventing Homer* (Cambridge, 2002) uses the early biographical tradition to explore Homeric poetry's ancient reception. Albert Lord's *The Singer of Tales* (Cambridge MA, 1960) documents the results of his studies with Milman Parry on oral poetics. For diametrically opposed, and highly trenchant, views on the Homeric question see Greg Nagy, *Homeric Questions* (Texas, 1996) and Martin West, *The Making of the Iliad* (Oxford, 2011). Michael Wood, *In Search of the Trojan War* (London, 1985), puts together a lively history of the search for Troy. For a study of Homeric society, and the problems of talking about it, see Moses Finley, *The World of Odysseus* (2nd Edition: New York, 1979), while Robin Osborne's 'Homer's Society' chapter, in Robert Fowler's *Cambridge Companion to Homer* (Cambridge, 2004), presents an excellent summary of the issues. In *The Returns of Odysseus* (Berkeley, 1998), Irad Malkin uses the *Odyssey* as a touchstone for the Greek experience of expansion and the development of identity.

Chapter 1

Jonathan Burgess explores *The Tradition of the Trojan War in Homer and the Epic Cycle* (Baltimore, 2001). Jenny Strauss Clay's *Hesiod's Cosmos* (Cambridge, 2003) describes epic poetry's structuring of the cosmos, while Barbara Graziosi and Johannes Haubold, *Homer: The Resonance of Epic* (London, 2005), discuss how the surviving poems trace the movement to a world of man. In his *The Mortal Hero* (Berkeley, 1984), Seth Schein compares the characters of Achilles and Hector to illustrate the poem's moral (and mortal) core. On the allusive importance of Thetis to the *Iliad*, see Laura Slatkin's *The Power of Thetis* (Berkeley, 1992). Bruce Heiden's *Homer's Cosmic Fabrication* (Oxford, 2008) shows how Zeus's plan brings structure to the narrative of the *Iliad*.

Chapter 2

Simone Weil's *The Iliad, or Poem of Force* has recently been republished with a new translation and an introduction on its influence (New York, 2006). For the *Iliad* constructing a political community, see Dean Hammer, *The Iliad as Politics* (Norman, 2002) and Elton Barker, *Entering the Agon* (Oxford, 2009). Johannes Haubold, *Homer's People* (Cambridge, 2000) discusses the role of Agamemnon and Achilles (among others) as leaders and shows the importance of the people to the epic. Caroline Alexander's *The War that Killed Achilles* (London, 2010) reads the *Iliad* as an evocation of war's destruction that still resonates in today's conflicts around the world.

Chapter 3

For the classic discussion of Homer's tragedy of Hector, see James Redfield, *Nature and Culture in the Iliad* (Chicago, 1975). Hilary Mackie's *Talking Trojan* (Lanham MD, 1996) investigates the language and community of Homer's Trojans, while Edith Hall's *Inventing the Barbarian* (Oxford, 1989) presents the long view of Greek representations of the east. Casey Dué's *Homeric Variations on a Lament by Briseis* (Lanham MD, 2002) uses the slave Briseis to explore the role of women in the *Iliad*. Barbara Graziosi and Johannes Haubold's commentary on Iliad *Book VI* (Cambridge, 2010) discusses in depth many of the themes raised here.

Chapter 4

Jasper Griffin's *Homer on Life and Death* (Oxford, 1980) considers the *Iliad*'s exploration of heroism and mortality. Michael Lynn-George's *Epos: Word, Narrative and the Iliad* (London, 1988) demonstrates the literary sophistication and emotional depth of Homer's poem. Oliver Taplin's *Homeric Soundings* (Oxford, 1995) traces the *Iliad*'s internal resonances and the interaction between scenes often separated by thousands of lines. The commentary on Iliad *XXIV* by Colin Macleod (Cambridge, 1982) remains unrivalled in its sensitivity to the structure, style, and big ideas of the last book.

Chapter 5

Richard Rutherford's *Homer* (Oxford, 1996) presents a handy guide to the Homeric poems, while Pietro Pucci's *Odysseus Polutropos* (Ithaca, 1987) analyses the engagement between them. Erwin Cook, *The Odyssey in Athens* (Ithaca, 1995), examines Zeus's justice through the poem's structure and relationship to other sources. Seth Schein's collection of essays *Reading the Odyssey* (Princeton, 1996) introduces many of the *Odyssey*'s key themes. For brevity and depth, Laura Slatkin's *Odyssey* essay in John Miles Foley's Blackwell's *Companion to Ancient Epic* (Oxford, 2005) is difficult to beat. Norman Austin's *Archery at the Dark of the Moon* (Berkeley, 1975) remains a classic investigation of literary issues in the *Odyssey*.

Chapter 6

For differing accounts of the poem's self-conscious exploration of storytelling, with particular attention to Odysseus as narrator, see Simon Goldhill's *The Poet's Voice* (Cambridge, 1991), Charles Segal's *Singers, Heroes and Gods in the* Odyssey (Ithaca, 1994), Douglas Olson's *Blood and Iron* (Brill, 1995), and Lillian Doherty's *Siren Songs* (Ann Arbor, 1995). George Walsh's *The Varieties of Enchantment* (Chapel Hill, 1984) explores early Greek views of poetry's seductive power. For the relationship of the *Odyssey* to other types of tale, see Denys Page's *Folktales in Homer's Odyssey* (Cambridge, 1973).

Chapter 7

Nancy Felson-Rubin's *Regarding Penelope* (Princeton, 1994) and Barbara Clayton's *A Penelopean Poetics* (Lanham, 2004) explore Homer's subtle and complex portrayal of Penelope. Best of all is Margaret Atwood's novel *The Penelopiad: The Myth of Penelope and Odysseus* (Canongate, 2005). Class issues are confronted by William Thalmann's *The Swineherd and the Bow* (Ithaca, 1998), while Sheila Murnaghan's *Disguise and Recognition in the* Odyssey (Princeton, 1987) unmasks the importance of recognition. Jonathan Shay's *Odysseus in America* (New York, 2002) is a compelling, and topical, account of reading the *Odyssey* in and against modern accounts of combat trauma and homecoming. Alex Purves's *Space and Time in Ancient Greek Narrative* (Cambridge, 2010) reads the signs of the ends of the *Odyssey*.

Epilogue

There have been a number of recent companions to the reception of Homer: Barbara Graziosi and Emily Greenwood's *Homer in the Twentieth Century* (Cambridge, 2007) has a chapter by Simon Goldhill on Mike Leigh's *Naked*; Martin Winkler's *Classical Myth and Culture in the Cinema* (Oxford, 2001) includes Hannah Roisman's analysis of *The Usual Suspects*; in her book *The Return of Ulysses: A Cultural History of Homer's Odyssey* (Baltimore, 2008) Edith Hall discusses Odyssean resonances in the Coen brothers' *O Brother, Where Art thou?*. Nick Lowe's *The Classical Plot and the Invention of Western Narrative* (Cambridge, 2000) sets out the argument that Homer's epics bequeath a dual template – in major and minor modes – for subsequent literature. The *Tabulae Iliacae* are the subject of a brilliantly illuminating new book by Michael Squire, *The* Iliad *in a Nutshell* (Oxford, 2012). Information about the Homer Multitext project is available from: http://chs.harvard.edu/chs/homer_multitext.

Index

Note: Italicised page numbers show illustrations